History

for the IB Diploma
The Move to Global War

Author and series editor: Allan Todd

Tilly Cox

Cambridge University Press's mission is to advance learning, knowledge and research worldwide.

Our IB Diploma resources aim to:
- encourage learners to explore concepts, ideas and topics that have local and global significance
- help students develop a positive attitude to learning in preparation for higher education
- assist students in approaching complex questions, applying critical-thinking skills and forming reasoned answers.

CAMBRIDGE UNIVERSITY PRESS

CAMBRIDGE
UNIVERSITY PRESS

University Printing House, Cambridge CB2 8BS, United Kingdom

One Liberty Plaza, 20th Floor, New York, NY 10006, USA

477 Williamstown Road, Port Melbourne, VIC 3207, Australia

314–321, 3rd Floor, Plot 3, Splendor Forum, Jasola District Centre,
New Delhi – 110025, India

79 Anson Road, #06–04/06, Singapore 079906

Cambridge University Press is part of the University of Cambridge.

It furthers the University's mission by disseminating knowledge in the pursuit of education, learning and research at the highest international levels of excellence.

Information on this title: education.cambridge.org

© Cambridge University Press 2015

This publication is in copyright. Subject to statutory exception and to the provisions of relevant collective licensing agreements, no reproduction of any part may take place without the written permission of Cambridge University Press.

First published 2011
Second edition 2015

20 19 18 17 16 15 14 13 12 11 10 9 8 7 6 5 4

Printed in Great Britain by CPI Group (UK) Ltd, Croydon CR0 4YY

A catalogue record for this publication is available from the British Library

ISBN 978-1-107-55628-7

Cambridge University Press has no responsibility for the persistence or accuracy of URLs for external or third-party internet websites referred to in this publication, and does not guarantee that any content on such websites is, or will remain, accurate or appropriate.

NOTICE TO TEACHERS IN THE UK

It is illegal to reproduce any part of this work in material form (including photocopying and electronic storage) except under the following circumstances:
(i) where you are abiding by a licence granted to your school or institution by the Copyright Licensing Agency;
(ii) where no such licence exists, or where you wish to exceed the terms of a licence, and you have gained the written permission of Cambridge University Press;
(iii) where you are allowed to reproduce without permission under the provisions of Chapter 3 of the Copyright, Designs and Patents Act 1988, which covers, for example, the reproduction of short passages within certain types of educational anthology and reproduction for the purposes of setting examination questions.

This material has been developed independently by the publisher and the content is in no way connected with nor endorsed by the International Baccalaureate Organization.

Dedication

For Karen

Contents

1 Introduction	**1**
Case Study 1: Japanese Expansion in East Asia, 1931–41	**18**
2 Causes of Japanese Expansion	**18**
2.1 How significant was the impact of nationalism and militarism on Japan's foreign policy?	19
2.2 What impact did Japan's main domestic issues have on foreign policy?	35
2.3 How significant was China's political instability?	43
3 Japan's Actions	**55**
3.1 What happened in Manchuria and northern China, 1931–36?	56
3.2 What were the main aspects of the Second Sino-Japanese War, 1937–41?	61
3.3 Why did Japan attack Pearl Harbor in 1941?	68
4 International Responses to Japanese Expansionism	**81**
4.1 How did the League of Nations respond to Japan's expansionism?	82
4.2 What political developments occurred within China as a result of Japanese aggression?	87
4.3 What was the international response to Japanese aggression?	88
Case Study 2: German and Italian Expansionism, 1933–40	**100**
5 Causes of German and Italian Expansion	**100**
5.1 What was the impact of Fascist and Nazi ideology on expansionist foreign policies in Italy and Germany?	101
5.2 What was the impact of economic issues on expansionist foreign policies in Italy and Germany?	120
5.3 How did conditions in Europe in the 1930s contribute to the collapse of collective security?	130
6 Germany's and Italy's Actions	**142**
6.1 How did Germany challenge the post-war settlements, 1933–38?	143
6.2 What were the main aspects of Italy's foreign policy, 1935–39?	151
6.3 How did Germany expand, 1938–39?	158
7 International Responses to German and Italian Expansionism	**169**
7.1 What was the international response to German aggression 1933–38?	170
7.2 What was the international response to Italian aggression 1935–36?	180
7.3 What was the international response to German and Italian aggression in 1939?	183

Contents

8 The Final Steps to Global War, 1939–41 — **193**

9 Exam Practice — **199**
  Paper 1 exam practice — 199
  Paper 2 exam practice — 216
  Further Information — 220

Index — 223

Acknowledgement — 227

Introduction

This book is designed to prepare students taking the Paper 1 topic, *The Move to Global War* (Prescribed Subject 3) in the IB History examination. It will examine the history of military expansionism and the move to global war in the period between the two World Wars, by looking at two case studies, from two different regions of the world.

Both of these cases studies must be studied. The first case study focuses on Japanese expansionism in East Asia from 1931 to 1941; the second case study explores German and Italian expansionism in the period 1933–39.

Each case study will examine **three** main aspects relating to these two examples of military expansionism in the period 1931–41:

- causes
- actions/ events
- international responses.

In particular, these case studies will examine the significance of nationalism and militarism, and the rise of right-wing and fascist regimes in Japan, Italy and Germany. In addition, economic developments will be examined, including the impact of the Great Depression. These case studies will also consider the problems arising from the peace settlements of 1919–20; and the various responses of the League of Nations, and of the main democratic states, to these developments which eventually led to the outbreak of the Second World War.

Overview

Themes

To help you prepare for your IB History exams, this book will cover the main themes and aspects relating to *The Move to Global War* as set out in the IB *History Guide*. It will also briefly examine some of the main political, economic, military and diplomatic developments in the period after 1919 which led to military expansionism in the years 1919–41. The major focus areas of the two case studies are shown below:

Japanese expansionism

- the political, economic and social problems of Imperial Japan in the years immediately before 1919 and, especially, between 1919 and 1941
- the rise of nationalism in Japan, and how this affected military affairs and expansionism in Asia after 1919
- the impact of the Great Depression on Japan, and the political instability in China after 1919

1 Introduction

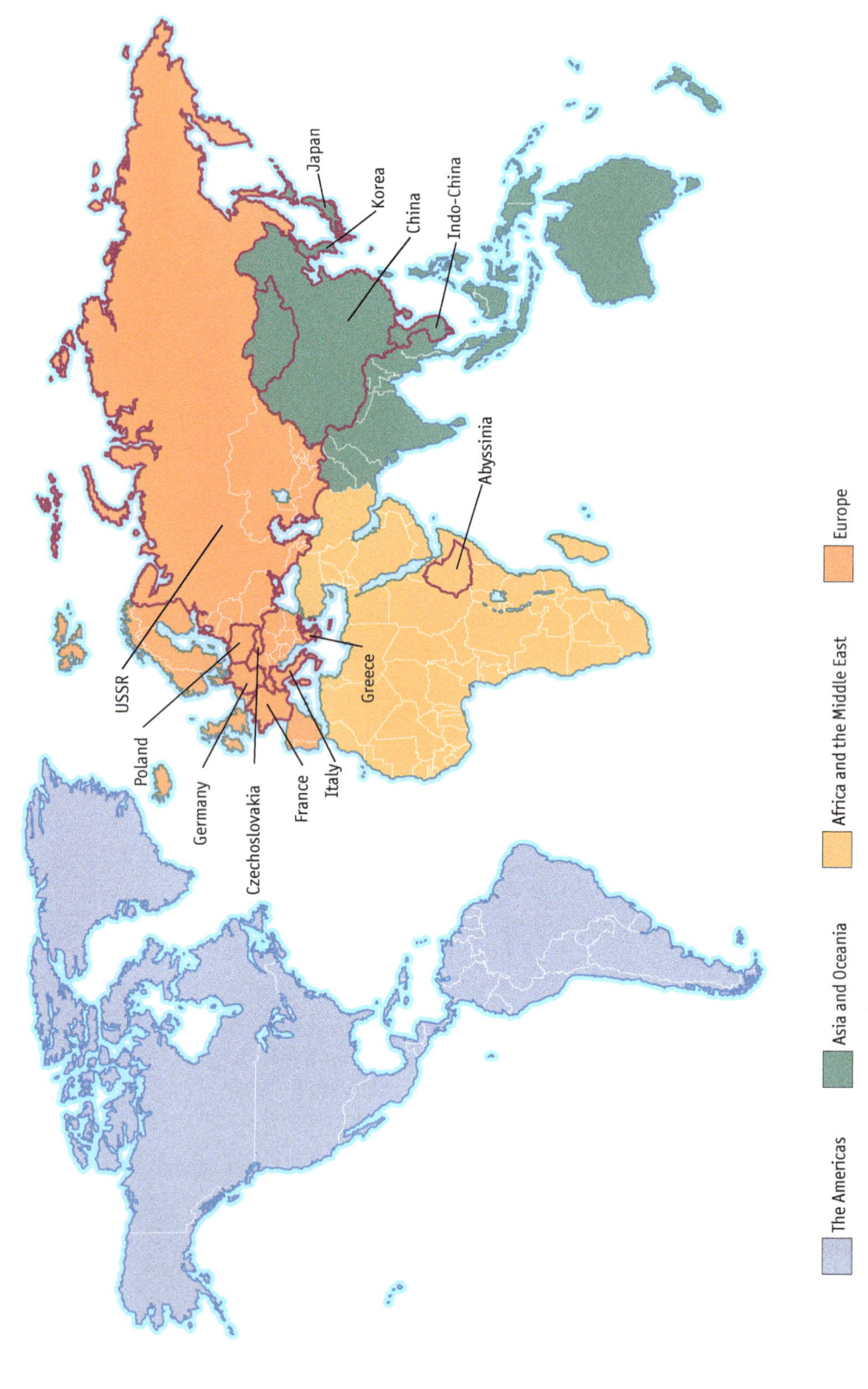

Figure 1.1 A map of the world, showing expansion by Germany, Italy and Japan in the period 1931–41

- Japan's military expansion in Manchuria 1931–36, and the Sino-Japanese War of 1937–41
- the responses of the League of Nations, China and the US to Japan's military expansionism in Asia during this period

German and Italian expansionism
- the political, economic and social problems of Italy and Germany in the years immediately before 1919 and, especially, between 1919 and 1939
- the rise of fascism in Italy and Nazism in Germany, and how this affected military expansionism in Europe and elsewhere after 1919
- the impact of the Great Depression on Italy and Germany, and the resulting European situation in the 1930s
- Italian and German challenges to the post-1919 peace settlements, and the development of the Axis alliances
- the responses of the League of Nations and the major states to Italian and German expansionism

Final steps to war
- how Japanese, Italian and German expansionism during the period 1919–41, and the international responses to it, finally led to the outbreak of war

Key concepts

Each chapter will help you focus on the main issues and compare the main developments relating to the two case studies. In addition, at various points in the chapters, there will be questions and activities which will help you focus on the six Key Concepts – these are:

- change
- continuity
- causation
- consequence
- significance
- perspectives.

Sometimes, a question might ask you to address two Key Concepts, for instance: Why did Japan attack the US pacific fleet at Pearl Harbor? What were the immediate consequences of this action for the countries in South East Asia?

It is immediately clear with this question that the Key Concept of Consequences must be addressed in your answer. However, it is important to note that although the word 'causes' doesn't explicitly appear in the question, words such as 'why' or 'reasons' are nonetheless asking you to address Causation as well.

To help you focus on the six Key Concepts, and gain experience of writing answers that address them, you will find a range of different questions and activities throughout these chapters.

Introduction

Theory of Knowledge

In addition to the broad key themes, the chapters contain Theory of Knowledge (ToK) links, to get you thinking about aspects which relate to History, which is a Group 3 subject in the IB Diploma. *The Move to Global War* topic has several clear links to ideas about knowledge and history. The topic is one that is much debated by historians – especially where it concerns responsibility for aggression and for the eventual outbreak of the most destructive war in history.

At times, the controversial nature of this topic has affected the historians writing about these states, the leaders involved, and the policies and actions taken. Thus, questions relating to the selection of sources, and to differing interpretations of these sources by historians, have clear links to the IB Theory of Knowledge course.

Fact: Apart from historians having different historical approaches – such as emphasising the role of individuals or the significance of economic developments – many historians have political beliefs and approaches. For instance, historians might be strongly attached to liberal principles, see capitalism as the best system, or have Marxist beliefs.

For example, when trying to explain aspects of the foreign policies followed by leaders, their motives, and their actions, historians must decide which evidence to select and use to make their case – and which evidence to leave out. The resulting question is, to what extent do the historians' personal views influence their decisions when they select what they consider to be the most important or relevant sources, and make judgements about the value and limitations of specific sources or sets of sources? Is there such a thing as objective 'historical truth'? Or are there just a range of subjective historical opinions and interpretations about the past, which vary according to the political interests and leanings of individual historians?

You are therefore encouraged to read a range of books offering different interpretations of the foreign policies pursued by different leaders, the actions of the three aggressor states, the responses of the League of Nations, and the significance of different historical events during the period covered by this book, in order to gain a clear understanding of the relevant historiographies (see Further Information, Chapter 9).

IB History and Paper 1 questions

Paper 1 and sources

Unlike Papers 2 and 3, which require you to write essays using just your own knowledge, Paper 1 questions are source-based. Whether you are taking Standard or Higher Level, the sources, the questions – and the mark schemes applied by your examiners – are the same.

To answer these questions successfully, you need to be able to combine the use of your own knowledge with the ability to assess and *use* a range of sources in a variety of ways. Each Paper 1 examination question is based on four sources – usually three written and one visual. The latter might be a photograph, a cartoon, a poster, a painting or a table of statistics.

Captions and attributions

Before looking at the types of sources you will need to assess, it is important to establish one principle from the beginning. This is the issue of ***captions and attributions*** – these are the pieces of information about each source provided by the Chief Examiner.

Captions and attributions are there for a very good reason, as they give you vital information about the source. For instance, they tell you who wrote it, and when,

Introduction

or what it was intended to do. Chief Examiners spend a lot of time deciding what information to give you about each source, because they know it will help you give a full answer, so they expect you to make good use of it! Yet, every year, even good candidates throw away easy marks because they do not read – or do not use – this valuable information.

Essentially, you are being asked to approach the various sources in the same way that a historian would approach them. This means not just looking carefully at what they say or show, but also asking yourself questions about how reliable, useful and/or typical they might be. Many of the answers you need to provide to these questions come from the information provided in the captions and attributions.

Types of source

Most of the sources you will have to assess are written ones, which are sometimes referred to as 'textual' sources. They might be extracts from books, official documents, speeches, newspapers, diaries or letters. Whatever type of source you are reading, the general questions you need to ask about them are the same. These questions concern the content (the information the source provides), its origin (who wrote or produced the source, when and why), and its possible limitations and value, as a result of the answers to those questions.

Although visual (or non-textual) sources are clearly different from written sources in some respects, the same questions and considerations are relevant.

Approaching sources as a set

As well as developing the ability to analyse individual sources, it is important also to look at the four sources provided *as a set*. This means looking at them **all** to see to what extent they agree or disagree with each other.

This ability to look at the four sources together is particularly important when it comes to the last question in the exam paper – the one where you need to use the sources *and* your own knowledge to assess the validity of a statement or assertion, or to analyse the significance of a particular factor. Here, you need to build an answer – along the lines of a 'mini-essay' – which combines precise knowledge with specific comments about the sources. Try to avoid falling into the trap of dealing with all the sources first, and then giving some own knowledge (as an afterthought) which is not linked to the sources.

Exam skills

If all this sounds a bit daunting, don't worry! Throughout the main chapters of this book, there are activities and questions to help you develop the understanding and the exam skills necessary for success. Before attempting the specific exam practice questions which come at the end of each main chapter, you might find it useful to refer *first* to Chapter 9, the final Exam Practice chapter. This suggestion is based on the idea that if you know where you are supposed to be going (in this instance, gaining a good grade), and how to get there, you stand a better chance of reaching your destination!

Questions and mark schemes

To ensure that you develop the necessary understanding and skills, each chapter contains questions in the margins. In addition, Chapter 9 is devoted to exam

---

Theory of knowledge

History and evidence: Winston Churchill (1874–1965) once said: *'History will be kind to me, for I intend to write it.'* In trying to reconstruct the past, historians are faced with several problems: apart from too little or too much material, how useful or reliable are the pieces of evidence with which historians deal? As an example of the relative value of a source for finding out about a particular event, ask yourself this question: is a recent history book *more* valuable than a speech made at the time of that event?

Introduction

practice. It provides help and advice for all Paper 1 questions and for Paper 2 essay questions, and sets out worked examples for Paper 1 judgement questions and for Paper 2 essays. Worked examples for the remaining three Paper 1-type questions (comprehension, value and limitations and cross-referencing) are to be found at the end of Chapters 2 to 7.

In addition, simplified mark schemes have been provided, to make it easier for you to understand what examiners are looking for in your answers. The actual IB History mark schemes can be found on the IB website.

Finally, you will find activities, along with examiners' tips and comments, to help you focus on the important aspects of the questions. These examples will also help you avoid simple mistakes and oversights that, every year, result in even some otherwise good students failing to gain the highest marks.

Background to the period

To fully understand developments in the period 1931–41, it is necessary to have some knowledge of the First World War and its more immediate impacts.

Figure 1.2 Ruins of the Belgian town of Ypres, on the First World War's Western Front in Europe, in 1918

Introduction

The First World War

Several factors contributed to the outbreak of the First World War, including a rise in nationalism, and economic and colonial rivalries between the world's most powerful nations. These rivalries were accompanied by arms races and secret diplomacy, as countries tried to strengthen their position in Europe and around the world.

By 1914, two major alliances had formed. On one side was the **Triple Alliance**: Imperial Germany, Austria-Hungary, and Italy; on the other side was the **Triple Entente**: made up of Britain, France and Tsarist Russia. In addition, Imperial Japan, an expanding power in Asia, was linked to the Triple Entente as a result of the 1902 Anglo–Japanese Alliance with Britain, which was renewed in 1905 and 1911. In June 1914, a clash of imperial interests and the rise of nationalism in the Balkans (south-eastern Europe) resulted in the assassination of the heir to the Austro-Hungarian throne. Within two months, the countries of the two rival alliances were at war with each other. The First World War – which lasted from 1914 to 1918 – was, at the time, the most destructive conflict the world had ever seen.

Revolutions and the end of empires

In addition to widespread physical destruction, the First World War also had significant political effects. In particular, the pre-war nationalist tensions led to the break-up of both the old Austro-Hungarian (or Habsburg) Empire, and the Turkish (Ottoman) Empire. In part, this process resulted from the emergence of nationalist groups demanding the right to form independent countries.

> **Triple Alliance:** In 1915, Italy switched sides and joined the Triple Entente; while, from October 1914, Turkey entered the war and fought on the side of the Triple Alliance.
>
> **Triple Entente:** 'entente' is French for 'understanding' or 'agreement' and is applied to diplomatic agreements between states. As well as Italy joining in 1915, Japan also supported the Triple Entente – but its activities were restricted to Asia and the Pacific. After the Bolshevik Revolution in Russia in 1917, Russia pulled out of the war; in the same year, the USA entered the war on the side of the Triple Entente.

Figure 1.3 The mutiny of the Petrograd garrison during the March Revolution in Russia in 1917

1

Introduction

The empire of Tsarist Russia also collapsed – before the end of the war – as a result of nationalism and revolution. In early 1917, Russian soldiers mutinied against the horrors of modern warfare, while workers and peasants rose up in a largely-spontaneous revolution which spread rapidly across Russia. In February/March 1917, the tsar (emperor) was overthrown and replaced by a Provisional Government which, however, kept Russia in the war on the side of the Allies. However, after a second revolution in October/November 1917 – led by the communist Bolsheviks – Russia withdrew from the First World War, and a revolutionary Marxist government was established. The Bolsheviks then called on soldiers and workers in countries around the world to overthrow their governments and so end the war. The new Russian government also called for self-determination for all national groups which had been forced to be part of the various European empires.

This Bolshevik Revolution also acted as an inspiration to other revolutionary groups, including soldiers who were angered and radicalised by the effects of the First World War. Such groups wanted to overthrow the capitalist system which – according to Marxist theories – had been responsible for plunging the world into such a destructive conflict. There was a short-lived rebellion in Hungary, but most significant was the outbreak of revolution in Germany, which led to the abdication of the German kaiser (emperor) and the emergence of a democratic government. The new German leaders were prepared to sign an armistice (ceasefire) in November 1918, thus ending the fighting. Later, a democratic constitution for Germany was drawn up in the town of Weimar; as a result, Germany in the period 1919–33 was referred to as Weimar Germany.

Post-war problems

As well as causing the break-up of old empires, the war had serious economic consequences – for both the victors and the defeated. Countries in Europe wasted both human and material resources, ran up massive debts, and lost trade to countries such as the USA and Japan. In addition, huge agricultural areas of Europe – in both the west and the east – had been destroyed, along with railways, roads and bridges.

After 1918, many of the politicians – and the ordinary people of Europe – who lived through the horrors of the First World War were determined to avoid any future conflict. It was in this context then that the victorious nations met in Paris in 1919–20, and attempted to conclude peace treaties that would ensure the First World War would be the 'war to end all wars'. Yet, in attempting to deal with so many issues, the peace treaties themselves actually created new problems, in both Asia and Europe. This is particularly true of the Treaty of Versailles, which was essentially imposed on the new democratic government of Germany.

In addition, Japan – despite fighting on the Allied side and helping Britain protect its imperial possessions in Asia from Germany during the war – was largely disappointed with its gains from the 1919–20 peace settlements. Italy, too, was another Allied state dissatisfied with its gains – which were less than what had been promised when it was persuaded to switch sides from the Triple Alliance to the Triple Entente by the Treaty of London in 1915.

> **ACTIVITY**
>
> Using the internet and any other resources available to you, carry out some research on the various treaties that were signed in 1919–20. Then make notes about:
>
> a the problems the peacemakers faced
>
> b the main decisions reached – including how Japan, Germany and Italy were treated.

Introduction

QUESTION
Look carefully at the cartoon. Can you identify **two** clues which show that the cartoonist was predicting war in 1940?

PEACE AND FUTURE CANNON FODDER

The Tiger: "Curious! I seem to hear a child weeping!"

Figure 1.4 A British cartoon from 1919 showing the Allied leaders Clemenceau (France), Wilson (USA), Lloyd George (Britain) and Orlando (Italy) after the peace conferences; the cartoon is predicting a new war in 1940

9

1 Introduction

Such a view of these treaties is not one simply proposed by historians with the benefit of hindsight. Several observers at the time recognised the problems being created – and warned of a future war.

The League of Nations

Against this background, the major European states attempted to construct a diplomatic approach which would both uphold the terms of the peace treaties and avoid a future war. To help achieve this, the victorious powers established the League of Nations, in which Britain and France were the most important members. Although the USA never joined, and major European states such as Germany and Russia were not at first allowed to join, the League had a number of successes before 1929. Particularly important were agreements such as the Locarno Treaty in 1925, and the Kellogg-Briand Pact of 1928 which attempted to achieve collective security (see 'collective security' in Terminology and definitions) by, respectively, guaranteeing the borders created by the peace treaties and getting countries to renounce aggression as a way of settling disagreements.

However, during this period, the League was often by-passed by the Conference of Ambassadors which, created to enforce the treaties, conducted direct diplomacy. Attempts by the League to achieve disarmament ultimately failed and, after the collapse of the US stock market in 1929 and the onset of the Great Depression, many states began to adopt more aggressive foreign policies. As a result, the League increasingly failed to maintain collective security in the years 1929–39. Conflicts such as the Japanese invasion of Manchuria in 1931, and Italy's invasion of Abyssinia in 1935 – as well as the increasing challenges to the peace settlements made by Nazi Germany after 1933 – showed the weaknesses of the League. At the end of that period, international diplomacy collapsed, and the world was plunged into another world war.

Terminology and definitions

In order to understand the history of the interwar years which eventually ended in another world war, you will need to be familiar with a few basic terms. These include terms relating to political ideologies, and also technical terms. Some of these terms can, confusingly, have slightly different meanings, according to who is using them and what beliefs they hold. Alphabetically, they are:

Appeasement

In the context of international diplomacy 1919–39, this refers, in particular, to the policy adopted after 1937 by the Conservative British prime minister, **Neville Chamberlain**. This was his strategy of attempting to avoid another war by negotiating with Nazi Germany on peaceful changes to parts of the Treaty of Versailles. Associated with this term is another term – 'revisionism' – which in this context means a willingness to 'revise' parts of the post-war peace treaties.

During the 1920s, some non-German politicians had begun to argue that the Treaty of Versailles had, in some areas, been unfair to Germany. Many Germans also felt this, referring to the treaty as a 'Diktat' (dictated peace), which had been imposed on them by the victorious Entente powers. Chamberlain shared this attitude – although French

Figure 1.5 Neville Chamberlain (1868–1940)

He was a Conservative politician, who became prime minister in 1937 and was the British politician most associated with the policy of appeasement. He believed that Hitler's demands were reasonable and at first totally rejected any idea of an alliance with the Soviet Union.

governments were less sympathetic, they felt compelled to go along with appeasement, in order to retain friendly relations with Britain, as they knew they could not fight another war without Britain's backing.

Collective security

Collective security refers to attempts by countries to act together in order to stop the use of military aggression as a way of solving problems. The League of Nations tried to ensure collective security through negotiation. If this failed, sanctions would be imposed on aggressor nations. Sanctions are actions taken to put pressure on a country (or individual) to force it to do – or to stop doing – something. For example, economic sanctions might include a trade ban or boycott, especially of vital products such as armaments, oil or coal. In the last resort, there was the option to apply military force.

One aspect of collective security in the interwar years was the attempt to uphold the peace treaties of 1919–20. In particular, France was determined to enforce the demilitarisation of the Rhineland: the German territory to the west of the River Rhine, between France and Germany. The Treaty of Versailles had stated that this region, along with a 50km belt of land to the east of the Rhine, should be demilitarised (that is, contain no German military units). Hitler's decision to break this agreement in 1936 – and the failure of Britain and France to take action against him – was, with hindsight, an important factor in the collapse of collective security.

In practice, the League's attempts to uphold collective security were undermined by the fact that several important countries – including Japan, Italy and Germany – regarded the organisation as a 'club of victors', whose main role was to enforce the unfair terms of the treaties.

Communism

Communism refers to the far-left political ideology associated with **Karl Marx** (1818–83) and Friedrich Engels (1820–95), which aimed to overthrow capitalism and replace it with a classless communist society. The first attempt to apply these theories was made by the Bolsheviks in Russia. Under the leadership of **Vladimir Ilyich Lenin**, the Bolsheviks encouraged workers' uprisings in other parts of Europe and, in 1919, established the Communist International (Comintern): this was an organisation which it was hoped would help spread revolution to other countries.

As the only workers' state, the Bolshevik regime was widely feared and hated by other countries and, in order to prevent the spread of revolution, the other major European states tried to overthrow the Bolsheviks. When this failed, the European powers applied economic and trade embargoes in an attempt to isolate and weaken Russia (known as the Soviet Union, or USSR, after 1924). For many European politicians – even after the Nazis came to power in Germany in 1933 – the communist Soviet Union posed the most serious threat to stability in Europe.

Communism should not be confused with socialism. Although the two ideologies have some common aims, socialism focuses on achieving these aims by peaceful means, such as holding elections.

Karl Marx (1818–1883)

Marx was a German philosopher and historian who developed the materialist conception of history, arguing that class struggle and conflict were the most important factors behind social and economic – as well as intellectual and political – change. Along with his close collaborator Friedrich Engels (1820–95, he wrote The Communist Manifesto in 1848, which urged the industrial working classes in developed capitalist states to bring about revolution in order to achieve a socialist and then a classless communist society, based on greater freedom and abundance. His ideas inspired many revolutionaries, including Lenin and Leon Trotsky.

Vladimir Lenin (1870–1924)

Lenin (real name Vladimir Ilyich Ulyanov) joined the Russian Social Democratic Labour Party (RSDLP) – a Marxist party – in 1898. He provoked a split in the RSDLP in 1903 and formed the Bolshevik faction. In exile from Russia until April 1917, he returned and pushed for the Bolsheviks to overthrow the Provisional Government in November 1917. He acted as prime minister of Russia from 1917 to 1924 and, just before his death, recommended – unsuccessfully – that Joseph Stalin be removed from positions of power.

1 Introduction

Conference of Ambassadors

This was an organisation set up by the victors of the First World War – Britain, France, Italy and Japan (the 'Big Four') – to resolve, by direct diplomacy, any problems arising from the peace treaties of 1919–20. It met in Paris throughout the 1920s, and frequently made decisions independently of the League. This was largely because of the various weaknesses of the League – but the work of the Conference of Ambassadors increasingly undermined the League.

Fascism

This term is derived from the Italian word *fascio* (plural *fasci*), meaning a group, band, league or union. In 1919, **Benito Mussolini** – who, in 1922, was the first Fascist dictator to come to power in Europe – applied it to his Fascio di Combattimento ('Fighting' or 'Battle Group'), which was set up to oppose socialists and communists (see section 5.1, Italian fascism). Mussolini later formed the far-right ultra-nationalist Fascist Party. After October 1922, he began to turn Italy into a one-party fascist dictatorship. Other far-right nationalist politicians in interwar Europe tried to follow his lead, including Hitler and his Nazi Party in Germany. The term 'fascist' was then used to describe this political ideology, and all groups holding such views.

Fascism is opposed to liberalism, which is tolerant of different viewpoints and seeks non-violent and democratic solutions. Fascism is particularly opposed to left-wing political groups and tends to act in the interests of capitalist firms, especially the larger ones.

Kwantung Army

This refers to the most important army group within the Imperial Japanese Army. After the Russo-Japanese War of 1904–05, the army established a Kwantung Garrison in Manchuria in 1906 – in 1919, this was re-organised as the Kwantung Army. It was extremely nationalistic, and many of its officers were members of the 'Imperial Way Faction' which strongly advocated an expansionist foreign policy. During the 1920s and 1930s, its officers often ignored instructions from Japan's governments – and even those from the Army General Staff. Instead, its officers were increasingly prepared to use its military strength to dominate and even overthrow Japan's civilian governments.

Left-wing and right-wing

The origin of these terms can be traced back to the French Revolution. In 1792, the most radical political groups (those wanting the most fundamental changes to the system) sat on the left side of the National Convention, while the most conservative groups (those opposed to change) sat on the right. In the centre were moderates, who wanted smaller-scale changes at a gradual pace. Since then, the term 'left-wing' has been applied to socialist or communist groups, while 'right-wing' has been applied to conservative or fascist groups; the moderate centre are referred to as liberals.

Meiji Restoration

This refers to the return in Japan of a political form of rule in which the emperor of Japan once again exercised direct political power. This took place in 1868, following the end of the Shogunate period, during which real power had rested with a shogun – the top military leader, appointed by the emperor. Over the centuries, this post had been

Figure 1.6 Benito Mussolini (1883–1945)

Benito Mussolini, born in 1883, followed an inconsistent political path in his early years. From 1904 to 1910, he developed a reputation as a socialist militant and, in 1911, was imprisoned for violent protests against the Italian government's imperialist war on Libya. However, the First World War led him to make a dramatic switch to extreme nationalism, and then to fascism. He ruled Italy from 1922–43, and his fascism served as the model for many other fascist parties which emerged elsewhere in Europe during the 1920s and 1930s – including for Hitler and his Nazi Party. In 1934, Mussolini set up a Fascist International, and gave funds to emerging fascist parties.

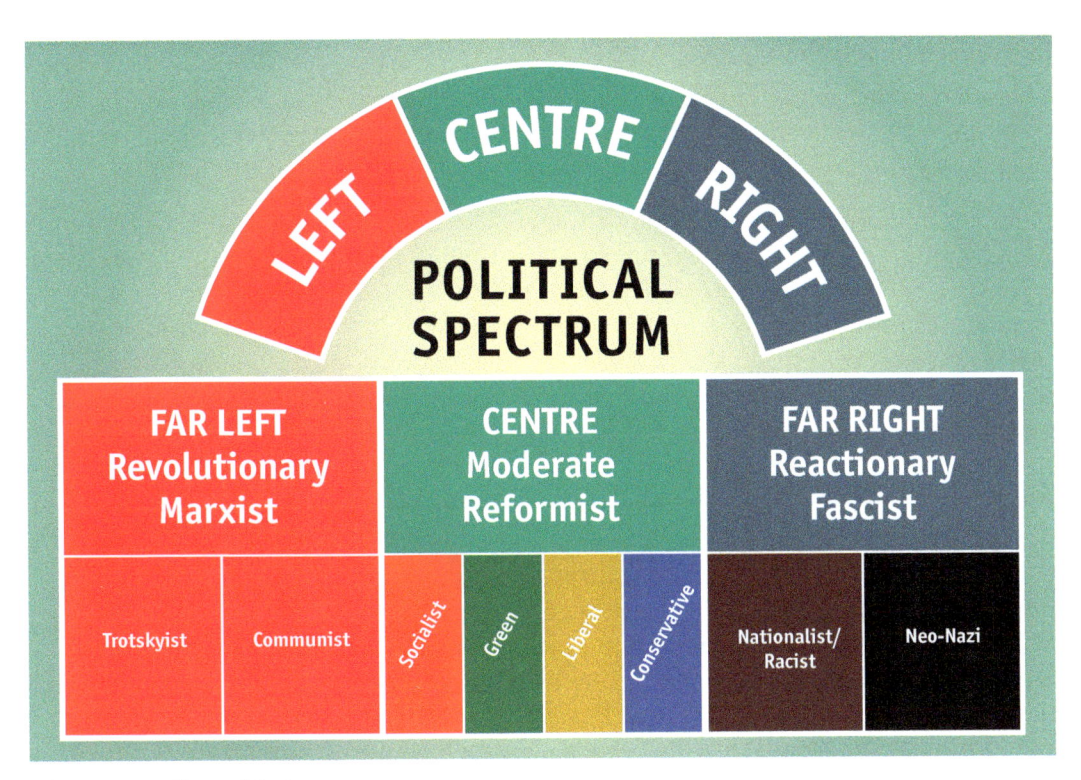

Figure 1.7 The political spectrum

held by various leaders of the most powerful feudal clans. This had been the form of rule for several centuries but, by the 13th century, the shoguns had taken most of the power from the emperors. The last shogun was the head of the Tokugawa clan, which had dominated Japan from 1603 until 1867. The restoration of imperial rule in 1868 was known as the Meiji Restoration because the emperor decided to give the name 'Meiji' – meaning 'enlightened rule' – to his period of rule.

Militarism

This term relates to the glorification of a nation's military forces and the belief that the nation should have a large and strong military capability, in order to defend, or even aggressively extend, national interests. It often results in a nation's military leaders being able to ensure that the armed forces dominate the civilian political administration of that country, and so dictate domestic and especially foreign policy. While this often exists in authoritarian states, militarism can emerge in democracies, too – especially at times of crisis – resulting in the elected government being unable to control the actions of the military. Sometimes, this can lead to the establishment of a military government.

Nationalism

This means a sense of belonging to, and identifying with, a nation or country: this involves feeling linked to all the other people who are part of the same nation. It involves feelings of sharing a common history, culture, values and language. In addition, there is a strong belief that the nation should have political self-determination. However, on occasions, nationalism can lead to the belief that the nation has the right to expand its territory at the expense of other nations. This is most likely to happen at times of economic or political crisis – and is often linked to increased militarism.

Introduction

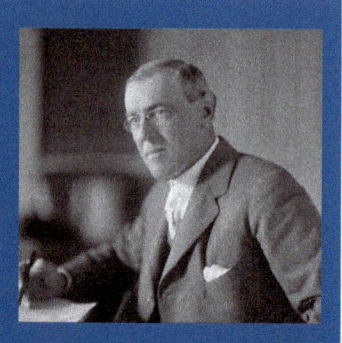

Figure 1.8 Woodrow Wilson (1895–1924)

Woodrow Wilson was elected Democratic president of the USA in 1912 and re-elected in 1916. His Fourteen Points, issued in January 1918, were the basis on which German civilian governments sued for peace in October and November 1918. His main aim was to establish a League of Nations to settle disputes between states peacefully, and to end secret diplomacy. In the end, though, the US never joined the League and, under the Republicans, adopted a policy of isolation as regards European developments. Although Woodrow Wilson wished to apply the concept of self-determination in Europe, he did not apply this to the countries of Central and Latin America. For instance, in 1915, he ordered the invasion of Haiti which, until 1804, had been a French colony. Following this US invasion, Haiti was occupied by the US until 1934, and the Haitian economy was opened up to increased investments by US corporations.

Self-determination

This refers to the idea that national groups should be able to live in independent countries – this was a principle particularly associated with US president **Woodrow Wilson** who defended this concept at the 1919–20 peace negotiations.

However, although self-determination was applied to some ethnic and national groups from the former Austro-Hungarian and Russian empires, the claims of others were ignored. For example, German-speakers in Austria and some of the newly-created 'successor states' were not allowed *Anschluss* (union) with Weimar Germany. In some areas, the decision about where such populations should be placed was taken by plebiscites (public referendums on a single issue), organised by the League of Nations.

Successor states

This term refers to the new states in central and eastern Europe that were created – or, in Poland's case, re-created – by the post-war peace treaties of 1919 and 1920. Apart from Poland (which, since the eighteenth century, had been divided between the pre-1914 German, Austro-Hungarian and Russian empires), two totally-new states were created: Czechoslovakia and Yugoslavia. In addition, Austria and Hungary became two separate states, with reduced territory. Finland and the Baltic States (Estonia, Latvia and Lithuania) also gained their independence, having previously been part of Tsarist Russia.

Most of these new states were economically and militarily weak, and many had significant minority ethnic groups as part of their populations. These ethnic groups often wanted to be ruled by another country, or felt unfairly treated. Because of their general insecurity, some of these states formed alliances. For example, Czechoslovakia, Yugoslavia and Romania formed the Little Entente in 1920–21.

Taisho democracy

This term refers to the period in Japanese history from 1912–26, during which there was an attempt to create a wider, more democratic and liberal political framework in Japan. The name 'Taisho' means 'Great righteousness', and the name was chosen by the new emperor who succeeded following the death of the Meiji emperor. The Meiji Constitution, drawn up in 1889 and which came into force in 1890, had placed considerable power in the hands of the emperor: this included supreme command of the military. During the new Taisho period the emperor suffered from ill-health: as a result, power shifted from the senior statesmen (often known as the *genro*) surrounding the emperor, to the Diet (parliament) of Japan and Japan's two main democratic parties. The main achievement of Taisho democracy was the granting of universal democracy in 1925. The Japanese governments during this period tried to control the influence of the military but, when the Taisho emperor died and was succeeded by Hirohito, Japan saw a rapid shift away from democracy and towards greater ultra-nationalism and militarism. The Hirohito years from 1926–89 are known as the Showa era ('period of Japanese glory').

Figure 1.9 A map showing the territorial changes made in Europe by the peace treaties of 1919–20

1 Introduction

The Wall Street Crash

Wall Street was, and still is, the location of the US Stock Exchange, where shares in companies are bought and sold. Because of over-speculation, followed by panic selling, share prices fell dramatically in October 1929, and investors lost large amounts of money. This collapse – known as the Wall Street Crash – caused a severe economic depression in the USA. As a result of this, the US ended its loans to other countries. Germany was particularly affected by the Wall Street Crash, as it relied on US loans to pay the reparations (compensation) imposed on it by the Treaty of Versailles.

Fact: The economic crisis that began in 2008, and which affected countries across the world, is regarded as the worst global economic crisis since then.

However, most countries were soon plunged into what became known as the Great Depression. This was a global economic event, resulting in widespread distress – high unemployment, inflation, industrial decline in production and trade, and poverty – in most capitalist countries in the 1930s.

One impact was to turn many of its victims towards supporting extremist political parties. Another was that during the 1930s, some countries – notably those with fascist or militaristic regimes – increasingly resorted to an aggressive foreign policy to solve their economic problems.

Zaibatsu

These were the large industrial companies which became increasingly powerful and influential in the interwar period. Many had close family and personal ties to those army officers in the Japanese Army who saw military conquest as a way of aiding Japanese development and, especially after the start of the Great Depression, of solving Japan's growing economic problems.

Summary

Chapter 8 describes the final steps towards war, marking the culmination of all the factors described in Chapter 2–7. By the time you have worked through this book, you should be able to:

- Understand the underlying economic, political and ideological causes behind the policies of military expansionism of Japan in the period 1919–41.
- Understand how Japan was able to take advantage of the condition of China in the 1930s to win imperial conquests.
- Show an awareness of the various responses of the League of Nations and individual states to Japan's expansion in the region.
- Understand why Japan came into conflict with the US as a result of its attempts to secure an empire in Asia in the 1930s.
- Understand how economic, political and ideological developments in Italy and Germany in the 1920s and 1930s led to the desire for military expansion in both countries.
- Show an awareness of the main examples of these two states' military expansion in Europe and Africa in the period 1919–39.

- Understand how the condition of Europe in the 1930s contributed to the growth of military expansionism as a way of dealing with the problems faced by Italy and Germany.
- Understand how the responses of the League of Nations and individual states contributed to the trend towards military expansionism by these two countries.
- Understand the special impact of the Great Depression on such developments in Japan.
- Show a broad understanding of how all these developments eventually led to the outbreak of war in both Asia and Europe, and what became known as the Second World War.

Case Study 1: Japanese Expansion in East Asia, 1931–41

2 Causes of Japanese Expansion

TIMELINE

- **1853 Jul:** US Commodore Perry arrives in Japan
- **1854 Mar:** Treaty of Kanagawa with the US
- **1868 Jan:** Meiji Restoration
  - **Apr:** Five Articles
- **1894 Aug:** First Sino-Japanese War begins
- **1895 Apr:** Treaty of Shimonoseki with China; Triple Intervention
- **1902 Jan:** Anglo-Japanese Alliance
- **1904 Feb:** start of Russo-Japanese War
- **1905 Aug:** Treaty of Portsmouth (USA)
- **1911 Oct:** 'Double Tenth' Revolution in China
- **1915 Jan:** 'Twenty-One Demands' presented to China
- **1916 Jun:** death of Yuan Shikai in China
- **1919 May:** May Fourth Movement protests in China
- **1921 Nov:** start of the Washington Conference
- **1926 Jul:** start of the Northern Campaign in China
- **1927 Apr:** Shanghai Massacre ends First United Front in China
- **1929 Oct:** Wall Street Crash in the US begins the Great Depression
- **1930 Nov:** assassination attempt on prime minister Hamaguchi
- **1931 Sep:** Japan starts invasion of Manchuria
- **1932 May:** assassination of prime minister Inukai
- **1933 Feb:** Japan leaves League of Nations
- **1936 Dec:** Second United Front in China
- **1937 Jul:** Japan invades China

Introduction

This chapter is the first of seven which examine the various factors involved on the road towards the Second World War which, on all levels, was far more destructive than even the First World War – which, it had been hoped, was the 'war to end all wars'. This chapter, and Chapters 3 and 4, will focus on the main developments in Asia and the Pacific, during the period 1931–41, which contributed to the outbreak of war in this region.

For these first three chapters, the focus will be on Japan and its role in the events leading up to the truly global Second World War. At times, though, there will be references to European developments – in particular, those involving Nazi Germany and Fascist Italy – which impacted on the decisions taken by Japan. These European aspects will be examined in more detail in Chapters 5, 6 and 7; Chapter 8 will then deal with the final steps which turned the growing aggression and expansionism of the 1930s into what is generally referred to as the Second World War.

From 1931, Japan launched a series of military campaigns across East Asia and the Pacific which, initially, were highly successful. Sometimes referred to as either the 'Fifteen-Year War' or 'The Greater Asia War', this Pacific War is more often seen as a part – though an important part – of the general Second World War. In some ways, it can be argued that the Second World War actually began in 1931 in Asia, rather than in 1939 in Europe.

KEY QUESTIONS

- How significant was the impact of nationalism and militarism on Japan's foreign policy?
- What impact did Japan's main domestic issues have on foreign policy?
- How significant was China's political instability?

Causes of Japanese Expansion

Overview

- In 1854 and 1858, the US had forced Japanese rulers to sign treaties which ended Japan's policy of seclusion, which had lasted for 200 years. These treaties were mainly designed to open up Japan to US trade.
- From the mid-19th century, nationalism became an increasingly significant force in Japanese politics. In large part, it was directed against Western powers (such as Britain, France and the Netherlands) which had already-existing colonies in Asia.
- In particular, during the late 19th century, tensions with both Tsarist Russia and the US developed as a result – especially as both states wished to expand their influence and control in Asia, thus coming into conflict with Japan's own ambitions.
- Such ambitions were revealed as early as 1876, when Japan forced Korea to sign the Japan-Korea Treaty, forcing Korea to open up to Japanese products.
- This was a first attempt to counter growing Russian aims on Korea. Later, in 1905, Japan declared Korea to be a Japanese 'protectorate'; then, in 1910, Japan formally annexed Korea, making it a part of the Japanese Empire. By occupying Korea, Japan was in a much better position to push its interests as regards mainland China.
- From the late 19th century, many nationalist groups were formed in Japan, which pushed for Japanese expansion in Asia. At the same time, the samurai tradition was increasingly stressed and, as a result, militarism grew. Military leaders increasingly pressed Japanese civilian governments to support an aggressive foreign policy.
- These pressures increased as a result of the impact of the Great Depression on Japan, which greatly increased Japan's long-term problems of limited raw materials and a rising population.
- As China experienced significant political instability for much of the 1920s and 1930s, Japanese expansionists saw this as offering an easy way of solving Japan's problems.

2.1 How significant was the impact of nationalism and militarism on Japan's foreign policy?

The scope of Imperial Japan's war in Asia and the Pacific was certainly impressive – but, before examining the main events in this war, and how the rest of the world reacted to its actions, it is important to establish the causes which led to Japan's imperial expansion after 1931. Two important factors behind the events from 1931–41 were clearly the often closely-associated emergence and development of Japanese nationalism and militarism.

2 Japanese Expansion in East Asia, 1931–41

> **SOURCE A**
>
> In this truly global conflict, Imperial Japan's war on Asia and then the Pacific encompassed a larger geographic area and affected a larger population than the war in Europe and Africa. Japan, with limited help from her colonies, Formosa and Korea, would overrun and subjugate a population over one and a half times larger than Germany did with the help of her six Axis partners… Japan's militarists would cause over half of all Allied civilian casualties.
>
> Gruhl, W. 2007. *Imperial Japan's World War Two, 1931–1945*. New Brunswick, USA. Transaction Publishers. pp. 25–6.

Japanese nationalism before 1900

There were several important elements within Japanese nationalism, which developed in its modern forms from the middle of the 19th century.

Seclusion and early nationalism

Before 1867, Japan was a strictly-segregated feudal society, with a structure very similar to that which predominated in most European countries during the Middle Ages. In Japan, though, this feudal structure lasted longer than in most European states – partly as a result of seclusion from the rest of the world.

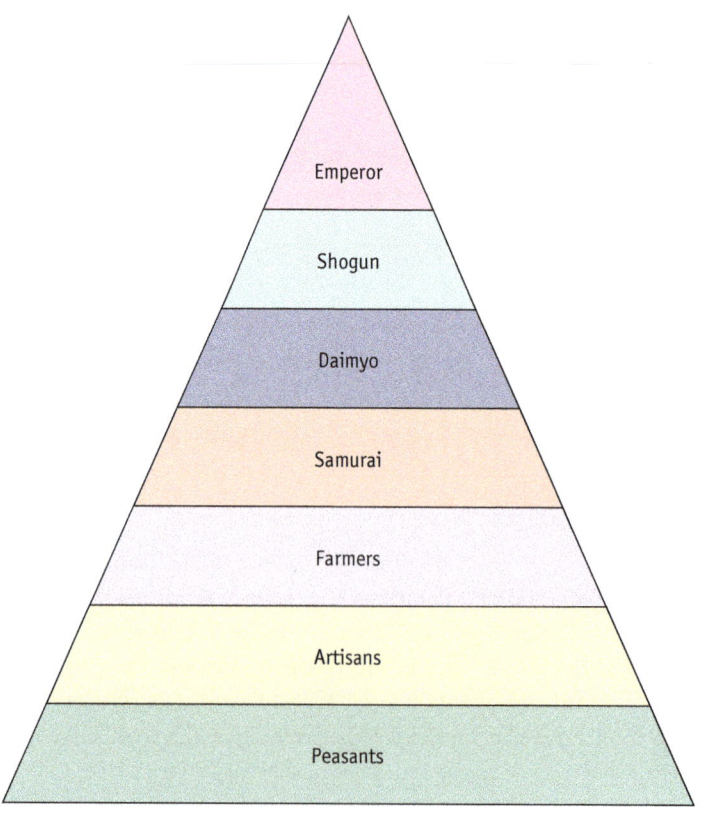

Figure 2.1 Diagram showing the social structure and castes during the Tokugawa shogunate

Causes of Japanese Expansion

Real power in Japan before 1867 increasingly rested with the largest of Japan's feudal landowning clans. Before 1600, various clans had come to dominate, only to be replaced – following military struggles – by another clan. From 1600 to 1867, Japan was ruled by the Tokugawa clan, which had become the largest and most powerful of Japan's various feudal **samurai clans**.

The head of the dominant samurai clan acted as the 'shogun', the commanding general of Japan's armies.

The Tokugawa clan used their domination to establish national unity; and, under the Tokugawa shogunate, Japan had followed a policy of seclusion from the outside world – including from China. This was partly based on an underlying nationalist belief in the superiority of Japanese culture – with a particular desire to assert Japanese culture against the earlier reliance on Chinese culture (for instance, Japan's writing system had been based on the Chinese system). However, it was also based on serious concerns regarding the growing influence and control of Western powers in Asia in the 19th century. The last shogun was **Tokugawa Yoshinobu**.

His attempts to modernise and strengthen Japan's government, and his failure to keep foreign states from increasing their contacts with Japan, led to the rise of opposition from amongst the Satsuma, Choshu and Tosa samurai clans. These feared that his reforms would transfer the emperor's powers to himself and his government. So they raised forces to oppose him, under the slogan: '*sonno joi*' ('revere the emperor, expel the barbarian'). The Tosa clan then suggested that Yoshinobu should resign as shogun and, instead, head a new national council made up of the leading daimyo.

However, although he did resign as shogun and returned all power to the emperor, a brief internal power struggle – the Boshin War – broke out in 1867, as the Satsuma and Choshu were opposed to the Tosa suggestion that Yoshinobu become the head of any new governing council, as they did not want him to have any political power at all in case he was able to dominate it.

Japan and the US

Apart from Britain (which sent a mission to Japan in 1818), one of the main Western powers increasingly interested in extending its interests in Japan was the USA. Its first attempts, in 1837 and 1846, at securing trading relations with Japan were beaten off by Japanese ships – despite the US sending, in a form of '**gun-boat diplomacy**', two warships in the latter year. However, on 8 July 1853, Commodore Perry arrived – with four warships – to repeat US requests for various commercial agreements, and 'promising' to return (with more warships) the following year to receive Japan's response.

Although some of Japan's political leaders – and the emperor's court – favoured national resistance, the Tokugawa shogunate, who were fully aware of China's humiliation in the Opium War of 1839–42, finally agreed to the Treaty of Kanagawa in March 1854, which opened up two of Japan's ports to US trade, and granted the US the position of 'most-favoured-nation'. Thus Japan's policy of seclusion, which had lasted for over 200 years, was finally ended. This was an important turning point in Japan's history: in particular, it led to the rapid emergence of Japan as an important regional and even international power.

The US followed up the 1854 treaty with other treaties further opening up Japan to US trade. In 1858, Japan's government signed the Treaty of Amity and Commerce with

---

samurai clans: Though Japan had an emperor as the nominal head of the political system, *samurai* clans had dominated Japan for centuries. The *samurai* were a special and privileged warrior caste – rather like knights in medieval Europe – who fought for feudal lords, known as *daimyu*. Their code of conduct did not permit surrender and did not respect those who did – these values were revived by nationalists and expansionists in 20th century Japan.

Tokugawa Yoshinobu (1837–1913)
Sometimes referred to as 'Keiki', he became the fifteenth – and last – shogun in 1866. The first Tokugawa shogun had been Tokugawa Ieyasu, who was appointed in 1600. Yoshinobu attempted to modernise various aspects of the Japanese system of government and its military forces. However, many other clans resented his reforms, and growing opposition forced him to resign in 1867. After his resignation, he retreated from the public eye; although, in 1902, the Meiji emperor gave him the rank of prince, for services to Japan – this was the highest rank in the peerage.

'gun-boat diplomacy': This was something much-practised by Britain in Asia – and especially in relation to China. Two 'Opium Wars' were fought against China in order to force the Chinese government to accept Britain's 'right' to sell opium in China. It was western acts such as these which contributed to Japan's nationalist policy of seclusion before 1868.

2 Japanese Expansion in East Asia, 1931–41

Fact: Following the Treaty of Amity and Commerce, similar treaties were soon signed with Britain, France and Russia. These soon became known as the 'unequal treaties' – in particular, as they granted extra-territorial rights to the citizens of the countries signing the treaties. Such western-imposed treaties were not just limited to Japan, but were also made with other Asian countries – and with China in particular. These led to much nationalist resentment in Japan and in other affected countries.

Figure 2.2 The landing of Commodore Perry and his 'black ships' at Yokohama, 8 March 1854

the US. However, this was opposed by the imperial court, which was dominated by nationalists who favoured continuing seclusion and instead advocated 'repelling the barbarians'. Nonetheless, Japan was gradually pressured into signing similar treaties with other Western nations.

SOURCE B

..., early in the nineteenth century, Sato Nobuhiro (1769–1850) asserted an ultranationalism derived from the dictum "Japan is the foundation of the world." In *Kondo hisaku* (*A Secret Strategy for Expansion*), written in 1823, Sato proposed making the whole world "provinces and districts" of Japan. His grand design began with the conquest of China. The first blow should be at Manchuria, "so easy to attack and hold"; then Japanese forces would occupy all of China. Sato laid out the strategy for conquering China in fine detail. The intellectual links, if any, between this ideology of military aggression shaped in a feudal society and concepts of international relations after the Meiji Restoration have not been fully established, However, there is an eerie similarity between the basic ideas of *A Secret Strategy for Expansion* and the concept of the Greater East Asia Co-prosperity Sphere. The ideology of military conquest was at least latently linked to the advocacy of an attack on Korea and other expansionist ventures in the early 1870s. I suspect it was the wellspring nourishing the aggressive [nationalist] ideologies that flourished in the 1920s.

Ienaga, S. 1978. *The Pacific War 1931–1945*. New York. Pantheon Books. p. 5.

KEY CONCEPTS QUESTION

Significance: In what ways did the arrival of US naval ships in the mid-1850s have a significant impact on developments within Japan?

Causes of Japanese Expansion

The Meiji Restoration, 1868

Because these treaties made important concessions to the Western powers, and were all signed without the emperor's consent, pro-imperial and anti-Western factions were able to stir up anti-government sentiments and movements. The main advocates of resistance were often fanatics who were prepared to kill and die for their cause – they were known as '*shishi*' (men of high purpose). Some of their main inspirations were thinkers such as Aizawa Seishisai and Sakuma Zozan – the latter favoured learning from Western science and technology, but stressed the importance of maintaining traditional moral values: 'Eastern morals and Western science'.

An important early shishi leader was **Yoshida Shoin**, a member of the Choshu clan – he wanted the old feudal system to be transformed in a way which, by establishing greater national unity, would enable Japan to resist the growing power of the western nations. He argued that the existing government was incapable of serving the emperor or expelling the Western 'barbarians'. His anti-government activities, and his involvement in an assassination plot, led to his execution in 1859.

Despite this, such feelings of nationalist resentment at Western interference and control continued to grow, and the Choshu clan leaders were able to persuade the emperor to adopt an anti-Western policy and, initially, to get the government to agree to a new seclusion policy. However, when Western vessels were fired upon from Choshu coastal territories, the Western powers retaliated. Though this persuaded the Choshu of the need to modernise their armies, it also led to political moves by the government against the Choshu and other anti-Western groups. This led to fighting in the 1860s. Eventually, however, the powerful Satsuma clan decided to switch its support to the Choshu against the government.

In 1866, the emperor died, and was replaced by emperor Meiji, who was only fifteen years old. He soon came under the influence of those opposed to the government; and the threat of a civil war finally persuaded the shogun, in 1867, to formally restore political authority to the emperor, in order to avoid a national crisis. After some limited fighting, the Satsuma-Choshu clans were victorious and, in January 1868, the emperor established the imperial court in Edo, which was renamed Tokyo. After 1868, the imperial system continued without interruptions in Japan, and one of the main aims of the new imperial government was to prevent Japan from suffering the fate of several other Asian nations: that is, coming even further under the control of Western powers. The policy which was followed was that of 'Enrich the country, strengthen the military' (*fukoku kyohei*). This idea – that, if Japan wanted to prosper, it needed to have strong military forces – would become increasingly influential in the 1920s and 1930s (see section 2.1, Japanese militarism).

Cultural nationalism

From the end of the 17th century, education in Japan was increasingly based on strong nationalistic and pro-imperial principles. In part, this new National Learning involved a rejection of the philosophical and political ideas of Chinese Confucianism, and a turn to Japan's own Shinto religion and philosophy. The influence of such thinkers as Motoori Noringa extended well into the 20th century. It stressed how Japan had been created by the **Sun Goddess** – and how Japan's imperial families were descended from the Sun Goddess, and that the emperor was the 'living god'. This belief became an official state belief after the Meiji Restoration in 1868; was an essential part of the pro-emperor nationalism which was pushed by the political new system; and was taught to all Japanese students until the end of the Second World War.

Figure 2.3 Yoshida Shoin (1830–59)

He set up a private school in order to train those who would be capable of leading the new Japan. Several of the students who attended this school later went on to be important future leaders of Japan in the Meiji period. His execution did not weaken the '*sono-joi*' ('revere the emperor, repel the barbarians') movement and, in fact, he became a martyr and hero of Japanese nationalists in the 1920s and 1930s.

Sun Goddess: Many Japanese before and after 1868 believed that Ameratasu O-mi kami, the Sun Goddess, had had sexual intercourse with Japan's first emperor, Jimmu – thus all subsequent emperors could claim divine origins. As a result, the rising sun became the symbol of Japan.

2 Japanese Expansion in East Asia, 1931–41

SOURCE C

Our country is known as the land of the gods, and of all the nations in the world, none is superior to our nation in morals and customs … [People] must be grateful for having been born in the land of the gods, and repay the national obligation … Now finally imperial rule has been restored,… If we repay even a smidgen of the honourable benevolence we will be doing our duty as the subject of the land of the gods.

Shigeki, T. 1991. *Meiji Ishin to Tenno.* Tokyo. Iwanami. pp. 91–5.

EMPEROR/ IMPERIAL PERIOD	DATES
Meiji	1868–1912
Taisho	1912–26
Showa	1926–89

Table 2.1 A table showing the imperial periods in Japan, from 1868–1989

Figure 2.4 Photo of Japanese troops with the rising sun flag

QUESTION

Why was the rising sun an important symbol in Imperial Japan?

In the early years of the Meiji Restoration, there were many areas of Japanese life and society which were modernised, in order to allow Japan to resist growing Western influence – and to enable Japan itself to become a more powerful nation. From the 1880s, there was a resurgence of cultural nationalism against many of these 'Westernization' developments. Much of this was directed against the more liberal principles – such as democracy and parliamentary government – which had begun to influence Japanese education since the early 1870s. Many saw these attempts to 'civilize and enlighten' the country as undermining traditional Japanese values. Increasingly, the government took control of the approval and printing of school textbooks, to ensure they stressed patriotism, loyalty and obedience to the emperor, and a national history. One of these traditionalists, Motoda Eifu (1818–91), was one of the new emperor's tutors. His influence played a major role in the Imperial Rescript on Education in 1890, which was a determined attempt to foster a **state nationalism**, which stressed the incompatibility between Eastern and Western values. Many were convinced that Western influences were corrupting, and even destroying, traditional Japanese culture and the very essence of Japan itself.

As well as these state-sponsored attempts to create a sense of Japanese nationalism, there were also various important individuals and groups which stressed cultural pride in all things Japanese as a reaction against Western influences and values. In an attempt to halt and even reverse these trends, Japanese nationalists began to revive aspects of Japan's traditional culture – such as Shintoism (Japan's ancient religion) and emperor worship. In addition, there was renewed interest in, and revival of aspects to do with, the samurai tradition and the bushido code.

Not all of those supporting cultural nationalism – for instance, in praising the achievements of Japanese art and poetry – rejected all Western aspects: several thought it would be sensible to adopt the best aspects of Western culture and technology. Such cultural nationalists – for example, Tokutomi Soho (1863–1957) – opposed political nationalism, and wanted Japan to follow peaceful foreign policies.

However, some eventually did become strong nationalists – Soho included. He adopted a much more militant nationalism following the Triple Intervention of April 1895 which saw Western powers force Japan to give up some of the concessions it had forced China to grant it after the First Sino-Japanese War of 1894–95 (see below). From then on, Soho was a strong supporter of Japanese militarism and imperialist conquest. Under emperor Taisho, 1912–26, there was a brief turn towards more liberal Western culture and values – at least, in the urban areas of Japan. But this largely came to an end during the more militaristic and nationalistic 1930s.

Nationalism and modernisation

Although there had been economic difficulties and social unrest before 1868, which had indicated problems within Japanese feudalism and which had created difficulties for the last shogun, it was undoubtedly the arrival of Western powers which finally led to the end of the shogunate. This increasing Western influence had led to a rise of Japanese nationalism which, after 1868, was expressed in several ways. After 1868, Japan's new rulers were determined to adopt Western science and technology, in order to make Japan strong. As early as April 1868, they introduced the Charter Oath of Five Articles: Article Five explicitly stated how the new Japan was going to seek knowledge throughout the world. In addition, the creation of a modern army and navy was a top priority. For the new army, conscription was introduced in 1873, to supplement the use of elements of the more important samurai sections; its training was to be based on the Prussian army which had just defeated France in the Franco-Prussian War, 1870–71.

state nationalism: When Japanese governments indoctrinated school children with nationalistic sentiments, many came to be extremely proud of Japan, and to believe that they were superior to other races. In particular, despite the enormous cultural debt Japan owed China, the Sino-Japanese War of 1894–95 led many to hold a very low view of Chinese people. Such feelings go some of the way in explaining – though not excusing – the behaviour of many Japanese troops in China after 1937.

Theory of knowledge

History, emotion and perception:
According to the philosopher David Hume (1711–76), *'Reason is always and everywhere the slave of the passions.'* Is 'nationalism' an essentially emotional, non-rational, political ideology? When reading and writing history, is it possible for people from different cultures, who have different cultural values, to study such aspects relating to another country?

2 Japanese Expansion in East Asia, 1931–41

Before 1868, Japan had no navy and, at first, the new government lacked the capacity to build naval ships. So, in 1875, three warships were purchased from Britain, and the new Japanese navy was based on the British navy.

Nationalism and imperialist expansion 1894 – 1914

Although the Meiji Restoration had largely been the result of nationalist resentment of Western influence and the 'unequal treaties' they had imposed on Japan, it soon became clear that the new Japan had imperialist designs of its own as regards its neighbours in Asia and the Far East. Its first designs were on Korea.

The First Sino–Japanese War, 1894–95

As early as 1876, Japan had forced Korea to establish diplomatic relations – and to agree to an 'unequal treaty' which gave special rights to Japanese people in Korea. When this led to nationalist protests in Korea, both China and Japan took advantage of the turmoil to send troops into the country. Immediate hostilities between China and Japan were avoided by the Li-Ito Convention of 1885, which was an agreement that both countries could station troops in Korea. But unrest continued and, in August 1894, tensions between China and Japan over rivalry in Korea led to the First Sino-Japanese War. The Japanese army and navy – both of which had been modernised since 1868 – inflicted defeats over the less-advanced Chinese forces. This compelled China to seek peace in 1895. The Treaty of Shimonoseki of April 1895 resulted in Chinese recognition of Korean independence, and saw Japan obtaining various territories, including Formosa (now known as Taiwan). China also had to sign a commercial treaty with Japan, as well as granting some manufacturing rights to Japanese firms.

Figure 2.5 A Japanese print of the Battle of Pyongyang, Korea, 1894. Following the Japanese victory here, Japanese armies then invaded Manchuria

This war – and Japan's victory – engendered strong nationalistic sentiments amongst the Japanese; even previously liberal intellectuals began to advocate continued militarism and imperialism.

Such feelings were increased by the reaction of Western powers to Japan's victory and gains. Tsarist Russia – which also had expansionist plans on both Korea and Manchuria – persuaded France and Germany to join it in forcing Japan to give up some of its mainland gains in China. This Triple Intervention forced Japan to give up the Liaodong (Liaodung) Peninsula, in return for financial compensation. This led to great public anger in Japan, and helped to further arouse support for Japanese militarism and imperialism. From then on, Japanese foreign policy became more nationalistic and aggressive. Initially, the Japanese government began to prepare its military forces for a conflict with Russia.

> **KEY CONCEPTS QUESTION**
> **Causation:** Why did the Triple Intervention of 1895 lead to increased nationalism in Japan?

The Russo–Japanese War, 1904–05

As both Russia and Japan wanted to increase their influence in Korea, after 1895 Japan had increased its economic interests in Korea, including building railways and developing Korea's timber industry in the Yalu River region. However, Russia – which also had growing designs on Manchuria – had similar plans and, in 1896, persuaded China to lease the Liaodong Peninsula to it for twenty years. The Japanese government was furious, as this was what it had just been forced by the Triple Intervention to give up. Russia also got the right to build the South Manchurian Railway, in order to link the Chinese Eastern Railway to Port Arthur. Because Russia wished to have a direct link between Valdivostok and Port Arthur, it wanted to have access through Korea and thus opposed growing Japanese influence there.

Then, using the Boxer Rebellion of 1900 (see section 2.3) as an excuse, Russia sent some of its troops into Manchuria. Although they should have been withdrawn following the defeat of the Rebellion, Russian troops remained. As a result, Japan decided to sign the Anglo-Japanese Alliance with Britain in January 1902. A Japanese proposal that Russia acknowledge its special interests in Korea, in return for recognising Russia's in Manchuria, failed. Consequently, in February 1904 – following a naval skirmish – Japan's government declared war on Russia. Once again, Japan's military and naval forces proved superior and, in 1905, Russia accepted the offer of the US – which had its own interests in the region – to mediate a peace.

In August 1905, the Treaty of Portsmouth (USA) saw Japan get Russia to recognise its special interests in Korea. Japan also got the southern half of Sakhalin Island, the Russian leasehold of the Liaodong Peninsula – and the South Manchurian Railway. However, while the war had aroused Japanese nationalist feelings, these gains were far less than the public in Japan were expecting. As a result, there were many protests by extreme nationalists, some of which resulted in violent clashes with the forces of law and order.

Nonetheless, Japan's victory over Russia made it a major political and military power in the Far East, which was likely to bring it into conflict with other Western powers, such as Britain and the US, which also had interests in the region. Also, as well as confirming its growing control over Korea, it gave Japan a significant interest in Manchuria. In 1905, both Britain and the US also recognised Japan's paramount interests in Korea – in return, Japan promised not to interfere in the US 'protectorate' of the Philippines. These agreements allowed Japan to consolidate its control of

2 Japanese Expansion in East Asia, 1931–41

Figure 2.6 Russo–Japanese War, 1904–05

Causes of Japanese Expansion

Figure 2.7 A cartoon about the Russo–Japanese War, 1904–05

Korea – in 1905, Korea was declared a Japanese protectorate. Five years later, in 1910, despite significant military resistance, Korea was formally annexed by Japan and made part of the Japanese empire.

The First World War and Japanese nationalism

Another factor which led to increasing nationalism in Japan was the First World War and its aftermath. The Anglo–Japanese Alliance of 1902 had been renewed in 1905 and, as soon as the First World War began, Japan entered on the side of the Triple Entente (see the Introduction). The main war aim of the Japanese government was to take over the German concessions in China – which was also on the side of the Allies. In a short space of time, Japan gained control of German holdings in the Shandong (Shandung) Peninsula, as well as the harbour of Jiaozhou (Kiaochow), which had been leased to Germany by the Chinese in 1898. In addition, it also occupied the Caroline and Marianne islands in the Pacific. As a consequence of the war, Japan had thus built up a strong position for itself in the Far East.

The Twenty-One Demands

In January 1915, Japan secretly presented China with the Twenty-One Demands – or 'Grievances'. These included demands that Germany's concessions be transferred to Japan, and for Chinese recognition of special Japanese interests in various areas, including south Manchuria. Others, however, demanded Japanese influence over aspects of China's political, financial and military affairs – including that China should accept Japanese 'advisors' in its government.

> **QUESTION**
>
> How did Japan's victory in the Russo–Japanese War of 1904–05 strengthen its position in Asia?
>
> Why did this victory present potential problems as regards Japan's relationships with other major world states?

Fact: Up to 1915, US relations with Japan had been quite good – for instance, the US had been generally supportive of Japan during its war with Russia, and had accepted Japanese control of Korea. But significant conflicts of interests in China then began to emerge. Japan wanted the US to recognise – as it had in relation to Korea – that it also had 'paramount interests' in China. Although, in 1917, the US recognised that Japan had special interests in China, it insisted that China's territorial integrity should be upheld. It also maintained that the USA's 'Open Door' policy should prevail in China – this explicitly opposed the establishment of any special spheres of influence.

2 Japanese Expansion in East Asia, 1931–41

> **QUESTION**
> According to **Source D**, what were Japan's main aims as regards Chinese territory in 1919?

> **QUESTION**
> What were the main reasons that Japanese nationalists were angered by the terms of the Treaty of Versailles?

Fact: Though concessions in Shandong were granted as a result of the Treaty of Versailles, Japan was eventually forced to agree in 1922, at the Washington Conference, to withdraw its troops from these areas and return them to China. Although Japan was allowed to retain the economic concessions, to many nationalists, this agreement of 1922 was an insult – and one of the factors behind Japan's expansionist policy towards China in the 1930s.

Fact: Despite proclaiming after 1941 that it wanted to create an 'Asia for the Asians', by 'liberating' Asian colonies from their Western rulers – and even establishing a Greater East Asia Co-Prosperity Sphere – the Japanese rulers never extended equal rights to the people of the lands they conquered. In particular, the army often treated the newly-liberated people extremely brutally.

These were opposed by the US, which, although it agreed that Japan had some rights for special recognition in China, was increasingly developing its own interests in China. Eventually, Japan was forced to agree to withdraw these more contentious items and China then signed the agreement.

The US was also concerned by Japanese actions in Russia, following the Bolshevik Revolution of 1917. Along with many other Western powers – including the US – Japan sent in an army of 72,000 to oppose the Bolsheviks. These were sent to Siberia and remained there until late 1922 – two years after the US had withdrawn its own troops from Soviet territory. Japan's slowness to withdraw was a clear indication that it also saw that part of the Far East as a potential area for expansion. Although Japan finally recognised the new Communist government of Russia in 1925, it continued to keep a watchful eye on this part of East Asia.

The 'Mutilated Victory'

Japan had been on the Allied side in the First World War, and it was disappointed with its gains from the 1919–20 peace settlements.

> **SOURCE D**
> At Paris, the Chinese delegates demanded that the German concessions in the [Shandong] province, and the port of Kiaochow, should be returned to China. Japan argued that Germany had yielded them up to her, and that she would negotiate about them not at the conference itself but in direct talks with the Chinese. Already in 1918, in an exchange of notes with the Chinese warlord government in Peking, the Japanese had laid claims to rights far in excess of those the Germans had enjoyed. They had also secured the agreement of the United States that 'territorial contiguity' assured Japan of a special position on the Chinese mainland, and her claims had received diplomatic backing from Britain and France during the war.
>
> Henig, R. 1995. *Versailles and After, 1919–1933*. London. Routledge. p. 28.

At first, US president Woodrow Wilson tried to pressurise the Japanese representatives at Paris into giving up their country's occupation of Jiaozhou and the Shandong Peninsular. However, he was eventually forced to recognise Japan's conquests of these areas; in fact, criticism of the agreements over Shandong was one of the reasons why the US eventually refused to ratify the Treaty of Versailles.

Yet, although its control of German concessions in the Shandong Peninsula, and of the Pacific islands, was eventually approved, Japan did not obtain all it had wanted. As regards Germany's former Pacific colonies, it was disappointed not to be given outright ownership. Thus, nationalists felt Japan had not been fairly treated. Another country which experienced similar disappointment was Italy which, like Japan, had fought on the Allied side. Italian nationalists felt Italy's legitimate territorial demands – despite earlier promises made by Britain in 1915 – had not been met (see section 5.1, Impact of the First World War and the Peace Treaties 1914–19). By 1939, these two 'disappointed losers' – Japan and Italy – had both become joined to Germany by various treaties and agreements in what became known as the Axis Powers; and all three were to fight on the same side in the Second World War.

Causes of Japanese Expansion

Racism and nationalism

Another aspect of the post-war settlements also helped increase national sentiments in Japan. In 1919, at the Paris Peace Conferences, Japan proposed a **'Racial Equality'** clause, to be part of the Covenant of the new League of Nations. This was mainly an attempt to secure equality for Japanese nationals, and to ensure that Japan would be treated as a great power and thus have the same rights as members – such as Britain and France – to establish an overseas empire. In the end, this was blocked by both the US and Britain. This refusal was widely reported in the Japanese media, and played a part in increasing nationalist feelings, and in turning Japan away from close cooperation with Western powers.

Japanese militarism

Many people in Japan had great national pride, in part based on their belief that Japan deserved a special status in view of the 'fact' that the Sun Goddess had selected Japan as her 'chosen land'. However, in addition, Japanese nationalism was also closely linked to the associated factor of militarism.

The samurai legacy

The military had enormous respect and prestige in Japanese society. This was, in part, the result of the **samurai legacy** of pre-1868 Japan. From the early 20th century and during the interwar years, the elements of loyalty to the emperor and self-sacrifice were given much greater prominence than they had had during the Tokugawa shogunate. In particular, the military – and civilian nationalists – consciously adapted and developed the samurai legacy and the bushido code to obtain the general public's support for their expansionist aims.

Militarism and politics after the First World War

During the 1920s, militarism increased – especially after the start of the Great Depression – and, along with more general nationalism, was increasingly associated with the idea of territorial expansion as a way both for solving Japan's problems and for making Japan a regional and even a world power.

In Showa Japan, before and during the Second World War, bushido was used by the military commanders to impress upon Japan's soldiers the ideas that war was 'purifying' and that death was a soldier's duty – along with the idea that bushido would provide soldiers with a 'spiritual shield' which would allow them to fight to the end. Eventually, these beliefs culminated in the **kamikaze suicide missions** in the closing stages of the war.

Throughout the 1920s, a new and more hardline officer class emerged and tried to influence the foreign policy adopted by Japanese governments. They increasingly acted outside the control of civilian politicians – especially in border areas, such as Manchuria. This was significant, as many of these officers became convinced that Japan had been unfairly treated by the Western powers in world distribution of territories and raw materials. As the economic effects of the Great Depression hit Japan, they became convinced that the only way to ensure Japan's survival as a great nation was to expand into new territories in order to obtain vital raw materials, and to gain access to new markets for Japanese goods. By the 1930s, views that overpopulation and lack of sufficient raw materials were the main cause of Japan's difficulties were frequently

---

samurai legacy: This included the bushido code: 'bushido' translates as 'samurai's way' – rather like the 'chivalric code' by which knights in medieval Europe were supposed to conduct themselves. This samurai bushido code was based on moral values such as loyalty, honour, self-sacrifice and fighting to the death. For instance, if a samurai failed to uphold his honour – e.g. by surrendering or being captured – he could only regain it by committing suicide. However, before 1868, bushido also had pacifistic elements and stressed compassion for members of the lower castes.

kamikaze suicide missions: In the final stages of the war in the Pacific, 'Special Attack Units' were formed by Japan's air force. Their role was to fly planes loaded with various explosives and crash them into Allied shipping. The first such kamikaze attacks took place in October 1944, during the battle of Leyte Gulf, after Japan had suffered several crucial military defeats. Later, the Japanese navy also developed such units. About 20% of such attacks were successful.

2 Japanese Expansion in East Asia, 1931–41

Toyama Mitsuru (1855–1944)

He became the main inspiration of right-wing nationalists who wanted Japan's governments to adopt an expansionist policy which would extend Japan's border up to the Amur River. In 1881, he had founded the *Genyosha* ('Black Ocean Society'), an ultra-nationalist secret society. Its aims were to honour the emperor and respect the Empire.

Okawa Shumei (1886–1957)

He founded many right-wing societies and his writings inspired many of the right-wing ultra-nationalist extremist groups which dominated Japanese politics in the 1930s. In 1919, he – along with Kita Ikki – formed *Yuzonsha*, a nationalist discussion group; and, in 1924, he founded the magazine, *Nippon*, which called for a military government for Japan and expansion into Manchuria. He was also involved in various assassination and coup plots in the 1930s.

Hiranuma Kiichi (1867–1952)

He had become Minister of Justice in 1923 and, in 1939, briefly served as president of Japan. After the attempted coup on 26 February 1936, in which several political and military leaders were killed, Hiranuma followed the request of the emperor and began to distance himself from the *Kokuhonsha* group; later on, he disbanded it.

Figure 2.8 A kamikaze attack on the aircraft carrier USS Essex, on 25 November 1944. Though the attack caused extensive damage (and fifteen deaths), the ship was quickly repaired

expressed in most Japanese publications on social and economic issues. As increasingly pointed out by many liberal and even radical Japanese professors and publications – who were otherwise critical of the growing influence of Japan's military leaders over civilian governments – the worldwide restrictions on Japanese immigration and goods – were contributing to Japan's economic and social difficulties, and to the growth of support for expansionist policies.

Developments in the 1920s and 1930s

Once Tokugawa Keiki had given up political power, the imperial system had been restored, with young Emperor Meiji at its head. Although the decades which followed are known as the Meiji Restoration, the emperor was in fact strongly guided by the leaders of the Satsuma-Choshu clans. After the First World War, militarism and nationalism became increasingly connected – and increasingly expansionist in outlook and aims.

Nationalist groups after 1918

Various groups emerged around the beginning of the 20th century. Some of the main leaders and activists were **Toyama Mitsuru**, Inoue Nissho and **Okawa Shumei**.

One event which served further to reinforce right-wing nationalist feelings was the great earthquake which hit Japan in 1923. In Tokyo, the earthquake caused a massive fire, in which over 100,000 people died. False rumours that the fire had been started by Koreans led to mob attacks, in which hundreds of Koreans were killed. This led to the attempted assassination of Hirohito, the imperial regent. The attack saw the Minister of Justice, **Hiranuma Kiichi** – along with Sadao Araki – set up *Kokuhonsha* (the National Foundation Society) in 1924, to strengthen the 'national spirit'. This was an extreme nationalist movement, partly inspired by Mussolini's fascism, which aimed to destroy liberalism, individualism and party politics.

Causes of Japanese Expansion

In 1927, General **Tanaka Giichi** became prime minister – his sentiments were very sympathetic to right-wing militant nationalists, who were beginning to become increasingly influential. Under him, earlier moves towards democracy and liberalism came to an end, to be replaced by increasing militarism and the road to war.

The Washington Conference

Both nationalism and militarism in Japan grew as a result of attempts by the Western powers to limit the expansion of Japan's navy. In 1921–22, the main powers had agreed naval arms limitations. In early 1930, the powers met again, in London – this time to negotiate reductions in other warships. Japan's government agreed to a 10 : 10 : 6 US : Britain : Japan ratio in heavy cruisers, and a 10 : 10 : 7 ratio in destroyers. For submarines, Japan was able to obtain parity with the US. However, Japan's naval leaders were strongly opposed to the London Agreement on heavy cruisers, wanting instead the same ratio as for destroyers. The *Seiyukai* party agreed, and attacked the Hamaguchi government, stating that no government had the right to overrule the naval general staff on matters of defence – instead, they argued, the supreme command were independent of the government (see section 3.1, The Mukden Incident).

These arguments were soon used by militarists and nationalists to challenge the civilian governments in the 1930s. In addition, those naval leaders who had signed the London Agreement became assassination targets – as did the prime minister, who was seriously wounded in 1930 and thus forced to resign; he died soon afterwards. The governments which followed were increasingly under pressure – and assassination attempts – from right-wing ultra-nationalists.

Nationalism, militarism and the Great Depression

As the economic crisis caused by the Great Depression hit Japan after 1929, these – and other – nationalists and militarists increasingly demanded Japanese expansion on the mainland of Asia. Like the German nationalists after the First World War, Japan's nationalists increasingly came to believe that their country needed to end its dependence on Western powers such as the US and should, instead, create its own empire which would ensure that Japan could be self-sufficient.

One civilian nationalist who favoured such imperial expansion was Ikezaki Tadakata.

> **Tanaka Giichi (1864–1929)**
> His government, which lasted from 1927–29, is generally seen as beginning what became known as 'Showa fascism', as opposed to the earlier period of 'Taisho democracy', which had existed between 1912–26. He adopted an increasingly aggressive foreign policy in relation to China.

SOURCE E

It is well known that Japan's overpopulation grows more serious every year. Where should we find an outlet for these millions? [The Western Powers have divided up the world] ... the only remaining area is the Asian mainland. Moreover, Japan's claim to the region is written in the blood and treasure of two wars. [Even if the United States opposed Japan's legitimate expansion in China]..., we should resolutely pursue or interests.

Extract from Ikezaki Tadakata's writings in 1929. Quoted in Ienaga, S. 1978. *The Pacific War 1931–1945*. New York. Pantheon Books. p. 11.

> **QUESTION**
> With reference to its origins purpose and content, assess the value and limitation of **Source E** for historians studying the reasons for Japanese expansionist aims in the 1930s.

2　Japanese Expansion in East Asia, 1931–41

Although the nationalist ideology of writers and politicians in the 1920s such as Ikezaki were clearly expansionist, on their own, they would not have been sufficient to take Japan into another world war. This only became possible as a result of two factors: the impact of the Great Depression, and the fact that Japan's military leaders increasingly adopted such views – and were prepared to act on them.

During the 1920s, these views were increasingly taken up by army officers – including those in the Kwantung Army in Manchuria, who feared the Chinese Nationalists, led by Jiang Jieshi, might be able to create a unified and strong government in China, which would then be able to resist Japanese incursions.

SOURCE F

In the 1930s what came to be emphasized was the sanctity of the Emperor system originating with the Sun Goddess, the inviolability of the national polity, the uniqueness and superiority of the Japanese race and its history, and the mission to bring the eight-corners of the world under one roof … The notion that Manchuria was important for Japanese interests persisted from the time of the Russo-Japanese war. Among civilian groups that favoured Japanese expansion into Manchuria and Mongolia was the Amur River Society, which was founded in 1901. After the Russo-Japanese War Toyama Mitsuru … became the leader of the Amur River Society… Another radical nationalist was Inoue Nissho (1886–1967) who organized extreme nationalist societies, including the Blood Brotherhood League whose object was to assassinate thirteen prominent leaders.

Hane, M. 2013. *Japan: A Short History*. London. Oneworld Publications. pp. 140–1.

From the late 1920s, young military officers began to organise nationalistic political circles. In part, this was the result of their opposition to the disarmament policies associated with the Washington Conferences. Others – especially those from rural areas – were angered by the lack of help given to poor peasants during the Depression, while politicians and industrialists lived in luxury in the cities. This was just one motive for the assassination of prime minister Inukai in 1932. Many felt that things had deteriorated since the death of Yamagata in 1922, since when the influence of the military in politics had declined. In particular, they came to believe that party politics was weakening Japan as a power in Asia.

Some of the groups formed included the *Issekikai* (One Evening Society), formed in 1929 by middle-level officers. Some of these – such as Tojo Hideki – later became national leaders in the 1930s. In 1930, the *Sakurakai* (Cherry Blossom Society) was formed – to overthrow the civilian government, and instead to establish a military dictatorship. Their fear was that, with the navy already reduced in strength, the next victim would be the army. They increasingly came to think that the whole political system needed 'clearing out' in order to restore Japan's traditional 'spiritual values' – these included belief in the superiority of the Japanese people and culture, and the 'emperor system', as opposed to parliamentary government.

These concerns were shared by civilian ultra-nationalists – although at first they were less interested in expansion on the Asian continent, they also favoured a totalitarian military government. These civilian nationalists were increasingly opposed to Western nations and all aspects associated with Western culture – including liberalism and democracy, which came to be seen as fundamentally opposed to their version of 'Japanism'.

An academic who had written that the emperor was just one element of the state – not above it – was dismissed from his post at the University of Tokyo in 1935, and was later nearly assassinated.

The anger at this academic's ideas led to such ultra-nationalist protests that the government was forced, in 1937, to issue the Fundamentals of Our National Polity. This re-asserted that the emperor was a descendant of the Sun Goddess, and that he was the head of Japan and its people. It also stressed loyalty, patriotism and the martial spirit; and stated that all undesirable thought and movements – such as democracy, socialism and communism – were caused by Western liberalism and individualism. These were all beliefs which formed part of Italian Fascism and German Nazism, although Japan never developed a fascist party which was able to come to power, as happened in these two other states.

2.2 What impact did Japan's main domestic issues have on foreign policy?

> **ACTIVITY**
> Carry out some further research on Japan's nationalist groups after 1918. Then write a couple of paragraphs to show what impact such groups had on Japan's domestic politics.

As well as the developments regarding the growth of nationalism and militarism, Japan also experienced important economic and political changes – both of which help explain Japan's expansionist foreign policy after 1931.

Japan's economy 1868–1929

The Meiji Restoration

Following the Meiji Restoration, Japan underwent extensive industrialisation, under the slogan of 'Enrich the country, strengthen the military'. This was an explicit recognition of the fact that a strong economy and military would ensure Japan would never again be bullied or dominated by Western powers. These developments bore fruit as early as 1905 when, much to the surprise of the West, Japan defeated Russia in the Russo–Japanese War of 1904–05.

Although Japan's economy was rapidly modernised after 1868, Japan had two major domestic problems: it lacked sufficient raw materials to support its aim of being a 'great power'; and there was insufficient land for its large and growing population. In addition to these long-term problems, Japan also experienced several short-term economic problems in the 1920s. For instance, in early 1927, there was a banking crisis, which resulted in many medium- and small-sized banks going bankrupt. One effect of these developments was to concentrate financial control in the hands of the bigger banks. In industry, too, the smaller industries folded and the larger ones were able to increase their monopolistic positions. The prime minister at the time, Tanaka, responded by increasing military spending and stepping up the economic exploitation of Japan's colonies. However, these did little to solve Japan's domestic economic crisis. Not long after, the Great Depression

2 Japanese Expansion in East Asia, 1931–41

Minseito political party: This political party was one of the two main political parties in Japan, and had been formed in 1927. It was a centrist, liberal and pro-democracy party, which first came to power in 1929. It tried to achieve better relations with the West, and to reduce the control of the military over the government. Its main rival was the *Seiykai* party, which was more conservative. In 1940, these two parties merged with the government-controlled party to form a wartime coalition.

began to have a catastrophic effect on the Japanese economy. After Tanaka's resignation in 1929 – because of his refusal to be open about who was responsible for the assassination of Zhang Zuolin, the Manchurian warlord – (see section 3.1, Manchuria, 1931), Hamaguchi, leader of the **Minseito political party**, became prime minister.

Economic impact of the Great Depression

Although Japan's industry had been modernising and expanding since 1900, it was not self-sufficient in coal, iron, oil, tin or rubber. Japan thus suffered badly during the worldwide Depression. In addition, the Japanese economy largely depended on exports. The important silk industry – Japan's main export – was particularly hit badly as sales of silk, which was a luxury product, fell dramatically as the Depression deepened and widened across the world. Much of Japan's total production of silk was exported to the US but, as the Depression began there and unemployment rose significantly, the demand for such luxury goods declined dramatically. During the first year alone, 1929–30, Japanese silk exports dropped by nearly 40%, with prices crashing by approximately 80% in the 1930s compared to the 1920s. In addition to Japan's silk industry, its cotton textile industries, and its mining and heavy industries, were also badly affected. Between 1929 and 1931, Japan's exports dropped by 50%, over 50% of the affected industries went out of business and production and employment in these industries declined by over 30%. By 1931, the Depression had led to 50% of all Japan's factories closing down. Japan's rice farmers were also badly hit.

These problems were made worse by the fact that Japan actually had few raw materials, so it relied heavily on the import of such resources from Manchuria. In addition, as the Depression worsened around the world, many countries reduced their imports and imposed tariffs on foreign goods, in order to protect their own industries. At the same time, during this period, Japan's population was increasing rapidly, at a rate of approximately 1 million per year. As much of Japan is mountainous, the amount of fertile agricultural land was relatively limited. Consequently, Japan was relatively overcrowded, and it proved increasingly difficult to feed Japan's expanding population; as a result, increasing poverty was soon accompanied by inadequate food supplies. By the late 1920s, there was considerable hardship in many rural areas. The situation was made worse by the adoption of racist immigration laws by the US and other states, which severely restricted the emigration of poor Japanese suffering from the effects of the Depression.

SOURCE G

The Depression hit the Japanese economy very hard. Unemployment rose, farm prices crashed, and exports shrank. The slump was blamed on the pro-Western policies of the Japanese democratic governments during the 1920s. In 1930, at the height of the Depression, a political crisis gripped Japan, which resulted in the growth of the influence of military factions and the collapse of parliamentary democracy. The Japanese army became a state within a state, which civilian government had difficulty controlling. The pro-Western Japanese democratic leaders who had influenced foreign policy during the 1920s were replaced – or in many cases assassinated – by anti-Western factions, who supported a rapid growth in military spending.

Comments made by a Western observer about the reaction in China to the terms of the peace treaties. Quoted in Lynch, M. 1996. *China: from Empire to People's Republic, 1890–1949*. London. Hodder. p. 33.

Prime minister Hamaguchi tried to deal with these economic problems by economic retrenchment (cutting government expenditure in order to stabilise the economy), but this was inadequate. The impact of these economic problems soon adversely affected the working class and the peasants, leading to some increased left-wing opposition.

The Depression: militarism and nationalism

At least as important as the economic impact of the Depression was the increasing discontent and hostility of right-wing militarists – these argued for an expansionist foreign policy, to replace the existing policy of international cooperation. The main advocate of this was Shidehara Kijuro (1872–1951) who had been foreign minister in several governments during the 1920s. Thus, in 1930, Japan had agreed to additional naval restrictions, in line with the earlier Washington Conference, at the negotiations in London. After Hamaguchi's shooting in late 1930, Shidehara took over as acting prime minister – but was continually attacked as a traitor. Eventually, Wakatsuki Reijiro – who had been prime minister from 1926–27 – became prime minister again in April 1931. He, too, though, was troubled by right-wing nationalists who plotted further assassinations. In September, he failed to deal with the Manchurian Incident (see section 4.1, Crisis over Manchuria), staged by the Japanese Kwantung officers, and was forced to resign. His replacement was Inukai Tsuyoshi (1855–1932), the leader of the *Seiyukai*. He, too, was attacked by right-wing ultra-nationalists, and became one of the names on their assassination lists.

> **QUESTION**
> Why did the Great Depression have such a serious impact on Japan's economy in the 1930s?

An aspect which played into the hands of those who advocated a more expansionist foreign policy was the fact that the Depression caused many nations – including Britain and the US – to protect their domestic industries by raising tariffs on foreign goods. Thus Japan was increasingly denied access to markets and sources of raw materials on equal terms. Increasingly, Britain and France – with their own empires in the Asian and African continents – acted as models for the expansionists in Japan who argued that Japan needed its own imperial market in order to protect Japanese industry. As the Depression's effects worsened, they thus began to argue for a crusade against the West and for a 'new order' in Asia – most immediately, Japanese expansionists looked to northern China as the most obvious target area for increasing Japan's empire.

Overall, the impact of the Great Depression arguably was the main factor in worsening relations between the major world states and thus ending the relative era of international cooperation which had existed for most of the 1920s. In Japan, as in many other badly-affected states, the economic and social impact of the Depression pushed increasing numbers towards aggressive nationalism and a growing hostility towards liberalism and parliamentary politics. As in both Fascist Italy (and later, in Nazi Germany), calls for a '**new international order**' in domestic politics in Japan were equally applied to the international scene. The most obvious impact of the Depression on Japan's foreign policy in 1930s can be seen by comparing the general attitude of that period to that prevailing in the 1920s. In the latter period, Japanese statesmen were prepared to operate within the Western international system – as long as Japan was treated as an equal. However, the 1930s industrial slump resulting from Depression saw Japanese goods discriminated against via tariffs, while Japan's equal access to markets and raw materials was increasingly restricted. This resulted in the growing influence of nationalists and militarists over Japanese foreign policy – these increasingly pushed for expansion which, they argued, was the only way Japan could solve its problems.

'new international order': Japan, along with Fascist Italy and Nazi Germany, was the most important state calling for a 'new international order'. According to Mussolini, such countries were 'have-not' or 'proletarian' nations, which were being deliberately and unfairly denied the vast territories and economic resources enjoyed by 'bourgeois' nations such as the US, Britain and France.

2 Japanese Expansion in East Asia, 1931–41

SOURCE H

A national consensus approved of an imperialist policy towards China, but there were sharp disagreements and differing emphases over implementation. At one end of the spectrum were the moderates who favoured enlarging Japanese interests by peaceful means: investment, opening new markets for Japanese goods, and co-operation with England and America. At the other end were the expansionists and militarists, who were prepared to go to war if necessary to suppress Chinese nationalism and resistance and drive England and America off the Asian continent. A variety of views and strategies lay between these two poles. Japan's policy towards China was not always asserted with military power.

Ienaga, S. 1978. *The Pacific War 1931–1945*. New York. Pantheon Books. pp. 9–10.

Political developments in Japan after 1918

Though in theory, Japan was a parliamentary state, real power lay with the emperor, the military leaders and the owners of the biggest industrial and banking firms.

Parliamentary democracy

Immediately after the First World War and the end of the power of the Meiji emperor and his oligarchy, there followed almost a decade of peaceful civilian and parliamentary government. **Shidehara Kijuro** was foreign minister of Japan from 1924–27 and again from 1929–31, in both the Kenseikai and Minseito parties' governments – and he was a supporter of international diplomacy and disarmament. In fact, his commitment to these principles led to the term 'Shidehara diplomacy'.

However, this attempt at 'normal' parliamentary government did not mean that Japan gave up expansionist ambitions. Even Shidehara himself was an expansionist. In 1928, he made a speech about the anti-foreign movement that was developing in China, and its spreading boycott of foreign goods, which aimed to raise Chinese national consciousness and end the unequal treaties. Whilst calling on the Chinese people to show restraint, he pointed out that Japan had ended the unequal treaties imposed on her by strengthening herself, not via illegal actions – and he urged China to do the same.

However, his expansionist views emerged in 1931 – just before the Japanese military unilaterally began their invasion of Manchuria – at a meeting with a Chinese diplomat over Manchuria, when he claimed that Japanese influence and control were justified.

SOURCE I

Chinese seem to think Manchuria is part of China but it used to be Russian. There is no doubt that if the situation had been left alone, Manchuria would soon have ceased to be under Ch'ing authority. The only reason the Manchu regime was able to hold this vast fertile region was a Japanese military presence. Since the Russo-Japanese War, Manchuria has enjoyed peace and prosperity unparalleled in any other Chinese area. Japanese are convinced that the development of the northeast region is at least partly due to our businesses and investment there.

Comments made by Shidehara Kijuro, in a meeting with the Chinese diplomat Ch'en Yu-jen in 1931, setting out his views concerning Japanese influence in Manchuria. These comments were made a month before the Manchurian Incident; at the time, Shidehara was Japan's foreign minister and did not support an expansionist foreign policy.

Quoted in Ienaga, S. 1978. *The Pacific War 1931–1945*. New York. Pantheon Books. p. 10.

Shidehara Kijuro (1872–1951)

He was appointed as Japan's ambassador to the US in 1919, but was extremely disappointed by the USA's adoption of racist immigration laws which discriminated against Japanese people. He was Japan's main negotiator at the Washington Naval Conference, which saw the major Pacific naval powers agree to some disarmament and to several international agreements intended to create stability in the Pacific. He favoured a liberal and peaceful foreign policy and, in particular, tried to maintain good relations with China. His opposition to expansion in China during the 1920s was bitterly opposed by sections in the military. He was forced to resign from office in 1931, because of his opposition to the actions of the Kwantung Army in Manchuria in 1931. At the end of the Second World War, he was prime minister during the US occupation of Japan from 1945–46.

Causes of Japanese Expansion

The influence of the zaibatsu

One result was that Japan's military forces – especially the army – played an increasingly important role in influencing the policies of Japanese governments. During the early 20th century, many military leaders also formed close ties with the owners of the large industrial and financial **zaibatsu**.

They had existed before 1900, but became increasingly dominant in the 1920s, and were increasingly able to influence Japan's national and foreign policies. For instance, corporations such as the Mitsui corporation – which had strong links to the Imperial Japanese Army – and the Mitsubishi group – connected to the Imperial Japanese Navy – were able to dominate the national and foreign policies of Japanese governments by their strong connections to various political parties.

Of the various *zaibatsu*, there were four main ones by 1900. These were as follows: Sumitomo, Mitsui, Mitsubishi and Yasuda. After defeating Russia in the 1904–05 Russo–Japanese War, other less-powerful zaibatsu were formed. By 1941, the 'Big Four' alone controlled over 30% of Japan's mining, metals and chemicals industries, and almost 50% of industrial equipment businesses.

As stated above, the end of the 1920s can be seen as the end of earlier attempts to develop a democratic system, and the start, instead, of the road towards increased militarism and eventual war. The first signs had come under the government of General Tanaka Giichi, the leader of the *Seiyukai* Party, and who was prime minister from 1927–29. In particular, he had met with army leaders to develop a China policy.

Opposition to liberalism and democracy

As Japan's economic situation worsened, the influence and activities of anti-democratic military and patriotic groups increased. Many right-wing nationalists believed that the crisis justified attempts to remove political leaders whose peaceful foreign policies blocked military expansion as a way of ending the economic crisis. In November 1930, a member of a patriotic society attempted to assassinate the then prime minister, Osachi Hamaguchi. In March 1931, a group planned a coup which was intended to put General Ugaki Kazushige in charge of the government, but he refused to cooperate with the plot. Later, in October, they hatched a similar plot – this time, to assassinate prime minister, Wakatsuki and to replace him with general Araki Sadao, who was widely known to be anti-foreign and a supporter of 'Japanism' and imperialism. However, he – like Ugaki, refused to agree – though significantly, in both cases, none of the plotters were punished.

Japan's economic difficulties were an important factor in the emergence of 'fascistic' elements which began to take an increasingly anti-liberal and anti-democratic stance. One important leader was Kita Ikki (1884–1937) who – like Mussolini – moved rapidly away from being a socialist and, instead, began to call for a form of 'national socialism', with greater power for the emperor. His ideas increasingly influenced many young army officers, and he was involved in the coup attempt of 26 February 1936 – for this he was executed in 1937. Also important was Inuoe Nissho (1886–1967), who organised several extreme nationalist societies, including the Blood Brotherhood League – this group planned the assassination of thirteen prominent Japanese leaders. Another important ultra-nationalist was Okawa Shumei (1886–1957) who founded many right-wing societies and was involved in several assassination plots in the 1930s. The *Kokuhonsha*, organised by Hiranuma Kiichi, was a nationalist society which included several leading political, business and military leaders.

In the late 1920s and early 1930s, young military officers organised political circles – initially, as many opposed the disarmament policies followed by government leaders

---

zaibatsu: This term translates as 'wealthy clique', and applied to the largest corporations and conglomerates which increasingly dominated the Japanese economy – especially after the end of the First World War.

QUESTION

Why were the *zaibatsu* able to exert such influence during the 1930s?

Historical debate:
Most historians – both Japanese and European – have tended to argue that, unlike Italy and Germany, Japan was not a fascist state. G. M. Wilson, for instance, saw the Japanese system of government in the 1930s as a statist, bureaucratic regime – not a form of 'fascism from above' or a 'military fascism' – which was based on the idea of a strong central government controlling economic planning. Others, such as R. Sims, have questioned this, and – while identifying certain differences – have nonetheless pointed out several shared features between the systems of rule in Japan, Italy and Germany during the 1930s.

during the Taisho and early Showa period. In these circles, right-wing civilians joined forces with military nationalists – both of which were increasingly opposed to democracy.

Political violence in the 1930s

In 1932, the Blood Brotherhood League (BBL) assassinated both the minister of finance and the director of the Mitsui zaibatsu – altogether, the group had an assassination list of thirteen possible targets. Although Inoue Nissho was sentenced to 15 years, imprisonment, the group continued with their plans. In conjunction with several right-wing nationalist naval officers who favoured an imperialistic foreign policy, they plotted the assassination of prime minister Inukai Tsuyoshi. Although, as leader of the then opposition *Seiyukai* party, he had at first criticised Wakatsuki's cooperation with the League over the military situation in Manchuria, once he had become prime minister, he decided to try to limit the actions of the Kwantung Army in Manchuria. However, the pro-war sentiment in Japan continued to grow, and conflicted with Inukai's attempts to get the Kwantung Army to withdraw to the zone of the South Manchurian Railway (SMR) and to start negotiations with the Chinese government, following the League's call for Japan to withdraw its troops from Chinese territory.

Figure 2.9 A photograph of part of the Kwantung Army, on parade in Manchuria in 1932

On 15 May 1932, army and naval officers of the BBL assassinated Inukai, who they saw as having betrayed his earlier statements when in opposition. His death was supposed to have been just one of many, but they only succeeded in killing Inukai. Many historians see this as a major turning point in Japan's move from democracy and party government towards militaristic extremism. From then on, party government effectively came to an end, and there was a rapid increase in military influence over both domestic and foreign policies.

Inukai's successor was Admiral Saito Makoto (1858–1936) – significantly, he was chosen by the emperor's main adviser, Saionji. Saito was seen as a moderate, and at first attempted to form a 'united national government'. However, he was not strong, and gave in to the army's insistence that Japan should withdraw from the League, following its acceptance of the Lytton Report in March 1933. He also allowed the Kwantung Army to advance into Inner Mongolia and south of China's Great Wall. However, war minister Araki managed to persuade the Kwantung Army to stop any further excursions and, in May 1933, China and Japan signed the Tanggu Truce, which saw the Jehol

Causes of Japanese Expansion

Figure 2.10 Map of Japan's gains after the Tanggu Truce of May 1933 gave it the province of Jehol (Rehe)

2

Japanese Expansion in East Asia, 1931–41

Province become part of Manchukuo, while the Kwantung Army gained control of the strategically-important Shanhaiguan Pass on the China-Manchukuo border.

Nonetheless, right-wing nationalist criticism of Saito continued and, in mid-1934, he was forced to resign. He was replaced by Admiral Okada Keisuke – again, on the recommendation of Saionji. This government complied with mounting right-wing nationalist pressure, and – much to the approval of the naval expansionists – ended Japan's acceptance of the Washington and London naval agreements in 1935.

Political influence of the military

In addition, the Japanese army used its prestigious position in Japanese society and politics to follow its own policies, increasingly independently from civilian governments which were often relatively weak. In particular, right-wing and nationalist officers began to pursue policies and actions which they believed would allow Japan to be self-sufficient – whether this was by moves towards autarky, or by trying to guarantee the supply of raw materials and agricultural products by a more aggressive foreign policy involving military expansion. Given the increasing poverty and economic problems in the early 1930s, Japanese governments found it increasingly difficult to control such military leaders. As Japan was increasingly denied full access to foreign markets and sources of raw materials, Japanese nationalists pressed for Japanese conquests and expansion.

In particular, such officers saw Manchuria – which was rich in raw materials such as coal and iron ore – as offering a relatively easy solution to Japan's economic problems. It was also agriculturally fertile, so could help feed Japan's expanding population while providing a market for Japan's export industries, and so would help revive the depressed Japanese economy.

Japan and the Western states

Given Japan's geographical position, Asia seemed the natural area into which it could expand. However, this would bring it into potential conflict with those European nations – such as Britain, France and the Netherlands – which already had colonies in the region. It would also lead to problems with the USA, which had been trying to expand its influence in the Pacific since the mid-19th century. By the end of the 19th century, US governments had come to see Asia and the Far East as crucially important for the expansion of US trade and interests. Consequently, the US tried to resist other nations expanding in these regions – whether they were the European nations (which already had colonies and dependencies there) or Japan.

As regards China, the US adopted the **'Open Door' policy** for China. Officially, this was based on espousal of free trade – and thus was opposed to imperial control, which tended to impose protectionist tariffs. However, the collapse of imperial rule in China led to internal instability, and to increased opportunities for foreign intervention. After the Boxer Rebellion had been defeated, the US pursued its 'Open Door' policy, in an attempt to prevent China being broken up by rival imperial countries.

In the late 1920s – and especially after the start of the Great Depression – the US continued its attempts to block Japanese expansion in China. One growing concern was that posed by the rapidly-expanding Japanese navy. Hence the US organised the Washington Naval Conference in 1921–22. This resulted in the Four-Power Act and the Five Power Naval Limitation Treaty. These attempted to limit the possibility of a naval

---

ACTIVITY

Carry out some further research on the increasing political violence in Japan in the 1930s. Then write a couple of paragraphs to explain how this impacted on the foreign policy pursued by different Japanese governments during this period.

'Open Door' policy: The 'Open Door' policy was first put forward by Secretary of State John Hay in 1899. In reality, because of the USA's more advanced industrial development, it meant US products could dominate local markets in less-developed economies.

Fact: China's '(in)ability to resist' external aggression had also been a factor in events in the 19th century, when China's relative military weakness and underdeveloped economy had meant European powers – along with Japan (which did modernise in the 19th century) and the US – had used force, or the threat of force, to obtain economic privileges at China's expense.

arms race – but also stated that the ratio of British, US and Japanese battleships in the Pacific should be, respectively, 5 : 5 : 3. The numbers of France and Italy's battleships was to be smaller. Though various nations tried to evade the practical limitations – for instance, by increasing the numbers of cruisers – these agreements remained in force until 1936, when Japan decided to end its involvement.

However, after 1930, the serious drop in exports led to a political crisis, and the army increasingly dominated or even ignored the civilian governments of Japan, and the various military factions began to exercise ever greater influence on foreign policy. Earlier attempts at establishing parliamentary democracy collapsed, and extreme nationalists resorted to the assassination of liberal political leaders.

2.3 How significant was China's political instability?

Another significant factor in Japan's increasingly aggressive foreign policy in the 1930s was the political turmoil in China. This made it appear an easy option for Japanese expansion, as it meant that China's 'ability to resist' any external aggression was greatly reduced. Crucially, when Japan took its first actions against China, in Manchuria in 1931, the Chinese Nationalist government took little effective action – mainly because Jiang Jieshi was involved in a bitter civil war in his attempts to crush the Chinese communists.

China's Nationalist Revolution, 1911

The first significant political turmoil in 20th century China began after the 'Double Tenth' Nationalist Revolution in 1911 (see section 2.3, The 'Double Tenth'). This had toppled the **Manchu Qing dynasty**, which was blamed by many Chinese for allowing China, during the 19th century, to become 'dominated by the European powers', which had exploited China's weakness and forced it to sign a series of 'unequal treaties'.

For example, from 1839–42 Britain had fought an 'Opium War' against China, to force China to buy the opium drug from British traders based in British-ruled India. In 1860, a combined Anglo-French force waged a Second 'Opium War' against China – during this war, Beijing itself was attacked.

The Manchus and the 'unequal treaties'

These treaties had given European powers control of China's sea-ports, along with special trading privileges. By the end of the 19th century, fifty of China's ports were 'treaty ports', which meant they were open to foreign trade and residence. In addition, these European countries also had their own 'spheres of influence' which meant that, in their respective spheres or zones, their national companies had the biggest share of business. As has been seen, other countries were also keen to obtain their own trading privileges in China. For instance, the US – keen not to be outdone by the European powers – had signed the Treaty of Wangxia with China as early as 1844. It was China's obvious weakness that had contributed to Japan's decision to launch the First Sino-Japanese War in 1894 – this had resulted in Japan gaining Korea, Taiwan (Formosa) and Lushun (Port Arthur).

Manchu Qing dynasty: The Manchu dynasty had been ruling China since the 17th century. The last effective Manchu ruler, before the dynasty was toppled in 1911, was the empress dowager Cixi. She had been the main concubine of the emperor Xianfeng and, on his death, had made their son emperor. On his death, she had made her nephew, Guangxu, the new emperor. In 1898, Guangxu had attempted to modernise the way the Chinese empire was run, in a three-month period known as the 'Hundred Days of Reform'. However, his aunt – who opposed these reforms – launched a coup against him in the same year, and had him imprisoned until his death.

Fact: In 1958, the Chinese government introduced the 'pinyin' system for transcribing Chinese names and place-names into the Latin alphabet used in the West. This was accepted internationally in 1982. As a result, the older spellings were superseded – though these are still frequently seen, especially in older sources and books. For instance, before 1958, Jiang Jieshi's name was: Chiang Kai-shek. **Note:** In this book, where Chinese names and place-names appear for the first time, the pre-pinyin spelling will be given in brackets.

2

Japanese Expansion in East Asia, 1931–41

As a result of the Treaty of Wangxia, the US established a presence in several ports. It then decided that the wealth and importance of its 'China trade' justified the establishment of a network of ports across the Pacific – in Fiji in 1844, Samoa in 1856, and the Marshall Islands in 1881. Then, in 1898, the US annexed Hawaii. It was in part the importance of trade with China which led the US to send ships to Japan in 1853 and it was the growing US presence in the Pacific which led to increased tensions between the US and Japan in the 1930s.

> **Boxer Rebellion:** The Boxer Rebellion was led by the *Yi-Ho Tuan* ('Righteous and Harmonious Fists') movement, which was an anti-foreign and anti-imperialist militia that had been formed in 1898. They were known as 'Boxers' because they practised martial arts – including boxing. The Boxers blamed the 'foreign devils' for all China's problems.

Various rebellions against the Manchus – and the foreign influence they had permitted – had broken out before 1911 – for instance, the Taiping Rebellion in 1850 (which lasted fourteen years) and the **Boxer Rebellion** in 1900. The Boxer Rebellion was brutally suppressed by the intervention of an international army, with forces from eight countries – including Japan and the US. The US was able to play an important part in the suppression of the Boxer Rebellion because of the large number of ships and troops already present in the Philippines, following its occupation of those islands in 1898. In 1901, China was forced to sign the 'Boxer Protocol' with these eight countries: agreeing to the execution of 10 Chinese officials associated with the rebellion, and to the payment of massive war reparations of $333 million. Although, following the suppression of the Boxer Rebellion, Cixi had at last agreed to some reforms, it was too late to save the Manchu dynasty. In particular, the failure of the Manchus to stand up to the foreign countries in 1900 led to a massive increase in political support for nationalist and republican groups.

The 'Double Tenth'

The movement – the *Tongmenghui* (Sworn Chinese Brotherhood) – which eventually toppled the Manchu dynasty was led by **Sun Yixian**.

> **Sun Yixian (1866–1925)**
>
> He was a doctor who was opposed to the Manchus, and who wanted a republic which would modernise China. He had formed several secret societies and, before 1911, had tried ten times to overthrow the Manchus. At the time of the 'Double Tenth' Revolution in 1911, which began on 10 October – hence 'Double Tenth' – he was actually in the US, raising funds for his latest secret society, which had been formed in 1905. He returned to China on 24 December 1911 and was elected president of the 'United Provinces of China' by an assembly of rebels at Nanjing. Before the modern system for spelling Chinese names was introduced, his name was spelt 'Sun Yat-sen'.

As early as 1898, he had announced his first version of the 'Three Principles of the People', modelled in part on the three famous slogans of the French Revolution: 'Liberty, Equality, Fraternity'. Sun's Three Principles were: national freedom, democratic government, and the people's livelihood (the latter is sometimes translated as 'socialism' or 'welfare'). These principles were restated on several other occasions during the rest of his life.

In September 1911, a rebellion had broken out in Sichuan province, and agents of Sun Yixian's group went there to help spread the revolt. On 10 October 1911, soldiers in Wuchang decided to join the rising and, because of the date, the revolt became known as the 'Double Tenth'. From there, it spread quickly to become a full-scale revolution – by the end of November, fifteen of China's eighteen provinces had joined the revolution. The rebels formed a provisional government in Nanjing, while the Manchus recalled **Yuan Shikai** from retirement to suppress the revolution.

The early years of the Chinese Republic

Although Yuan quickly defeated the rebels, he then turned against the Manchus and decided instead to support the rebels – in return for being elected their president, he promised to force the Manchus to abdicate. Although the rebels wanted Sun Yixian as president, Yuan's military strength won out and Sun, who had been elected as president in December 1911, eventually resigned, in order to prevent a possible civil war. This then paved the way for Yuan to be elected as president in his place in February 1912. At the same time, the Manchus finally abdicated and China became a republic.

Although the new republic established in 1912 was supposed to be a democracy, Yuan soon made it clear he intended to rule in an autocratic way. In 1913, elections for a National Assembly were held – the majority of seats were won by Sun Yixian's *Guomindang* (GMD – People's National Party), which he'd formed in 1912. The GMD was based on Sun's Three Principles, but Yuan had no intention of sharing power with a parliament dominated by Sun's party. In 1913, Yuan ordered the assassination of a GMD leader – Sun's attempted 'Second Revolution' in July 1913 was easily suppressed, and Yuan then banned the GMD and Sun fled into exile in Japan, where he remained until 1917. In January 1914, Yuan made himself president for the next ten years and then dismissed the National Assembly. By the end of 1915, he controlled twelve of the eighteen provinces and, in December 1915, he decided to make himself emperor. This was opposed by some of the other military leaders, by the GMD – and by the Japanese, who wanted to gain control of large parts of China, and feared the emergence of a strong ruler in China would prevent this. Yuan's acceptance of most of the Twenty-One Demands, and his plans to make himself emperor, led to revolts within his armies and then, in June 1916, he died.

The Warlord Period, 1916–28

Yuan had been able to hold most of China together but, on his death, the new republic was soon plunged into the chaos of the 'Warlord Period', in which rival local military leaders fought for control of the country. From 1916–27, the central government, based in Beijing, only controlled a small area around the capital. Sun's GMD set up a rival government in Guangzhou in the south; while various army generals set themselves up as 'warlords' and proceeded to fight each other over the following eleven years for control of China. This chaotic, and extremely violent, period meant the complete collapse of any centralised and strong government in China; these were ideal conditions for any power wishing to establish or extend its interests in the country.

The First World War and political turmoil

Although Chinese forces did little fighting, China sent almost a million labourers – organised in 'Labour Battalions' – to help the Allied armies in France, Turkey and Africa. However, its forces did seize German ships at anchor in Chinese ports, and confiscated various German businesses in China.

Hence, at the end of the First World War, although China had been on the side of the Allies, it soon discovered that its nationalist expectations – such as ending the 'unequal treaties', regaining the German concessions, and the withdrawal of Japan's Twenty-One Demands – were going to be ignored in the peace treaties of 1919–20. Given the political and military turmoil inside China, there was nothing much the government could do about these decisions – although the Chinese delegation did refuse to sign the Treaty of Versailles.

However, when news of the terms of the Treaty of Versailles – especially those by which the Allied powers in Paris agreed to Japan retaining possession of the former German concessions in China – became known in China, it led to nationalist protests. On 4 May 1919, a mass demonstration, organised by students, took place in Beijing.

As the protests spread, the movement became known as the 'May Fourth Movement'. From early June, workers and businessmen in Shanghai, China's main port, went on strike. As well as demonstrations and strikes, the movement also organised a widespread and successful boycott of Japanese goods – this was particularly annoying for Japan's government and for Japanese businesses.

This May Fourth Movement gave added strength to a largely intellectual political movement known as the 'New Tide', which had been formed in 1916. Like the May Fourth Movement, it wanted to modernise China and free it from foreign interference and control.

Yuan Shikai (1859–1916)

He had been a famous general who had overseen the modernisation of China's armed forces after 1895. After crushing the rebels of 1911, he then allied with them, promising that if they supported him as president of a new republic, he would get the Manchu rulers to abdicate. After becoming president of the new republic in February 1912, he quickly began to rule as an autocrat and, in 1915, he declared himself China's new emperor. However, this was opposed by many different sections within China – yet, until his death in 1916, he was able to hold China together. From 1916–27, China experienced a period of great political instability, which became known as the time of the warlords.

Guomindang (GMD – People's National Party): Sun set this political party up in an attempt to bring together China's many reforming groups. Its ideas were a mixture of Western ideas about democracy and various elements of socialism. Thus Sun had no problem later on with working alongside the Chinese Communist Party, or accepting advice from Soviet Russia. After his death, though, Jiang Jieshi – increasingly advised by Chinese bankers and businessmen – moved the GMD in a much more right-wing direction.

2 Japanese Expansion in East Asia, 1931–41

Fact: Earlier in 1915, the Japanese government had presented the 'Twenty-One Demands' to China, demanding control of many aspects of China's economy and territory. When Yuan accepted most of these, rather than risk a war with Japan, many more Chinese turned against him.

Fact: It was the size of the May Fourth Movement's protests which led Sun to return to China and re-found the GMD in 1920.

Chinese Communist Party (CCP): This had only been formed in 1921, in part as a result of the efforts of an assistant librarian at Beijing University named Mao Zedong. Most leaders of Soviet Russia actually thought the much larger GMD were the group to back – and even advised the CCP to cooperate with the GMD in a junior capacity. Although, in its early years, the CCP remained relatively small, it had many supporters amongst the left-wing of the GMD, which was led by Wang Jingwei. This support increased as a result of its role during its participation in the Northern Expedition of 1926–27 against the warlords.

Figure 2.11 Photograph of student demonstrators from Beijing's Tsinghua University. Some of their slogans were: 'Do away with the Twenty-One Demands' and 'Don't sign the Versailles Treaty.'

SOURCE J

This [4 May] movement is the strongest move of its kind that the Chinese have made… Already it has caused great alarm in Japan. This boycott is different to all others. On previous occasions it has been the Chinese merchants who have been the mainstay of such attempts, but this time it is the consumer who is carrying it on…. Millions of dollars have been collected to start making articles which have heretofore been purchased from Japan. It will not surprise me if this boycott within the next eighteen months does not cost the Japanese four hundred million dollars.

Extracts of comments made by a US journalist in 1919. Quoted in Lo Hui-Min (edited), 1978, *The Correspondence of G.E. Morrison, vol 2, 1912–1920*.

The First United Front

Meanwhile, Sun had been reorganising the GMD which, since 1917, had established its control of the southern province of Guandong. In 1922, one of Soviet Russia's most able diplomats was sent to help Sun further modernise the GMD. Very quickly, it became a mass party and Sun agreed that members of the **Chinese Communist Party (CCP)** could also belong to the GMD. Although their aims were different, both the GMD and the CCP wanted to unite China and free it from foreign control. Working together thus seemed sensible and, in 1923, what became known as the First United Front was formed between the GMD and the CCP. The Russians then sent other advisers to help Sun modernise and strengthen his armed forces so that they could defeat the warlords.

Causes of Japanese Expansion

Figure 2.12 A map of the GMD-CCP Northern Expedition of 1926, showing the different warlord areas of China

2 Japanese Expansion in East Asia, 1931–41

In 1924, at a GMD conference, Sun issued the latest version of his Three Principles and announced his aim of creating a united China free from foreign interference. However, to achieve victory over the warlords, he needed outside help. Western powers, such as Britain and France, refused, so Sun turned to Soviet Russia, where a Communist government had come to power in 1917.

The Northern Campaign

However, in 1925, Sun died and **Jiang Jieshi** (see section 3.1, Manchuria, 1931), his son-in-law, soon rose to eminence within the GMD. Jiang had been in charge of the GMD's military academy at Huangpu and had become commander-in-chief of the newly-improved GMD army. In July 1926, having established GMD control of the provinces of Guandong and Guangxi, Jiang began a march to the North – often known as the Northern Campaign – to take on the warlords. These had formed a very loose coalition, and had established Beijing as their centre.

This political and military Northern Campaign of 1926–27 was relatively easy, as many Chinese were fed up with the turmoil and violence of warlord rule, while many warlord armies mutinied and joined the nationalists. A GMD army led by communists established a GMD government in Hankow in September 1926, while another GMD army captured Nanjing in early 1927 and set up another government there. By the end of 1926, GMD-CCP forces – numbering over 250,000 – had established control over half a million square miles, with a combined population of 170 million people.

The end of the First United Front

However, just as the GMD had established its control in southern China, Jiang decided to break the alliance with the CCP. During the Northern Campaign, the GMD had become increasingly divided along left-wing / right-wing lines – while Jiang increasingly resented the success of CCP military units. In April 1927, as his forces had approached Shanghai, a communist-led rebellion had taken control of the city. When his troops entered the city, Jiang had the communists rounded up and at least 5,000 communists and communist sympathisers were slaughtered in the Shanghai Massacre. This attempted destruction of the CCP then spread to other areas where the communists were strong. Although these actions meant Jiang could establish his control of south China and establish a Nationalist government in Nanjing, his actions in Shanghai proved to be the start of a protracted civil war which did not finally end until 1949.

However, in April 1928, GMD leaders put Jiang in charge of a second Northern Campaign – this time with the aim of capturing Beijing and establishing GMD control over the north of China. After a short campaign, Jiang was able to defeat several warlord forces, and to 'take Beijing'; the GMD government then moved the capital from there to their base at Nanjing, which was in the richest part of the country. It was there the GMD established their National Government which then entrusted the power to rule to a Council of State – and Jiang was appointed as the chairman of this council, thus making him the new ruler of China.

Civil War in China

China did, however, not remain at peace, and political disunity and turmoil continued in the years immediately before and during the start of Japan's wars of aggression against China. In 1929, two northern warlords who had originally surrendered to Jiang

---

Figure 2.13 *Jiang Jieshi (1887–1975)*

He was a professional soldier, and had trained in Japan. He supported reform, and had taken part in the 1911 Revolution. Sun sent him to Soviet Russia for political training, and then appointed him commander of the GMD's newly-created Military Academy at Huangpu. He later used his military power to become head of the GMD government after defeating the last of the warlords but, although he did at times militarily-oppose Japanese incursions, his many campaigns against the forces of the CCP resulted in China experiencing two more decades of internal political instability and military conflict. To help him 'exterminate' the communists, he received help from many military 'advisers' and armaments from Nazi Germany.

QUESTION

Why were Japanese expansionists concerned about the ending of the 'Warlord Period' in China at the end of the 1920s?

Causes of Japanese Expansion

Figure 2.14 Some of the Nationalist GMD troops involved in the Northern expedition against warlord forces in August 1926

decided to rebel and, for the next two years, northern China was once again gripped by fighting and political instability. This was just the opportunity that Japan's nationalists and military leaders wanted. In addition, even in some of the provinces nominally under GMD control, gangs of bandits – used to the plunder opportunities they had enjoyed during the warlord period – often terrorised whole districts, making their living from robbery and kidnapping.

More seriously, the communists who had survived the Shanghai Massacre of 1927 had fled to Jiangxi province, where they had established a 'Chinese Soviet Republic' to rule the province. This Jiangxi Soviet, as it became known, was headed politically by Mao Zedong, while the leader of their Red Army was Zhu De. Whilst there, they quickly gained widespread support from the peasants through their land reform programmes and, amongst other reforms, their establishment of schools. Jiang saw the CCP as his most serious threat – even after Japan had occupied Manchuria. This was despite the fact that, for most Chinese, the invasion was seen as a national insult.

Fact: The communist-led rebellion had been planned in discussions between Wang Jingwei, the leader of the GMD's left-wing faction, and communist leaders. An important role in the uprising was played by communist-led trade unions. In order to undermine the communists' influence, Jiang allied himself with the leaders of the 'Green Gang', an underworld criminal organisation which was opposed to communist influence in Shanghai's trade unions. Jiang also decided to marry a daughter of the wealthy and powerful Sung family, which owned many businesses and financial institutions in Shanghai.

Fact: Ironically – given that Japan was unhappy about the idea of a single and strong Chinese government – Jiang's task of establishing GMD control in the north was made easier as a result of the assassination of Zhang Zuolin, the ruler of Manchuria and the most powerful of the warlords, as he was leaving Beijing by train. His son, Zhang Xueliang, soon accepted Jiang and his GMD as the true government of a united China. This was something that Japanese expansionists did not want – and Jiang's successes were one reason why Japan decided to invade Manchuria in 1931, before Jiang could fully establish his control of all China.

SOURCE K

The conquest of Manchuria fanned the fires of Chinese nationalism to a white heat. Japanese goods were boycotted in Shanghai as part of the anti-Japan protest movement, and relations between the two countries grew more tense.

Ienaga, S. *The Pacific War 1931–1945*. New York. Pantheon Books. p. 65.

2 Japanese Expansion in East Asia, 1931–41

Fact: Jiang – like his wealthy backers – feared the growing influence and popularity of the CCP. Thus, even when carrying out some limited military actions against Japanese forces after the formation of the Second United Front between the GMD and the CCP in 1936, sections of his armies were still directed against the communists.

Fact: Most of Jiang's main troops in the northeast were Manchurians, who wanted to fight the Japanese much more than they wanted to fight the communists, who were already carrying out guerrilla attacks against the encroaching Japanese forces. In addition, Zhang himself was keen to avenge the murder of his father. As a result, he had made an unofficial agreement with the communists not to fight them.

Jiang's 'Extermination Campaigns'

From 1930–34, Jiang conducted a series of what he himself called 'Extermination Campaigns' in order to destroy the communists. During these military campaigns, more than a million Chinese were either killed or starved to death. Despite Japan's growing military incursions into Chinese territory after 1931, Jiang decided to prioritise his campaigns against the communists.

This thus presented Japan with a golden opportunity to expand into Chinese territory: with China distracted by an increasingly bitter war, there was little likelihood of any serious opposition from China's military forces.

The fifth – and biggest – Extermination Campaign was launched in the autumn of 1933, and was largely based on the advice of two military advisers sent to Jiang by Nazi Germany. Though ultimately successful, in that the CCP's Red Army was forced to retreat to the remote northern province of Shaanxi, this did not end the political and military instability in China. It was this continuing disorder which allowed Japanese forces to cross over from Manchuria into several northern Chinese provinces: in 1933, they occupied the province of Rehe, and then continued to advance southwards in 1934. By the end of 1936, Japanese forces had also occupied the provinces of Chahaer and Suiyuan, along with parts of Hebei and Shanxi.

The Second United Front

While this was taking place, Jiang decided to continue with his Extermination Campaigns against the communists, rather than resisting Japanese incursions and, in 1936, he launched yet another extermination campaign against the communists in the north. In doing this, he ignored the growing demand from ordinary Chinese people, and the CCP (whose slogan from 1935 was 'Chinese do not fight Chinese'), to stop the internal fighting and form a united front against the Japanese who were taking over more and more of China – and even demanding that northern China be permanently separated from the south. Jiang's argument was that the communists were more of a threat than the Japanese and that war could not be declared against Japan until the communists had been defeated and national unity established.

However, he had ignored the demands for a united front for too long – even though, Zhang Xueliang, the commander of Jiang's main forces in the northeast, pleaded with him to turn his forces against the Japanese. Jiang decided to fly to Zhang's base in Xian the capital of Shaanxi province to persuade him to attack the communists, as ordered. However, on 12 December 1936, Jiang was taken prisoner and, after two weeks of resisting, was forced to agree to the formation of what became known as the Second United Front. This was an agreement between the GMD and CCP to join forces to fight the Japanese – in return for his release, Jiang was recognised as the commander-in-chief of all the Chinese forces; while Stalin agreed to provide Jiang's forces with Soviet weapons. Ironically, this agreement played a big part in Japan's decision to launch all-out invasion of China in July 1937. This was because they feared that the political instability in China – which had allowed them to occupy significant amounts of Chinese territory since 1931 – might be coming to an end. Thus the formation of the Second United Front ironically acted as a spur to further Japanese attacks on China.

Causes of Japanese Expansion

SOURCE L

Sun Mingzhiu hailed him, and the Generalissimo's [Jiang Jeshi] first words were, 'If you are my comrade, shoot me and finish it all'.

To which Sun replied, 'We will not shoot. We only ask you to lead our country against Japan… The past is the past', Sun said to him. 'From now on there must be a new policy for China. What are you going to do?… The one urgent task for China is to fight Japan. This is the demand of the men of the North-East. Why do you not fight Japan, but instead give the order to fight the Red [Communist] Army?'

'I am the leader of the Chinese people.' Chiang [Jiang] shouted. 'I represent the nation. I think my policy is correct…'

Extract from a British journalist's account of discussions with Captain Sun Mingzhiu, who had led the capture of Jiang Jeshi in the Xi'an Incident on 12 December 1936. Quoted in Brooman, J. 1988. *China Since 1900*. Harlow. Longman Group. p. 19.

> **QUESTION**
>
> What connections do you think exist between the formation of the Second United Front in China in 1936 and Japanese plans to expand at China's expense?

Activities

1. Write a newspaper article about the main nationalist groups which were active in Japan in the 1920s and 1930s. Try to summarise their various aims and actions. In your final paragraph, explain what impact all this had on the foreign policies pursued by different Japanese governments during this period.

2. Draw up a summary chart, showing Japanese territorial expansion before 1931. Place the names of the various agreements or wars on the left-hand side, and details of the territorial gains on the right.

3. Find out more about Japan's growing concerns about US activities in Asia and the Pacific before 1931. Then write a couple of paragraphs to show whether Japan's concerns were justified.

2

End of chapter activities

Summary

You should now have a good understanding of how and why nationalism and militarism developed in Japan in the period before 1931.

You should also be able to explain the short-term impact of the Great Depression on both Japan's economy and its political system. In addition, you should be able to show how and why this influenced Japan's foreign policy.

Finally, you should be able to understand why political instability in China during much of this period made this country seem a tempting target for Japan's expansionists.

Summary activities

Copy the diagram below. Then, using the information in this chapter and from any other available sources, make brief notes under the headings shown. Remember to include information on historical debate / interpretations – including names of historians – where relevant.

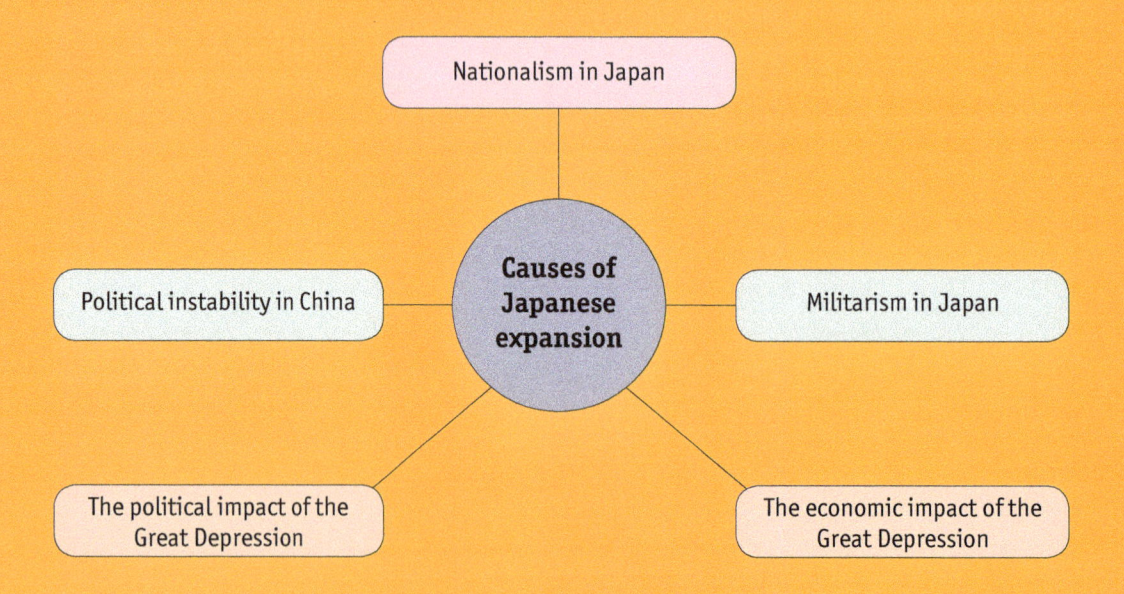

```
                    Nationalism in Japan
                            |
Political instability ─── Causes of ─── Militarism in Japan
     in China             Japanese
                          expansion
                         /        \
      The political impact of    The economic impact of the
         the Great Depression       Great Depression
```

Paper 1 exam practice

Question

> **SOURCE A**
>
> At Paris, the Chinese delegates demanded that the German concessions in the [Shandong] province, and the port of Kiaochow, should be returned to China. Japan argued that Germany had yielded them up to her, and that she would negotiate about them not at the conference itself but in direct talks with the Chinese. Already in 1918, in an exchange of notes with the Chinese warlord government in Peking, the Japanese had laid claims to rights far in excess of those the Germans had enjoyed. They had also secured the agreement of the United States that 'territorial contiguity' assured Japan of a special position on the Chinese mainland, and her claims had received diplomatic backing from Britain and France during the war.
>
> Henig, R. 1995. *Versailles and after, 1919–1933*. London. Routledge. p. 28

Why, according to **Source A**, might Japanese nationalists have assumed that, after the First World War, Japan's influence in China would be greater than before the war? [3 marks]

Skill

Comprehension of a source

Before you start

Comprehension questions are the most straightforward questions you will face in Paper 1. They simply require you to understand a source *and* extract two or three relevant points that relate to the particular question. Before you attempt this question, refer to Chapter 9 for advice on how to tackle comprehension questions, and a simplified mark scheme.

Student answer

*According to **Source A**, Japanese nationalists might have thought Japan's influence and territorial possessions in China would have expanded after 1918 because the US had already agreed that Japan had a 'special position' in China.*

Examiner comments

The candidate has selected **one** relevant and explicit piece of information from the source that clearly identifies a reason. This is enough to gain one mark. However, as no other reason has been identified, this candidate fails to get the other two marks available.

Activity

Look again at the source, and the student answer above. Now try to identify **one or two** other comments in the source which suggest other reasons why Japanese nationalists might have expected an expansion of Japanese influence in China, and try to make an overall comment about the source's message. This will enable you to obtain the other two marks available for this question.

Paper 2 practice questions

1 Examine the role of militarism in contributing to the creation of an aggressive foreign policy in Japan by 1931.

2 Compare and contrast the influence of nationalist ideology and the impact of the Great Depression as factors in the emergence of an expansionist foreign policy in Japan by 1931.

3 Evaluate the importance of ultra-nationalist societies in Japan in the period 1900–31.

4 'Political instability in China was the main reason for the emergence of Japanese expansionist aims before 1931.' To what extent do you agree with this statement?

Japan's Actions

3

Introduction

Having examined, in the previous chapter, the various causes – economic, diplomatic, political and cultural – which contributed to the development of strong nationalistic and militaristic attitudes within Japan, this chapter explores Japan's increasing expansionist actions in China – in Manchuria and northern China from 1931–36, and then during the Second Sino-Japanese War which began in 1937 – and in the Pacific during the period from 1931–41. In addition, the chapter will look at the various diplomatic developments which were connected to the move towards Japan's aggressive expansionist foreign policy during this period. As well as the growing ties between Japan and the fascist states of Italy and Germany – which culminated in the formation of what was known as the Rome-Berlin-Tokyo Axis – the deterioration in relations between Japan and the US during the 1930s will be seen as a crucial factor. Ultimately, this led to the attack on Pearl Harbor on 7 December 1941 – it was this which finally led to the entry of the US into the Second World War. Up till then, the US had been the only major state not directly caught up in the fighting which, in Asia and the Pacific, had been going on for ten years before.

KEY QUESTIONS
- What happened in Manchuria and northern China, 1931–36?
- What were the main aspects of the Second Sino-Japanese War, 1937–41?
- Why did Japan attack Pearl Harbor in 1941?

Overview

- As the impact of the Depression caused even greater problems for Japan's economy and political system, Japan's armed forces became increasingly political.
- Many military leaders came to the conclusion that only territorial expansion would solve Japan's problems. Increasingly, they tried to influence civilian governments – and even to establish independence from civilian political control.

TIMELINE
- **1928 Jun:** Assassination of Zhang Zuolin in China
- **1931 Sept:** Japanese invasion of Manchuria
- **1932 Jan:** First 'Shanghai Incident'
  - **Mar:** Manchuria becomes Manchukuo
- **1933 Feb:** Eastern Monroe Doctrine announced; Japan leaves the League of Nations
- **1936 Feb:** attempted military coup in Japan
  - **Sep:** Japan signs anti-Comintern Pact with Nazi Germany
- **1937 Jul:** start of Second Sino-Japanese War
  - **Dec:** 'Rape of Nanjing'
- **1938 Jul:** start of 'Border War' with the Soviet Union
- **1939 Aug:** Japan defeated at battle of Khalkhin-Gol; ceasefire in 'Border War'
- **1940 Jul:** 'Main Principles of Fundamental National Policy' announced
  - **Aug:** 'Greater East Asia Co-prosperity Sphere' announced
  - **Sep:** Tripartite Pact signed; Japanese forces enter north Indo-china; US announces economic sanctions against Japan
- **1941 Apr:** Japanese-Soviet Neutrality Pact
  - **Jun:** Nazi invasion of Soviet Union begins
  - **Jul:** Imperial Conference; Japan invades south Indo-china; US trade bans on Japan, and Japanese assets in US frozen
  - **Dec:** Japanese attack on Pearl Harbor

3

Japanese Expansion in East Asia, 1931–41

- The first aggressive action came in September 1931, when Japan's army – which was in the Chinese province of Manchuria, guarding the Japanese-owned South Manchurian Railway – staged an 'incident' at Mukden, in order to justify occupying the rest of Manchuria.

- Initially, Japan's civilian government tried to get the army to withdraw, and said it was willing to cooperate with the League of Nations. However, the army officers in Manchuria ignored the government in Tokyo and went on to occupy the whole of Manchuria.

- In February 1932, Manchuria was renamed Manchukuo and became part of the Japanese Empire. Almost immediately, Japanese army officers in Manchukuo began to make incursions into the north of China itself.

- Between 1932 and 1936, there were several 'incidents' but all-out war was avoided as China – caught up in the turmoil of civil war – made concessions rather than risk war with Japan.

- However, in July 1937, Japan launched a full-scale invasion of China, and soon occupied large parts of northeast China. However, as the war continued, it proved a growing strain on Japan's resources.

- For much of the 1930s, Japanese foreign policy was undecided as regards expanding further north (into Siberia and other Soviet areas), or expanding south (into Asia and the Pacific). However, defeats at the hands of the Soviet Union's Red Army in border clashes during 1938–39, helped push the decision towards 'going south'.

- During 1940, Japan formulated a clearer policy for expansion in Asia and the Pacific – including the announcement of its 'Greater East Asia Co-prosperity Sphere'. It also signed the Tripartite Pact with Nazi Germany and Fascist Italy.

- In 1941, having signed a Neutrality Pact with the Soviet Union, Japan moved troops into north Indo-china – this led the US to impose some economic sanctions on Japan.

- Finally, in July 1941, an Imperial Conference in Japan decided on expansion to the south – even if it led to war with Britain and the US.

- When Japan's army almost immediately invaded south Indo-china, the US imposed a total ban on all vital supplies (including oil) to Japan, and froze all Japanese assets in the US.

- The Japanese government and military concluded they needed to invade the Dutch East Indies to secure oil supplies. To do this without serious US opposition, they decided to destroy the USA's Pacific fleet in Pearl Harbor.

KEY CONCEPTS QUESTION

Significance: Why was Manchuria seen as being so important for the Japanese economy? Remember: for questions like this, you usually need to try to identify a range of different reasons – AND to try to establish which factor (or factors) was most significant.

3.1 What happened in Manchuria and Northern China, 1931–36?

Japan's nationalists had long had hopes of expanding into Manchuria and, before 1931, Japanese companies had made considerable investments there. In addition, during two wars, Japan had secured an important position in Manchuria – and the Japanese army was determined to maintain that position. From 1931, Japan adopted an increasingly expansionist policy – initially aimed at securing control of Manchuria but which, by 1936, was quickly turned against mainland China.

Manchuria, 1931

Japanese nationalists, who argued that Japan needed an empire in order to become a self-sufficient nation, initially looked to Manchuria. This was close to Japan and rich in raw materials, such as coal, iron ore, and bauxite. In addition, Manchuria was seen as possessing people who, as well as buying Japanese goods, could be a source of cheap labour. In fact, the use of Manchurians as cheap labour was already well-established before the invasion of 1931. For instance, there were enormous differences in average monthly salaries for employees of the **South Manchurian Railway**.

In 1926, the monthly salaries of Japanese regular and temporary employees were, respectively, 7.6 and 4.2 times higher than the wages of Chinese temporary workers. Thus it is no wonder that the SMR was such a highly profitable venture.

Given China's relative weakness – and the profits already being made in Manchuria – this Chinese province was seen by Japanese nationalists in the 1920s as a province which Japan could easily – and profitably – take over.

In 1927, after sixteen years of turmoil, China had finally achieved something like a unified national government, under the leadership of Jiang Jieshi, who was determined to extend his government's control of all areas of China. One of those areas was Manchuria which was under the control of the warlord Zhang Zuolin, who had ruled Manchuria since 1916.

However, officers in Japan's Kwantung (Guandong) Army in Manchuria, and other army officers, were determined to prevent China's new Nationalist government from regaining control over Manchuria. At first, they worked with Zhang Zuolin but when, in 1928, he retreated rather than fought to stop the advance of Jiang Jieshi's Nationalist forces, some Kwantung Army officers decided to kill him – and seize control of the whole province. Having successfully carried out the assassination of Zhang Zuolin in June 1928, they next became angry when it looked like his son, Zhang Xue-liang, was preparing to cooperate with China's Nationalist government. Their fears were soon confirmed – Zhang Xue-liang announced his support of Jiang Jieshi, put his troops at the disposal of China's Nationalist army, and started to draw up plans to develop Manchuria without any Japanese input. The Kwantung Army officers – along with the support of some army leaders in Japan – decided to overthrow him and, instead, to bring the whole of Manchuria under Japanese control. The main leaders of the Kwantung Army were: Ishiwara Kanji (1886–1949) and Itagaki Seishiro (1885–1948), and they had soon drawn up a plan to effect this – and to extend Japanese control into Mongolia as well.

South Manchurian Railway: The South Manchurian Railway company was an important element in Japan's growing economic and imperialist control of the province. As well as significant salary differences between its Japanese and Chinese employees, the SMR also operated coal mines. As with salaries, there were huge differences in working conditions and safety between Japanese and Chinese workers. From 1909–30, just over 3,800 Japanese were killed or injured working in these mines, compared to almost 115,000 Chinese. By 1930, around 45 million tons of coal had been extracted from the Fushun and Yent'ai mines alone – but over 100,000 Chinese workers had been killed or injured during that period.

Fact: Japan's prime minister, Tanaka Giichi, promised to take disciplinary action against the officers involved in the assassination of Zhang Zuolin, but the Army ministry blocked his attempts. As a result, Tanaka and his government were forced to resign. Once the plot had become public knowledge, it inflamed Chinese nationalist sentiments – and played a big part in Zhang's son's decision to support Jiang Jieshi and his Chinese nationalists.

SOURCE A

In the spring of 1931, a "Proposal Regarding the Problems of Manchuria and Mongolia" was drafted at Kwantung Army headquarters. It called for a "covert operation in the four northeast districts and a fabricated pretext for military action" in order to "overthrow the [Zhang Xue-liang] government and occupy Manchuria and Mongolia." On May 29 Kwantung staff officer Itagaki Seishiro argued that making Manchuria and Mongolia Japanese territory was an urgent priority. These plans came to fruition on the evening of September 18, 1931, when Japanese forces blasted the tracks of the South Manchurian Railway outside Mukden. Army units, "in response to the explosion," immediately attacked Chang Hsueh-liang's troops at the North Barracks and occupied the area.

Ienaga, S. 1978. *The Pacific War 1931–1945*. New York. Pantheon Books. pp. 59–60.

3 Japanese Expansion in East Asia, 1931–41

The Mukden Incident

The first step was to 'manufacture' an attack on part of the South Manchurian Railway (SMR) in Mukden, and then to blame it on Chinese troops.

Fact: Though at the time the Chinese troops were blamed for the Mukden Incident, most of them were sleeping in the North barracks when the explosion on the SMR in Mukden took place. Although the official story blamed them, the true facts emerged after the war. Hanaya Tadashi, one of the main plotters along with Ishiwara Kanji and Itagaki Seishiro, admitted later how the incident had really occurred. According to Hanaya, the plot also included several unit commanders in the Shimamoto Regiment, a Mukden independent guard unit.

Figure 3.1 A photograph of soldiers of the Kwantung Army interrogating a Chinese prisoner, after the Mukden Incident in Manchuria, 1931

When prime minister **Wakatsuki Reijiro** – following the advice of foreign minister Shidehara – ordered the Kwantung Army not to go into areas beyond the SMR, he was bluntly informed by the Army General Staff that the civilian government had no right

Wakatsuki Reijiro (1866–1949)

He first became prime minister in January 1926 but, in April 1927, was forced to resign because of the Showa financial crisis. He was made a baron in April 1931 – and, in the same month, he became prime minister again. This time, though, he was only in office for eight months. He was in favour of disarmament, which made him highly unpopular with Japan's military and the various ultra-nationalist political groups. His attempts to prevent the invasion of Manchuria and to restrain the army increased opposition to him and he was eventually forced to resign. He was opposed to the Second Sino-Japanese War, and to extending the war to the Pacific.

SOURCE B

Although Japan has undoubtedly acted in a way contrary to the principles of the Covenant by taking the law into its own hands, she has a real grievance against China. This is not a case in which the armed forces of one country have crossed the frontiers of another in circumstances in which they had no previous right to be on the other's soil. Japan owns the South Manchurian Railway and has been entitled to have a body of Japanese guards upon the strip of land through which the railway runs. Japan's case is that she was compelled by the failure of China to provide reasonable protection to Japanese lives and property in Manchuria in the face of attacks by Chinese bandits, and of an attack upon the line itself, to move Japanese troops forward and to occupy points in Manchuria which are beyond the line of the railway.

Extract from a memorandum by British Foreign Secretary, Sir John Simon, to the British Cabinet, 23 November 1931. Quoted in Fellows, N. 2012. *Peacemaking, Peacekeeping: International Relations 1918–36*. Cambridge. Cambridge University Press. p. 184.

to intervene, as this was a question of the independence of the supreme command – and that therefore, the staff of the field armies had the right to take whatever military action they considered necessary. Eventually, in December 1931, Wakatsuki and his government resigned over their failure to control the military and to solve Japan's economic problems.

The formation of Manchukuo

Despite attempts by the new Japanese prime minister, Inukai Tsuyoshi, who had replaced Wakaysuki, to get the Kwantung Army to comply with the League's ruling to withdraw its troops back to SMR territory, the Kwantung Army officers decided to capture key cities such as Jinzhou and Harbin, and to move north into Amur Province. In January 1932, Chinese anger at Japan's actions in Manchuria led to a clash between Chinese and Japanese troops in the international concession zone in Shanghai. Japan responded by bombing a heavily-populated civilian area of Shanghai.

Though this act helped turn world opinion against Japan, Inukai was forced to follow the advice of his war minister, **Sadao Araki**, and sent two army divisions to Shanghai – these drove all Chinese troops from Shanghai. Fighting continued during February, when Chinese forces launched an unsuccessful counter-attack. On 4 March, the League of Nations condemned the fighting and demanded a ceasefire – though the Chinese accepted this, Japan did not and intermittent fighting continued in and around the city. Finally, on 5 May, China and Japan signed the Shanghai Ceasefire Agreement.

Japan forced China to accept that, with the exception of some Japanese military units, Shanghai should be a demilitarised zone; whilst Chinese forces should be permanently withdrawn from the areas surrounding Shanghai, Suzhou and Kunshan. However, this first 'Shanghai Incident' aroused increasingly nationalistic feelings in Japan, which supported the Kwantung Army's decision, in February 1932, to transform Manchuria into a puppet state, called Manchukuo: this came into existence in March 1932, with the former Chinese Manchu emperor, Puyi, on the throne.

Japanese incursions in Northern China after 1932

The conquest of Manchuria was not the end of the aims and ambitions of Japan's nationalists. Almost immediately after 1931, a series of increasingly significant 'incidents' took place between Chinese and Japanese forces in parts of northern China along the border with Manchuria.

The continuing political disorder within China, resulting from Jiang's 'Extermination Campaigns' against the Chinese communists allowed Japanese forces to cross over from Manchuria into several northern Chinese provinces. In 1933, they occupied the province of Rehe (Jehol), and then continued to advance southwards in 1934. By the end of 1936, Japanese forces had also occupied the provinces of Chahaer and Suiyuan, along with parts of Hebei and Shanxi. Jiang, still determined to crush the communists, was not prepared to resist these increasing Japanese encroachments on Chinese territory.

> **QUESTION**
> What light does the invasion of Manchuria in 1931 shed on the relationship between Japan's civilian government and its military leaders?

> **Sadao Araki (1877–1966)**
> He was a general in the Imperial Japanese Army before and during the Second World War, and was appointed as minister of war in December 1931. He was also an important right-wing nationalist writer on imperial expansion, and supported those involved in an attempted coup in May 1932 which became known as the May 15 Incident. This involved both naval and army cadets, along with civilian members of the ultra-nationalist League of Blood. During the attempted coup, Inukai Tsuyoshi, the prime minster, had been assassinated. Despite his public sympathy for the plotters of the coup, he remained as minister of war; and, from September 1932, became increasingly outspoken in favour of totalitarianism at home, and militarism and expansionism abroad.

3 Japanese Expansion in East Asia, 1931–41

ACTIVITY

Carry out some additional research into Japan's incursions into Northern China between 1932 and 1936. Then create a chart to show these various steps, year by year, providing as much additional information as possible. Finally, write a paragraph to explain why you think Japan was able to take these actions without provoking a war with China.

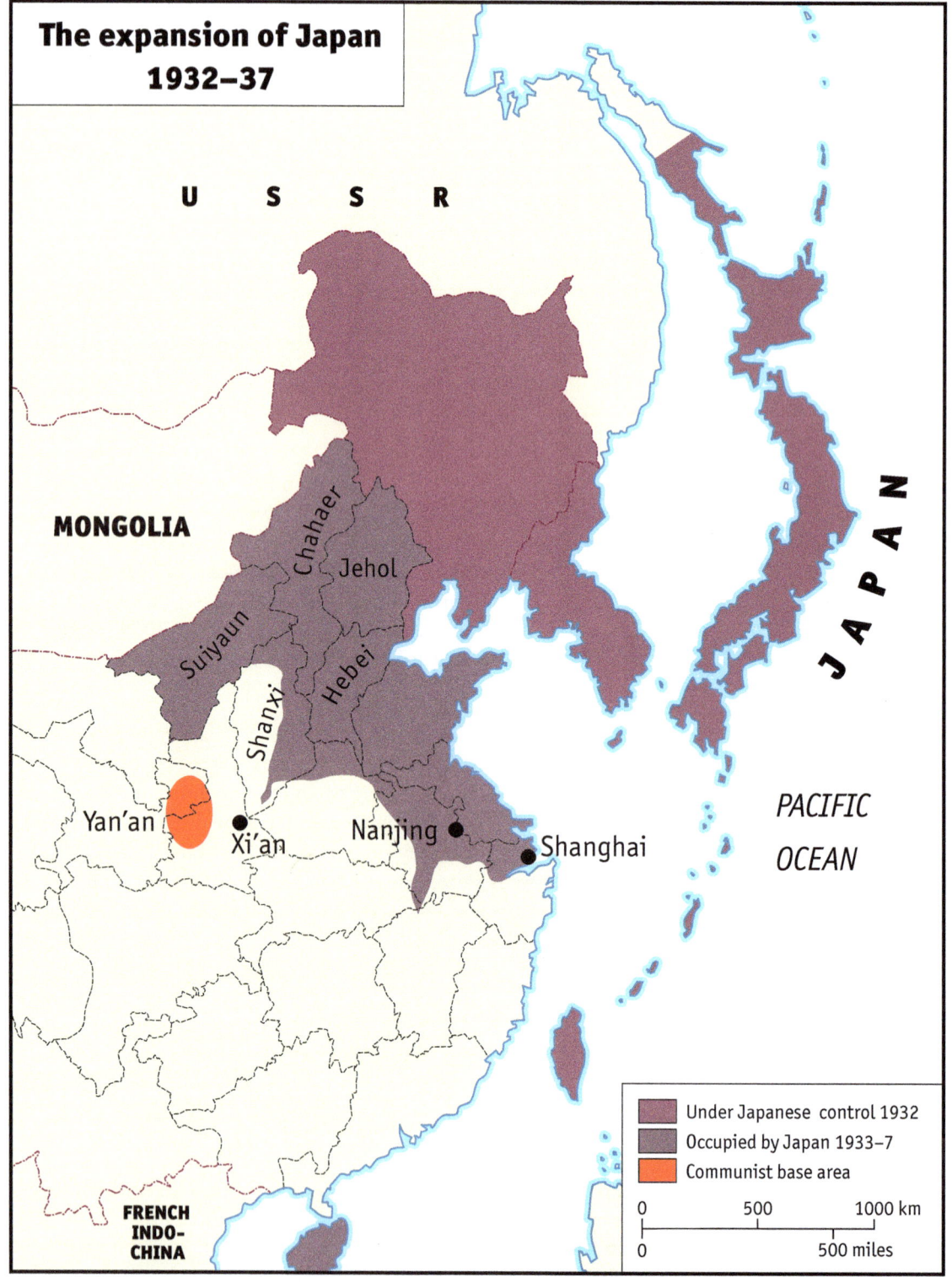

The expansion of Japan 1932–37

Legend:
- Under Japanese control 1932
- Occupied by Japan 1933–7
- Communist base area

Figure 3.2 Map showing Japan's conquests in China, 1932–37, before the Second Sino-Japanese War

3.2 What were the main aspects of the Second Sino-Japanese War, 1937–41?

To a considerable extent, the Japanese incursion into Manchuria was simply the prelude to war with China – referred to as the 'China Incident' by the Japanese. This war, which began in July 1937, is often known as the Second Sino-Japanese War. The First Sino-Japanese War was in 1894–95. This second war was the culmination of decades of Japanese imperialist policy which had as its aim the domination of China and access to its food supplies and raw materials – including potential labourers. Japan felt it was one of the 'have-not' nations and, by the mid-1930s, Japan's nationalists were determined to end this state of affairs.

SOURCE C

Japan may be regarded, along with Germany and Italy, as one of the three major dissatisfied 'have-not' powers of the world. It was in Italian Fascist intellectual circles that the idea first found expression that there could just as logically be a 'class struggle' between rich and poor nations as between the 'bourgeoisie' and the 'proletariat' in a single nation. German National Socialist [Nazi] leaders have displayed an increasing tendency to attribute their countries' economic difficulties largely to the lack of colonial sources of essential raw materials. Japan sees itself confronted with a similar problem, despite the acquisition of Manchukuo. So the spokesman of the Foreign Ministry, Mr. Amau, recently remarked:

'Unfortunately the territories which now feed Japan's population are too small. We are advised to practice birth control, but this advice comes too late, since the population of the Japanese Empire is already about 100,000,000. Japanese work harder and longer than people in Western countries; their opportunities in life are more restricted. Why? We need more territory and must cultivate more resources if we are to nourish our population.'

Extract from Chamberlain, W. H. 1938. *Japan over Asia*. Quoted in Overy, R. J. 1994. *The Inter-War Crisis 1919–1939*. Harlow. Longmans. p. 124.

The road to war

While it is clear now that the invasion of Manchuria was in many ways the first step towards Japanese military aggression and expansion at the expense of China, it did not seem an inevitable step to everyone at the time. For instance, in June 1937 – a month before the war on China began – **Konoe Fumimaro** was persuaded to become Japan's new prime minister. He was seen by some as a moderate who could achieve some kind of political consensus and stability within Japan.

However, he had also been expressing expansionist views as regards foreign affairs, and was prepared to abandon the policy of international cooperation. In particular, he was convinced that Japan had to adopt a policy for its own 'autonomous bloc' – in effect, Japan's own empire. He thus supported the idea of an '**Asiatic Monroe Doctrine**'.

This had been proclaimed by the Japanese delegation to the League of Nations in February 1933. In fact, many Japanese politicians and nationalists felt this concept had been recognised much earlier by the US, via the Lansing-Ishii Agreement of

---

Konoe Fumimaro (1891–1945)
He was a prince and was related to the most influential families and clans in Japan. He was widely respected by many different sections of Japanese society and his ideas for bringing all the different groups in Japan together seemed to mark him out as a moderate. However, in October 1940, he became the founder and leader of the Imperial Rule Assistance Association – this was a semi-fascist organisation, designed to promote the aims of the 'New Order' movement. To achieve this, he believed the Empire of Japan needed a totalitarian single-party state. This would allow Japan to successfully conclude the war against China, and to further expand Japan's empire.

Asiatic Monroe Doctrine: As early as 1905, just after the Russo-Japanese War, US president Theodore Roosevelt had informally suggested that, at some point in the future, Japan could have a 'Japanese – or Eastern – Monroe Doctrine' for Asia, designed to block European expansion in northern China and Korea. The announcement, in February 1933, was just another version of other similar Japanese claims: 'Asia for the Asiatics', 'paramount interest', 'special interest', 'Japanese leadership', and the 'right to live'.

3 Japanese Expansion in East Asia, 1931–41

Figure 3.3 Cartoon about the announcement of the Japanese Monroe Doctrine in February 1933

Fact: The belief that Japan's actions were no different from those taken in the Americas was particularly true of retired army officers and nationalist theoreticians. These advocated what they saw as Japan's 'Pan-Asia Mission' – with Japan as the leader of an Asia from which 'white imperialism' should be expelled. As noted by W. H. Chamberlain, the Tokyo correspondent for the *Christian Science Monitor* in the 1930s, such nationalist views had a quasi-religious hold over many Japanese.

Anti-Comintern Pact: This was an anti-communist alliance – its name comes from 'Comintern': an abbreviation for the Communist International, which the Bolsheviks and other communists had set up in 1919 to help spread a global revolution. This agreement eventually saw Japan joined in a common alliance with Nazi Germany and Fascist Italy. It was eventually followed up in 1940 with the Tripartite Pact which joined these three Axis powers together.

1917, when the US had accepted that Japan had 'special interests' in China, especially where there were common borders – though the US saw these interests as essentially economic rather than political. However, Japanese imperialists saw no real difference between their claims and actions in Korea and Manchuria in Asia, and those of the US in Latin and Central American, and in Caribbean countries such as Mexico, Nicaragua, Haiti and the Dominican Republic. In the latter case, the US had frequently intervened militarily to protect US investments and to ensure 'peace and stability'.

Not surprisingly, however, China was not willing to accept the 'independence' of Manchukuo. At first, in the early 1930s, Japanese governments continued to call for friendly relations in the area – but under 'Japanese leadership'. In 1935, Nationalist China established diplomatic relations with Japan. However, the Kwantung Army was determined to establish Japanese control over Northern China. In mid-1935, they used anti-Japanese protests as an excuse to insist that the Nationalist government withdraw its troops from the provinces of Hebei and Chahar, which were north of Beijing. They then tried to force the nationalists to make these provinces an autonomous zone, largely independent of China.

When Koki Hirota became prime minister, his Fundamental Policy was based on the need to focus on the Soviet Union – consequently, in September 1936, he signed the **Anti-Comintern Pact** with Nazi Germany. Though this was not a military pact, it served to bring Japan closer to Nazi Germany; in 1937, Fascist Italy also joined, and so Japan began to align itself to the fascist powers in Europe.

Japan's Actions

The Second Sino-Japanese War begins

On 7 July 1937 – just one month after Konoe had become prime minister – Japanese troops provoked a relatively minor clash between themselves and local Chinese forces at the Marco Polo Bridge, a railway junction just outside **Beijing**.

The Marco Polo Bridge Incident

This incident became the trigger for the Second Sino-Japanese War. Claiming that the Chinese had fired on them outside Wanping – a small town near Beijing, and close to the Marco Polo Bridge – the Japanese launched an attack on several Chinese army bases around Beijing. When Japanese troops attacked the small Chinese force defending the Marco Polo Bridge (sometimes known as the Lugouqiao Bridge), they met stiff resistance. At first, Japan's government began negotiations with the Chinese government. However, this time, hardliners in the Japanese army wanted more than a settlement along the lines of those made between 1931 and 1937 and war minister Sugiyama Hajime proposed sending extra divisions to China.

Yet those such as Ishiwara, who were more concerned about the Soviet Union, were reluctant to get involved in a full-scale war against China. Though they tried to persuade Hirota – who, in February 1937, had been replaced as prime minister and, instead, had become foreign minister – to oppose these steps, he finally agreed with the military hardliners. Konoe supported this – he then publically blamed the Chinese for the incident and announced the sending of more troops.

These announcements led to protests in China and, despite a ceasefire, several more military clashes took place. In the main, this was because the officers in Japan's North China Army, and the militarists in the General Staff of Japan's Imperial Army were determined to provoke a clash which would justify a full-scale invasion

Beijing: From 1928–49, this city was known as 'Beiping' and was the 'Northern Capital'; previously, it had been the official capital of China. During this period, however, the official capital of China was Nanjing (the 'Southern Capital'). Between 1932–37, Japanese forces had occupied most of the area to the north of Beijing – this took place whilst Jiang Jieshi was busy attacking the Chinese communists (see section 4.2). The Marco Polo Bridge was the boundary between the Japanese-held territory and that still under Chinese control. From 1937–45, Beijing was under Japanese occupation and became the capital of the puppet regime the Japanese set up, following their conquest of Northern China.

Figure 3.4 Japanese troops invading China, after the Marco Polo Bridge Incident

3 Japanese Expansion in East Asia, 1931–41

> **SOURCE D**
>
> First, and most immediately, it seemed likely that any compromise settlement would involve his [Jiang's] government formally ceding control of the former capital. This was not like giving up Manchuria. The establishment of Manchukuo had been a huge blow to China's prestige, but not a disaster. Chiang [Jiang] had all but recognized the Japanese client state by 1933. Beiping was a different matter. Under its former name of Beijing, the city had been a national capital for centuries. Although its political importance had waned, it was still a place of immense cultural and emotional significance to many Chinese. The city also had strategic importance: it was the major rail interchange for northern China, connecting the north of China to the inland commercial city of Wuhan, and allowing rail traffic to travel in all four directions of the compass … If Chiang surrendered the city, he would cede north China for a generation, and put the Nationalist heartland in great danger.
>
> Mitter, R. *China's War with Japan, 1937–1945: the struggle for survival.* London. Penguin Books. p. 75.

Previously, the various 'incidents' which had broken out between Japan and China in the period 1931–37 had been settled by 'compromise' – most of which involved Japan forcing China to make certain concessions. However, given Beijing's strategic and emotional importance for China, Japan's decision to attack it proved to be a turning point in Japan's relations with China.

Another 'incident' in Shanghai – China's most important port – led the Japanese navy to push for troops to be sent there, as it was an area of special interest to Japan. The army agreed, and by mid-August, there were armed clashes in Shanghai. When Nationalist China ordered a general mobilisation, Japan's government decided to begin an all-out war; Konoe's government then gave permission for the invasion of China. In Japan, there was much

Figure 3.5 An injured and terrified Chinese child amongst the ruins of Shanghai's South Railway Station. This was just one of the many civilian victims of the Japanese bombing of Shanghai on 28 August 1937

nationalism and popular patriotic support for their government's actions; and Japan's press openly supported the military hardliners, and called for China to be punished for its actions.

Japan had been modernising its armed forces since 1868, but China had only had a unified government since 1927 – and even then, China had been torn by conflicts with warlords, and by the civil war the Nationalists had launched against the Chinese communists. Given these factors – and the effective loss of control of Manchuria and various concessions made in north China – Japan met little serious resistance. By November 1937, Japan had occupied Shanghai, after a campaign which included bombing a civilian area of the city. In December 1937, following a three-month siege, Japanese forces captured the capital of China, Nanjing.

The 'Rape of Nanjing'

One of the most notorious aspects of the early part of the Second Sino-Japanese War was what happened in Nanjing. The commanding Japanese general, Matsui Iwane, made no attempt to control the behaviour of his troops in the city. In part, this was undoubtedly the result of the sense of **racial superiority** which had been an important part of the Japanese schooling system and which had been a strong element in Japanese nationalism for many decades.

While these Japanese atrocities in Nanjing in 1937 were not the only ones committed by Japanese troops in China, they were certainly the worst. One of the few Japanese commanding officers who did try to prevent such acts was General Hata Shunroku, who led the campaign against Hanguo on the central Yangzi River – he specifically issued strict orders to his troops *not* to commit atrocities.

racial superiority: The ideas and attitudes of racial superiority in Japan were very similar to those held by Italian fascists and German nazis – both these groups, respectively, used their racist views to justify their expansionist foreign policy against such countries as Abyssinia, Poland and the Soviet Union.

However, the reasons for atrocities such as those in Nanjing are undoubtedly more complex than this. For instance, as shown by several more recent wars, war requires brutal actions – and this clearly has a brutalising effect on those directly involved in the fighting, thus leading to vicious atrocities and abuses of human rights at times.

SOURCE E

[T]here were many cases of rape. Death was a frequently [sic] penalty for the slightest resistance on the part of a victim or the members of her family who sought to protect her … Many women were killed after the act and their bodies mutilated. Approximately 20,000 cases of rape occurred within the city during the first month of the occupation.

Extract from the judgement of the International Military Tribunal for the Far East, held in Tokyo after the war, on what Japanese troops did in Nanjing. Quoted in Boister, N. and Cryer, R. (eds). 2008. *The Tokyo International Military Tribunal: a Reappraisal.* Oxford. Oxford University Press. p. 191.

Fact: The Japanese atrocities in Nanjing still cause problems today between China and Japan, with many in China believing that Japan has not sufficiently apologised for what their troops did to civilians in Nanjing – or in so many other parts of occupied China during the Second Sino-Japanese War.

Figure 3.6 Some of the bodies of civilian victims during the 'Rape of Nanjing'

3

Japanese Expansion in East Asia, 1931–41

Theory of knowledge

History, ethics and writing history:

The Roman playwright, Publius Terentius Afer (186–159 BCE – and usually referred to as 'Terence'), once wrote: '*I am human and therefore indifferent to nothing done by humans.*' Is it possible for historians – and history students – to write about or study such incidents as the 'Rape of Nanjing' impartially, without making moral judgements? Even if it is possible, do you think it is either desirable or morally correct NOT to make moral judgements about such actions and those responsible for them? Or should we – as fellow humans – reject Terence's position, and instead remain 'indifferent'?

The war continues

After the capture of Nanjing, Japanese forces were able to take effective control of most of North China by the end of 1937. These developments forced Jiang to retreat and to establish a new wartime capital at Chonqing. By the start of 1938, there were over 1 million Japanese troops in China, and Japan controlled all the main cities and lines of communication in the provinces around the Yangzi River – China's most fertile and densely-populated area. Later in 1938, Japanese forces captured the important cities of Wuhan and Guangzhou, as well as occupying the island of Hainan.

Nazi Germany – which wanted Japan to focus on the Soviet Union, rather than get involved in a war in the Pacific – offered to mediate between Japan and China. But Japan insisted on such hard terms that China at first prevaricated. Konoe then took this as evidence of rejection, and ended all further negotiations. He then ordered the war in China to continue. Japanese forces soon controlled the whole coastal area from north to south, and

Figure 3.7 Map showing Japan's conquests in China, 1937–45

began to move inland. The new capital, Hango, was one target – another was Chongqing. However, the Nationalist government put up determined resistance and, over the next five years, Japanese forces were unable to push any further into the interior. From then on, there was a 'war of attrition' fought out in the mountainous areas of China. From 1938 onwards, Japanese forces managed to maintain their control of the large cities, and the main railways, airfields, ports and roads – but the countryside stayed mostly in Chinese hands.

In the south, the Japanese concentrated their efforts on destroying Jiang's new capital of Chongqing – it was bombed so frequently, that it became known as 'the most bombarded city in the world'. It has been estimated that the city suffered over 5,000 separate bombing raids.

An attempt to politically and militarily weaken Nationalist China, by persuading Wang Jingwei to leave the nationalists and instead become head of a Japanese puppet government in China in early 1940, had little significant effect on Chinese resistance to Japanese troops. However, the situation began to change after December 1941. By then, Japan had over 2 million troops in China – these amounted to almost 50% of Japan's army. But the decision of Japan's government to attack the US naval base at Pearl Harbor in December 1941 began to create increasing problems for Japan's armed forces in China, thus easing the pressure on Jiang's forces (see section 4.2, The Second Sino-Japanese War after Pearl Harbor).

Fact: Part of Japan's inability to make further progress was because it had a much smaller population than China and thus had insufficient forces to invade and occupy the whole of China. Even in the areas they did control, they never had total control: as they moved south from Manchuria, they had to leave many of the areas they had already conquered unguarded. This allowed Chinese forces – especially those of the Communists' Red Army – to move back into these northern and eastern areas and take control of the countryside. In August 1940, the CCP launched their massive 'Hundred Regiments' offensive against the Japanese in central China. This involved 115 regiments, numbering over 400,000 soldiers: after some great successes in August and September, the Japanese launched counter-attacks and, in December 1940, the CCP's offensive was called off.

KEY CONCEPTS ACTIVITY

Consequences: Carry out some additional research on developments in the Second Sino-Japanese War after 1938. Then write a couple of paragraphs to explain what impact the following two developments had on Japan's war in China: (a) The Second United Front between the GMD and CCP; and (b) Japan's decision to attack Pearl Harbor.

Figure 3.8 A photograph of some of the civilian victims in July 1941, after one of the many Japanese bombing raids on Chongqing

3

Japanese Expansion in East Asia, 1931–41

3.3 Why did Japan attack Pearl Harbor in 1941?

While several factors behind Japan's decision to attack the US Pacific naval base in Pearl Harbor originate in the 19th century, there were also some important short-term factors. These include the increased influence of Japan's military leaders and the signing of the Tripartite Pact in 1940 – less than a year before the attack on Pearl Harbor.

Military factions and foreign policy 1937–40

In November 1937, some hardline Japanese army officers tried to start a war with Britain and the US by attacking their gunboats off the Chinese coast – but the Japanese government quickly apologised and paid compensation.

By 1935, there were several rival factions in the Japanese army. They were to prove crucial for the extension of Japan's expansion into the Pacific - and thus for its eventual clash with the US. There was the Imperial Way Faction, whose members were ultra-nationalists, led by generals Araki Sadao and Mazaki Jinzaburo – these believed in the supremacy of Japanese soldiers if they were imbued with 'spiritual power' (the Yamato spirit). They advocated the 'Imperial Way' (*Kodo-ha*), and those officers who tended to favour violent action to overturn the existing system looked up to them. This faction included supporters of the 'Strike-North' Faction, which wanted to expand into Siberia (and beyond) at the expense of the Soviet Union.

The other main faction – known as the 'Control' Faction (*Tosei-ha*) did not favour individual acts of political violence – instead, they wanted to modernise the Japanese army – especially as regards tanks and planes. They saw modern war as requiring the total mobilisation of the nation's resources – which they felt should come under the control of the army's central command. Leaders of this faction included Nagata Tetsuzan and a future prime minister, Tojo Hideki. This faction included members of the 'Strike-South' Faction, which believed Japan should solve its lack of resources by military expansion in southeast Asia and Oceania.

Conflict between these two factions erupted in mid-1935, when General Hayashi Senjuro, the war minister, removed general Mazaki from his post of Inspector General of Military Education. This was one of the top three army positions – the other two were war minister and army general chief of staff. Mazaki's supporters saw this as an attempt to weaken their *Kodo-ha* faction, following the discovery in 1934 of a conspiracy by *Kodo-ha* officers to assassinate leading statesmen and set up a military government. They particularly blamed the chief of military affairs, Nagata; and, as a result, a *Kodo-ha* officer killed him. The assassin was portrayed as a patriot, and the *Kodo-ha* officers decided to put their plan into action anyway. This had the implicit support of Mazaki and several other generals, and received financial support from right-wing businessmen and politicians.

Several of the plotters were attached to the First Division, which was due to go to Manchuria – so they decided to strike before they were sent off. On 26 February 1936, the troops of the First Division were ordered to occupy key positions in the capital,

---

Fact: There were two main factions in the 1930s and these, and others, were to prove crucial for the extension of Japan's expansion into the Pacific – and thus for its eventual clash with the US. The 'Imperial Way' Faction included supporters of the 'Strike-North' Faction, which wanted to expand into Siberia (and beyond) at the expense of the Soviet Union. The 'Control' Faction, on the other hand, included members of the 'Strike-South' Faction, which believed Japan should solve its lack of resources by military expansion in southeast Asia and Oceania. Because some members of the 'Strike-North' Faction were involved in the attempted coup on 26 February 1936, they lost influence – one result was that the 'Strike-South' Faction began to dominate planning for strengthening the military and for territorial expansion.

ACTIVITY

Briefly summarise the main differences between the 'Strike-North' and the 'Strike-South' Factions in the Japanese military. Then list the most important likely consequences of each proposed policy of expansion.

while assassination squads were despatched to kill prominent political and government officials. Those to be killed included prime minister Okada, former prime minister Saito, minister of finance Takahashi Korekiyo, and general Watanabe Jotaro – the last three were all killed. The officers of the army were undecided as to whether to go along with the plans of the plotters, or to crush them. In the end, the emperor made it clear he would not support the attempted coup. So martial law was proclaimed and the plotters decided to surrender – two committed suicide, while nineteen were eventually executed.

This failed coup marked the end of the *Kodo-ha* group, and those generals associated with it were placed on the inactive list and military regulations were revised so that none of them could serve as war minister in the future. Leadership thus passed to the *Tosei-ha* officers, who believed in a disciplined centralised order. However, they were certainly not against the army intervening in politics – just against individual acts of violence. One effect of the 26 February plot and the response of the *Tosei-ha* officers was to make political leaders very wary of opposing the military. Thus the result of the attempted coup was to greatly increase army influence over the government. As the army would choose the war minister, they had a kind of veto power over any government – if they refused to name one, a new cabinet could not be formed. Thus, if they disliked a potential prime minister, they could prevent him from heading a government. An early example of this came when the emperor chose Hirota Koki to form the next government. The army chose general Terauchi Hisaichi as war minister – and he made sure that Hirota did not appoint any liberal cabinet ministers: one of those rejected by him was Yoshida Shigeru, who had opposed the army's actions in Manchuria. From then on, the army continued increasingly to use its power to approve or disapprove all future cabinets.

The Fundamental Principles of National Policy

One of the first acts of Hirota's government was to proclaim 'The Fundamental Principles of National Policy' – this affirmed the need to consolidate Japan's position in East Asia, and to advance into the South Sea region.

Although it suggested a more moderate policy towards China, it advocated a stronger stand against Soviet Russia.

Hirota was later forced to resign, and Saionji's next choice was blocked by the army. Then, in June 1937, Saionji was able to get Prince Konoe Fumimaro appointed as the next prime minister. Although initially seen as something of a moderate, he had begun increasingly to take a hardline position as regards foreign affairs, and became opposed to the idea of continued international cooperation. In particular, he believed that Japan needed to follow its own foreign policy objectives, and form a bloc – like other nations – to push its interests forward. He saw Japan as a 'have-not' nation which would now make it clear to the 'have' nations – such as Britain, the US and France – that Japan now intended to become a 'have' nation too. His attitude certainly played an important part in the outbreak of war with China just one month after he became prime minister.

By then, the industrial-financial *zaibatsu* were ready to cooperate with the militarists in pursuing an expansionist imperialist foreign policy. In particular, Mitsui and Mitsubishi cooperated with the military to build up heavy industries linked to strategic war industries. Mitsubishi produced 30% of all ships, and also began to

Fact: Advances in the South Sea region were advocated by the navy, which wanted to gain access to the important oil deposits in southeast Asia. Although this was meant to be achieved by peaceful means, it eventually was an important factor in the invasion of China and the Dutch East Indies, and so contributed to the outbreak of the Pacific War. Consequently, Hirota was found guilty of being a Class A war criminal by the post-war International Military Tribunal, and he was executed in 1948.

QUESTION

Why were the Dutch East Indies increasingly seen as a vital area for Japanese expansion?

QUESTION

What do you understand by the term 'have-not' nations'?

3 Japanese Expansion in East Asia, 1931–41

produce the Zero fighter plane. In addition, their links to the military ensured they had access to vital raw materials, which were denied to medium- and small-sized enterprises. Thus their moves to establish even greater monopolies were advanced by war preparations.

Ever since Manchuria, there had been growing pressure for a greater concentration on war production. While others saw expansion on the mainland as a valuable outlet for Japan's impoverished and growing population – and a way of overcoming the impact of the Depression. In fact, the *zaibatsu* had been active in investing Japanese capital in Manchuria, in order to develop its economy. By 1940, Japanese businesses owned almost 85% of all capital investments in Manchuria – and they imposed an extremely harsh exploitation on Chinese labourers there, in order to increase their profits (these Chinese workers were paid only one-third of the wages paid to Japanese workers).

The growing regional influence of the US

Another reason for Japan's decision to attack Pearl Harbor was resentment at growing US influence in Asia and the Pacific. In fact, the US had increasingly adopted an expansionist foreign policy towards the Pacific, as well as Central and Latin America. In 1899, Theodore Roosevelt – a year before he was elected US vice-president – made a speech calling for the US to adopt a more aggressive and expansionist foreign policy. Such a policy was also based on the view that stronger more 'advanced' peoples should take charge of 'less-developed' non-white peoples and nations, in order to 'civilise' them.

In 1901, Roosevelt became president, following the assassination of President McKinley. His ideas were to have a big influence on US foreign policy in the Pacific.

Fact: Such views to 'civilise' non-white peoples and nations were also used to justify the expansion of the US westwards, which involved the takeover of the lands belonging to the Native Americans. By 1890, this was mostly complete.

Fact: The US establishment of control over the Philippines was only achieved after a tremendous loss of life. According to some estimates, US troops and forces commanded by them were responsible for the deaths of well over 100,000 Filipino people who tried, from 1899–1902, to resist seeing US control substituted for Spanish control.

SOURCE F

If we Americans are to be a really great power we must strive to play a great part in the world. If we shrink from hard contests, then bolder and stronger peoples will pass us by and win for themselves the domination of the world.

Extracts from a speech made by Theodore Roosevelt in 1901. Quoted in: en.wikiquote.org

This US expansionist approach as regards Asia and the Pacific was shown after the Spanish-American War 1898, which saw the US establish control over the Philippines in the Pacific Ocean, as well as dominating the newly 'independent' Cuba. Given the distance from the US, this US expansion in the Pacific was to be based on the rapid growth of its naval power.

In addition to the Philippines, the US also took over Hawaii and Guam in 1898. In the decades that followed 1898, US businesses and military presence in the region had continued to grow – and increasingly came into conflict with Japan's own interests in the region.

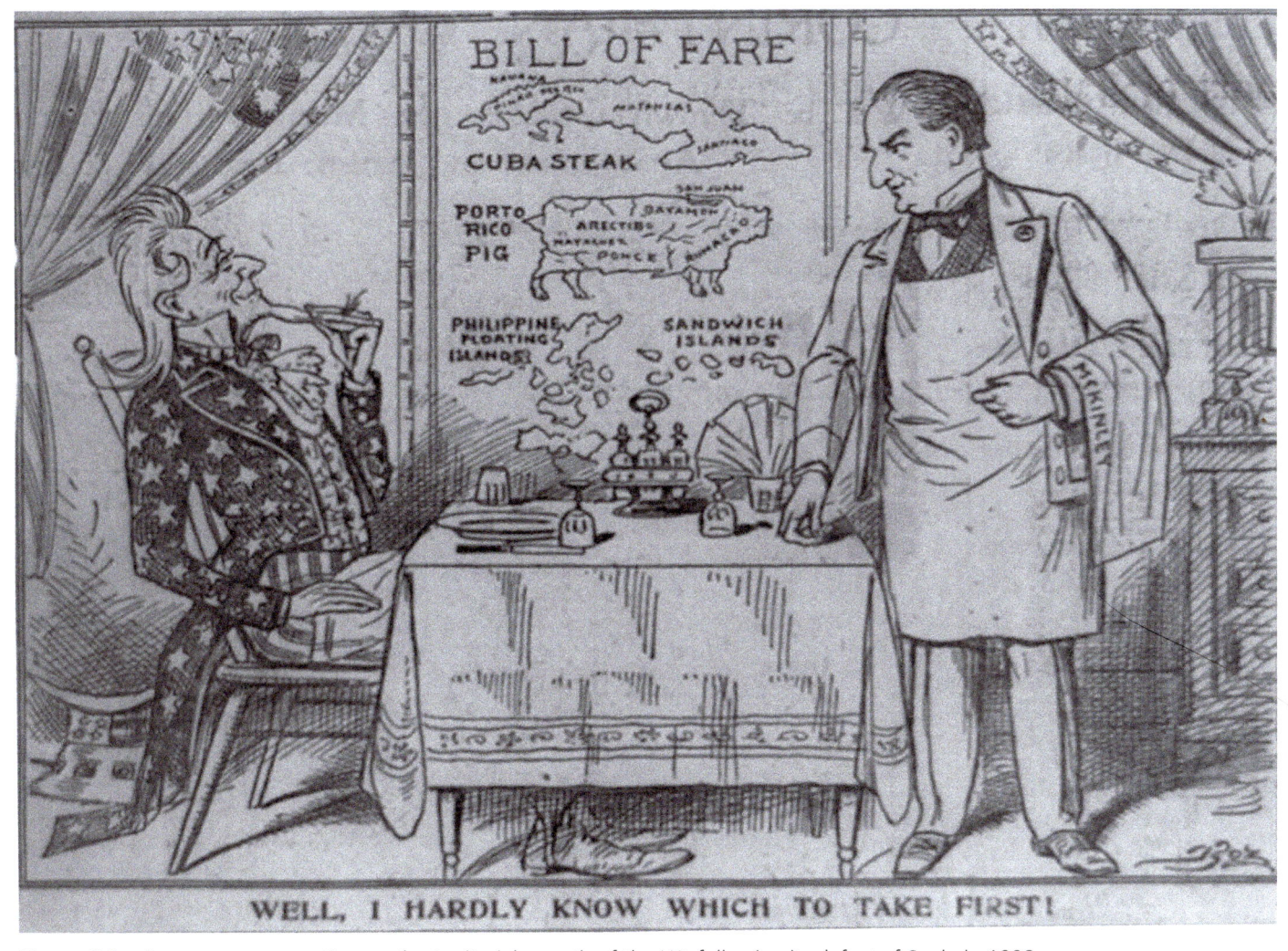

Figure 3.9 A cartoon commenting on the territorial growth of the US, following its defeat of Spain in 1898

Japan and the Soviet Union

Another factor which proved decisive in turning Japan's attentions to southeast Asia and the Pacific as an area for expansion was the growing realisation that any attempted advances into Soviet territory would prove much more difficult than previously thought. In July 1938, while the war in China was progressing, some army officers who were concerned about the Soviet Union's position in East Asia, precipitated a military clash at Changkufen, on the Siberia/Manchuria/Korea border. Although they had expected an easy victory, Japanese forces were decisively defeated and, after being forced to withdraw, they had to accept a negotiated settlement. In May 1939, the Kwantung Army provoked another clash in Nomonhan, on the border between Manchuria and Outer Mongolia. This quickly developed into a major conflict. In August 1939, at the battle of Khalkhin-Gol, the Soviet Union once again inflicted a crushing defeat on Japanese forces, and a cease-fire was called. By then, the invasion of China was

> **QUESTION**
>
> Look at **Figure 3.9**. What point is the cartoonist trying to make – and how do they achieve it?
>
> What are the value and limitations of this source for an historian trying to establish US foreign policy aims in the Pacific during the 1920s and 1930s?

3 Japanese Expansion in East Asia, 1931–41

proving costly for Japan, and an increasingly large army was needed in China. These developments served to strengthen the case of those who argued that expansion in southeast Asia and the Pacific would be an easier option.

The significance of the Tripartite Pact, September 1940

After 1937, hardline nationalists in Japan began to push for closer links to Germany and Italy – especially after Hitler's quick conquests in Europe in the period 1938–40.

At first, the three 'have-not' states – Japan, Germany and Italy – did not draw up any combined action plans for a concerted effort to challenge those aspects of the world order to which they objected. In fact, for much of the 1930s, it was clear that Fascist Italy was initially very distrustful of Nazi Germany's intentions in Europe; while, for some time, Nazi Germany tended to support China rather than Japan. As a result, these three countries – despite signing various bilateral agreements with each other – did not at first conclude any joint tripartite political alliance or military agreements.

However, the first significant step towards such a **three-way alliance** was taken in May 1939, when Germany and Italy signed the Pact of Steel.

In July 1940, Konoe formed a government, which had the support of the militarists and ultra-nationalists. He quickly formulated 'The Main Principles of Fundamental National Policy'. At the same time that this policy document was revealed, the principles of **Hakko ichiu** were also officially endorsed – though, as early as February 1933, these ideas were partly behind the announcement of Japan's 'Monroe Doctrine' (see section 3.2, The road to war).

The Greater East Asia Co-Prosperity Sphere

The Fundamental National Policy document called for the establishment of a 'New Order' in Greater East Asia, which, in particular, would be based on the 'Greater East Asia Co-Prosperity Sphere'. In late July, the Fundamental National Policy document was approved at a combined conference of the cabinet and the supreme command – even if it involved military conflicts with Britain and the US. Consequently, emphasis was placed on building up the armed forces, trying to conclude the war against China, and greater economic planning. On 1 August 1940, Japan's plans for a 'Greater East Asia Co-Prosperity Sphere' were publicly announced.

Japan's government had been angered by the announcement of the Nazi-Soviet Non-Aggression Pact in August 1939, and had initially withdrawn from the Anti-Comintern Pact. However, relations with Nazi Germany eventually began to improve once more. Consequently, two months after the announcement of Japan's Greater East Asia Co-Prosperity Sphere, Konoe's new government concluded the Three-Power Axis Alliance with Germany and Italy, by signing the Tripartite Pact, in September 1940.

The Tripartite Pact (sometimes also referred to as the Three-Power or the Berlin Pact) was signed in Berlin on 27 September 1940. In general, it confirmed the three countries' intentions to establish 'new orders' in their respective regions. It was essentially a defensive military alliance, though it was also intended as a warning to the US – which, at that time, was still officially neutral – that, if it attacked one of its members, the others would assist that country. It was hoped this would persuade the US not to intervene in any of the on-going military conflicts in Asia and Europe.

---

three-way alliance: Although a firm tripartite agreement binding these three countries together in the three-way alliance was relatively late in coming, they all shared a feeling that the existing international order was unfair to their respective countries. They also saw the 1930s as a 'window of opportunity', given the economic impact of the Great Depression and the reluctance of the Western democracies to oppose aggression.

Hakko ichiu: These principles were based on the belief that Jimmu, Japan's legendary first emperor, had said that *'I shall cover the eight directions and make them my abode.'* In the 1930s, these words were interpreted by Japan's ultra-nationalists to mean that Japan was divinely ordained to expand until it had united the whole world, with the 1930s' version of *Hakko ichiu* being: 'eight corners of the world under one roof'.

Figure 3.10 The signing of the Tripartite Pact, between Japan, Germany and Italy, on 27 September 1940. Those seated, from left to right are: Saburo Kurusu (Imperial Japan), Galeazzo Ciano (Fascist Italy) and Adolf Hitler (Nazi Germany)

SOURCE G

The first three articles of the Tripartite Pact of September 1940.

Article 1. Japan recognizes and respects the leadership of Germany and Italy in the establishment of a new order in Europe.

Article 2. Germany and Italy recognize and respect the leadership of Japan in the establishment of a new order in Greater East Asia.

Article 3. Japan, Germany, and Italy agree to co-operate in their efforts on aforesaid lines. They further undertake to assist one another with all political, economic and military means if one of the Contracting Powers is attacked by a Power at present not involved in the European War or in the Japanese-Chinese conflict.

From: http://avalon.law.yale.edu/wwii/triparti.asp

However, the Tripartite Pact *did not* include the provision that its members would actually declare war on the attacking country or countries, as opposed to just giving assistance to any member being attacked. In fact, the three powers did not work closely

3 Japanese Expansion in East Asia, 1931–41

with each other. This was especially true of Japan and Germany: Japan hoped Britain's problems in Europe would give it a free hand in Asia, while Germany saw Japanese expansion in Asia as a way of weakening both Britain and the US. As far as Japanese actions were concerned, the signing of the Tripartite Pact was soon followed by its decision to send troops into northern Indo-china.

Nonetheless, after the Japanese attack on the US in December 1941, both Italy and Germany also declared war on the US, on 11 December, at a Tripartite Pact Conference in Berlin. In addition, that Conference saw these three Axis powers agree that none of them would sign a separate peace with the US.

Invasion of Indo-china, September 1940

Another reason for the attack on Pearl Harbor was Japan's decision to move into French Indo-china – and the reaction of the US to this move. In late September 1940, following France's defeat by Nazi Germany in June 1940, a small Japanese force entered and occupied the northern part of French Indo-china – partly after having reached an agreement with the Vichy French authorities. This occupation was in part linked to the Second Sino-Japanese War, as it was aimed at stopping the Nationalist government of China from importing arms and fuel through French Indo-china along the Sino-Indo-china Railway, which ran from the Indochinese port of Haiphong, through Hanoi, to the Chinese port of Kunming. Previously, Japan had asked the French authorities to close the railway – which was China's only land access to the outside world – but this had been refused.

Initially, some Japanese politicians believed this move into north Indo-china could be done without provoking war with the US. In addition, at this stage, the final debates over strategy between the 'Strike-North' and the 'Strike-South' Factions in the Japanese military were still taking place. The former were still interested in extending Japanese control beyond Manchuria into Siberia – but there were concerns over what actions the Soviet Union might take. Thus – apart from not wishing to provoke Britain and the US at this stage – Japan decided against committing large numbers of troops in Indo-china, until the picture as regards the Soviet Union's intentions was clearer. Consequently, Japan decided not to occupy the southern half of Indo-china. Nonetheless, the US responded to Japan's moves in Indo-china by imposing economic sanctions against Japan – these reduced exports, amongst other things, of oil, iron and machinery. The US also made it clear that further Japanese aggression in the region would result in much tougher sanctions. As these items were vital for Japan's war in China, the military began to put pressure on the Japanese government to sanction action for obtaining alternative supplies.

Ruling out the 'Strike North' option

At the time of the decision to send troops into Indo-china, the final decision about whether to attack the Soviet Union or the US had still not been formally made. However, on 13 April 1941, the Japanese government and military concluded the **Japanese–Soviet Neutrality Pact** with the Soviet Union. This formally ended the Soviet-Japanese Border War, which had existed from 1938–39. Prior to these border clashes with the USSR's Red Army, Japan's military had assumed that Stalin's purges had seriously weakened the Red Army. Now, however, Japan decided that it would not be wise to take on the Soviet Union. This agreement allowed Japan to consider implementing the decisions of the July 1941 Conference by moving south. This was another important step on the road to the attack on Pearl Harbor, and to the wider Pacific War.

Japanese–Soviet Neutrality Pact: This pact – also known as the Japanese–Soviet Non-Aggression Pact – was important in several ways. In particular, it meant that the differences between the two main factions – the 'Strike-North' and the 'Strike-South' Factions – in the Japanese government and military were being resolved in favour of leaving the Soviet Union alone and instead of preparing for war in the Pacific against Britain, the US, France and the Netherlands. In addition, it allowed the Soviet Union to withdraw troops from East Asia – especially after December 1941, when Japan's attack against Pearl Harbor resulted in the US declaring war on Japan – in order to resist the German invasion which had begun in June 1941.

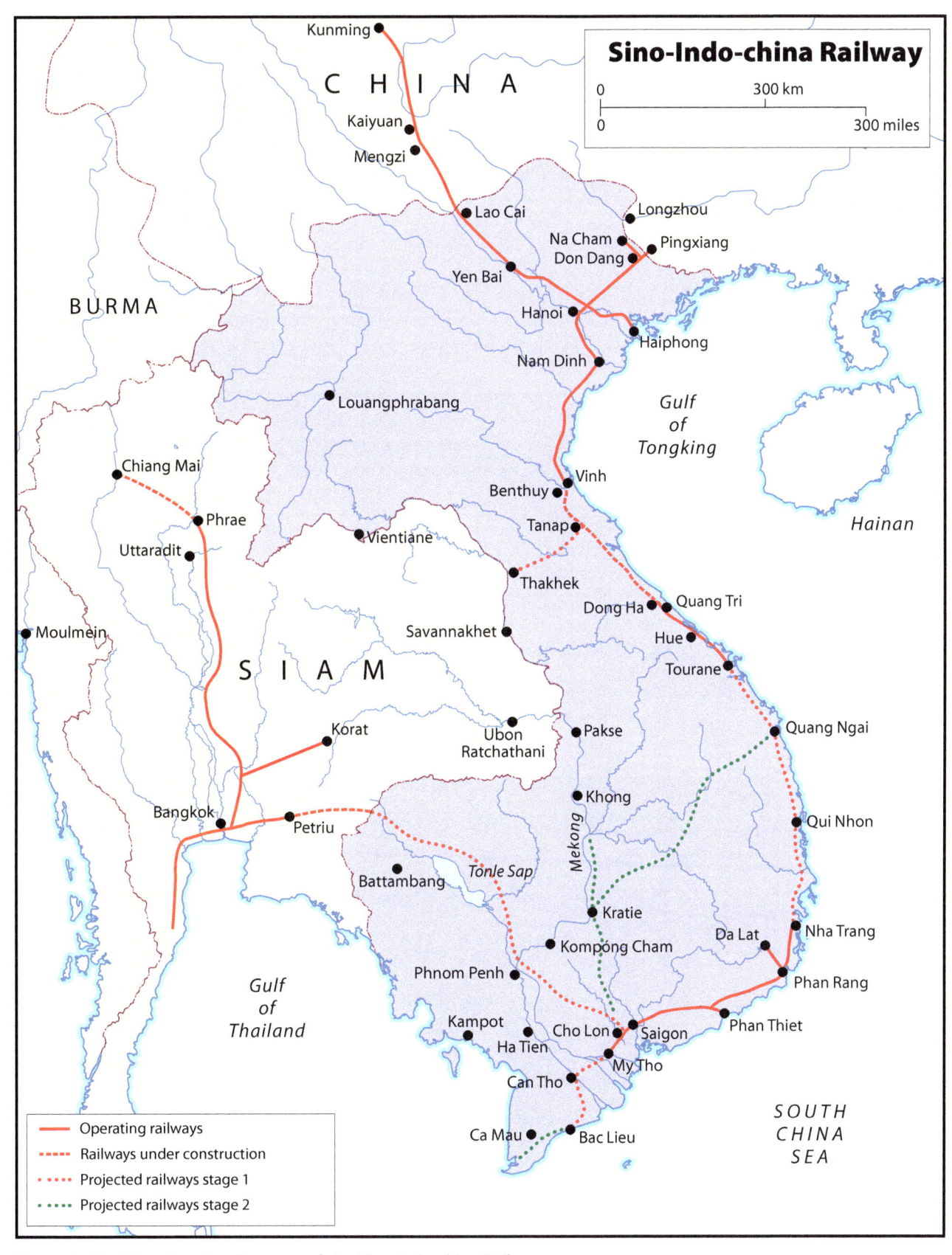

Figure 3.11 Map showing the route of the Sino–Indo-china Railway

3

Japanese Expansion in East Asia, 1931–41

After Hitler had launched the invasion of the Soviet Union in late June 1941, Japan concluded that there was no longer any Soviet threat to Manchuria. Consequently, in July 1941, the Japanese government held an Imperial Conference, which finally decided on significant expansion in southeast Asia and the Pacific – even if it meant war with the US and Britain.

So, on 28 July 1941, a large Japanese army moved into southern Indo-china.

> **SOURCE H**
>
> 1. Our Empire is determined to follow a policy that will result in the establishment of the Greater Asia Co-Prosperity Sphere and will thereby contribute to world peace …
>
> 2. Our Empire will continue its efforts to effect a settlement of the China Incident [Japan's invasion of China] and will seek to establish a solid basis for the security and preservation of the nation. This will involve steps to advance south.
>
> 3. Our Empire is determined to remove all obstacles in order to achieve the above-mentioned objectives.
>
> In order to achieve the above objectives, preparations for war with Great Britain and the United States will be made … In carrying out the plans outlined above, our Empire will not be deterred by the possibility of being involved in a war with Great Britain and the United States.
>
> Extract from the Minutes of the Japanese government's Imperial Conference, held in Tokyo on 2 July 1941. Quoted in Overy, R. J. 1987. *The Origins of the Second World War*. London. Longman. p. 114.

QUESTION
Study **Source H**. What do you think were the most significant decisions made during this Imperial Conference?

Figure 3.12 Japanese troops moving into Saigon, in southern Indo-china

The Japanese attack on Pearl Harbor, 7 December 1941

The US reacted to this latest example of Japanese expansionism by almost immediately imposing a total ban on vital supplies such as oil, iron and aircraft to Japan – and freezing all Japanese assets in the US. These US actions, which were much tougher than the 1940 embargo, helped push Japan into deciding to extend its 'Greater East Asia Co-prosperity Sphere' (see section 3.3, The Greater East Asia Co-Prosperity Sphere) in order to have access to the plentiful supplies of oil and rubber in the Dutch East Indies, the US-controlled Philippines, and British Malaya.

Fact: As well as the US Pacific naval base at Pearl Harbor, there were also Japanese attacks on two US bases in Oceania: Guam and Wake Island. In fact, the attack on Pearl Harbor did not inflict that much of a loss on the US, as its aircraft carriers – which proved to be the most important ships in the Pacific War – were at sea, on manoeuvres.

Historical debate: Although most historians reject the idea that US officials, because Japanese naval and diplomatic codes had been broken, knew of the impending attack on Pearl Harbor – but decided not to inform the base commanders – there have been several contrary arguments (including comments by retired US Navy Rear Admiral Theobald). Most of the 'advance-knowledge' conspiracy theories are also based on the fact that several senior figures at the time – such as US Vice Admiral Beatty and US Secretary of War Stimson – are on record as having said that the US government knew it was pushing Japan into war; wanted Japan to attack first; and hoped that the attack, when it came, would not be too costly. Such theories also point to the fact that US aircraft carriers (the most important ships in modern warfare) were not at Pearl Harbor at the time, but were at sea on manoeuvres.

SOURCE I

The United States government responded by freezing the Japanese assets in America and imposed a total embargo on exports to Japan except for cotton and food. Britain and the Dutch East Indies followed suit. This in effect meant a total economic blockade by the countries that Japan was heavily dependent upon for imports. In 1939 66.4% of Japan's imports came from regions under Anglo-American economic control. Japan was heavily dependent on the United States for oil, a commodity crucial for the navy. In 1939 eighty-five percent and in 1940 eighty percent of Japan's oil came from the United States. Without access to the major source of oil the Japanese navy's oil reserves were expected to last two years, and a year and a half if Japan were to engage in a full-scale war. This turned the navy leaders, who had been opposed to a military conflict with Britain and America, into advocates of military action to gain access to the oil fields of the Dutch East Indies. They realized this meant war with the United States and Britain but if the blockade continued the navy would be immobilized.

Hane, M. 2013. *Japan: A Short History*. London. Oneworld Publications. pp. 162–3.

In order to achieve this extension of the Greater East Asia Co-prosperity Sphere, Japan's military government decided that it would first be necessary to knock out the USA's Pacific fleet which was currently being reinforced. It was this that led to the surprise attack on Pearl Harbor.

This action – and the simultaneous Japanese attacks on British and Dutch colonies in the region – widened what the Japanese government referred to from December 1941 as the 'Greater East Asia War'. This included its on-going war in China (which they referred to as the 'Japan–China Incident'), as well as its new conflict with Britain and the US. The Japanese government argued that the Asian nations would, with the help of Japanese armies, be able to gain independence from the Western powers.

The Japanese government assumed that, having suffered a rapid knock-out blow, the US would agree to accept further Japanese expansion in southeast Asia. However, it was soon apparent that the US was only temporarily inconvenienced by the attack – before long, the superior industrial capacity and raw material supplies of the US turned Japan's 'Greater East Asia War' into a war of attrition. This prolonged warfare – as opposed to one of quick victories – was one that Japan's economy, already under strain from the Depression and its war against China, could not sustain.

Japanese Expansion in East Asia, 1931–41

Activities

1 Using the information in this chapter, and any other available sources, construct a timeline showing all the main military actions undertaken by Japan between 1931 and the end of 1941.

2 Write a newspaper article explaining why Japan saw expansion into Manchuria as a sensible course of action.

3 Produce a spider diagram which shows all the different factors which led to Japan finally deciding on the 'Strike-South' expansion policy. Then write a paragraph to explain which factor you think was most significant.

4 'The USA deliberately provoked Japan into attacking it, in order to be justified in entering the Second World War, and to further its own interests in Asia and the Pacific.' With a partner, produce two discussion papers (or speeches): one of you should support the statement and the other one oppose it. Then swap your work, and assess each other as regards: (a) clear argument and (b) precise supporting evidence.

End of chapter activities

Summary

You should now have a sound knowledge of the main foreign policy actions taken by imperial Japan in the period 1931–41, prior to the outbreak of war with the USA in December 1941.

You should also be able to explain why Japan finally decided to pursue expansion in Asia and the Pacific, rather than against the Soviet Union.

Finally, you should be able to understand the reasons for the diplomatic steps which ended with Japan signing the Tripartite Pact with Nazi Germany and Fascist Italy in September 1940.

Summary activities

Copy the table below and, using the information from this chapter and any other materials that you have available, summarise:

- the military actions undertaken by Japan in the period 1931–41
- the main reasons for those expansions of Japanese territory
- what the material and diplomatic outcomes were.

JAPANESE EXPANSION 1931–41

	Actions	Reasons	Outcomes
Manchuria			
Northern China			
China			
Indo-china			

Paper 1 exam practice

Question

> **SOURCE A**
>
> Although Japan has undoubtedly acted in a way contrary to the principles of the Covenant by taking the law into its own hands, she has a real grievance against China. This is not a case in which the armed forces of one country have crossed the frontiers of another in circumstances in which they had no previous right to be on the other's soil. Japan owns the South Manchurian Railway and has been entitled to have a body of Japanese guards upon the strip of land through which the railway runs. Japan's case is that she was compelled by the failure of China to provide reasonable protection to Japanese lives and property in Manchuria in the face of attacks by Chinese bandits, and of an attack upon the line itself, to move Japanese troops forward and to occupy points in Manchuria which are beyond the line of the railway.
>
> Extract from a memorandum by British Foreign Secretary, Sir John Simon, to the British Cabinet, 23 November 1931. Quoted in Fellows, N. 2012. *Peacemaking, Peacekeeping: International Relations 1918–36*. Cambridge. Cambridge University Press. p. 184.

3

With reference to its origin, purpose and content, analyse the value and limitations of **Source A** for a historian studying why Japan was able to successfully occupy Manchuria in 1931.

[4 marks]

Skill

Value and limitations (utility/reliability) of a source

Before you start

Value and limitations (utility/reliability) of a source questions require you to assess a source over a range of possible issues – and to comment on its value to historians studying a particular event or period in history. You need to consider the **origin, purpose and content** of the source *and* then use these aspects to assess the **value and limitations** of the source. You should link these in your answer, showing how origin/purpose/content relate to value/limitations.

Before you attempt this question, refer to Chapter 9 for advice on how to answer these questions, and a simplified mark scheme.

Student answer

Source A has good value for explaining why Japan was able to conquer Manchuria because it is from the British foreign secretary at the time of Japan's occupation.

Examiner comments

The response here has only limited comments on the origin and thus the value of the source. In addition, there is nothing on content or possible purpose, and nothing on the limitations of the source. The candidate has only done enough to get into Band 1, and so be awarded 1 mark.

Activity

Look again at the source, the simplified mark scheme, and the student answer above. Now try to write a paragraph or two to push the answer up into Band 1, and so obtain the full 4 marks. As well as assessing content and purpose, try to make developed comments on the limitations of the source as well as its value.

Paper 2 practice questions

1. Compare and contrast the nature of Japanese expansionism in China before and after 1937.
2. Examine the significance of the Marco Polo Bridge Incident as a cause of the Second Sino-Japanese War.
3. Evaluate the consequences of the Tripartite (Three Power) Pact as regards Japan's expansion in Asia and the Pacific in the period after 1940.
4. 'The main cause of the Japanese attack on Pearl Harbor in December 1941 was the influence of the military on Japan's government.' To what extent do you agree with this statement?

International Responses to Japanese Expansionism

4

Introduction

Between 1931 – when Japan launched the first of its expansionist military campaigns – and 1941, there were a number of different international responses to this aggression. While most history books correctly point out that the responses of the League of Nations were limited and ineffective, an examination of this period shows that the responses of individual nations were not much better.

Western European nations – such as Britain and France – were struggling to cope with the economic effects of the Great Depression and, after 1933, were more concerned with the challenges to the peace settlements of 1919–20 and collective security increasingly posed by Nazi Germany and Fascist Italy. The Soviet Union increasingly despaired of an alliance with Britain and France to limit the aggressive foreign policies of Germany and Japan, and thus began to make unilateral agreements in an attempt to bolster its own security. While the US, despite occasional statements, was at first more concerned to protect its own interests in Asia and the Pacific. It was not until 1940 that it began to take any meaningful action to limit Japanese aggression.

KEY QUESTIONS
- How did the League of Nations respond to Japan's expansionism?
- What political developments occurred within China as a result of Japanese aggression?
- What was the international response to Japanese aggression?

Overview

- In 1931, Japan's invasion of Manchuria presented the League with a serious test of its role to maintain collective security.
- However, both Britain and France were struggling with the economic effects of the Great Depression and both had colonies in Asia. They were thus reluctant to provoke a clash with Japan.

TIMELINE
1931 Sept: Japan invades Manchuria
Dec: Lytton Commission appointed
1932 Mar: Japan transforms Manchuria to 'Manchukuo'
Oct: Lytton Commission reports to League of Nations
1933 Feb: League votes to accept the Lytton Report
Mar: Japan leaves League of Nations
1936 Nov: Anti-Comintern Pact (Germany and Japan)
Dec: Second United Front formed in China
1937 Jul: Japan invades China
Sep: China appeals to League; Sino-Soviet Non-Aggression Pact
Oct: League gives China 'spiritual support'; Nine-Power Treaty Conference; Roosevelt's 'Quarantine Speech'; Italy signs Anti-Comintern Pact (Rome-Berlin-Tokyo Axis)
Dec: Britain, France and US grant loans to China
1939 Aug: Japan defeated by Soviet forces at Khalkhin-Gol
1940 Sep: Tripartite Pact
Oct: US restricts trade with Japan
1941 Apr: Japanese-Soviet Non-Aggression Pact
Jul: US imposes total ban on trade with Japan, and freezes Japanese assets

81

4 Japanese Expansion in East Asia, 1931–41

- Consequently, although the League set up the Lytton Enquiry at the end of 1931, it did not accept the report until February 1933, by which time Japan had conquered the whole of Manchuria. The following month, Japan formally left the League.
- During the early 1930s, Japan made several incursions into China and, in July 1937, began its invasion of China. Once again, the League did virtually nothing.
- Although the Soviet Union signed a non-aggression pact with China and began to provide China with military supplies, the other major states did little beyond holding a Conference of the Nine-Power Treaty signatories.
- Although US president Roosevelt made his 'Quarantine Speech' in October 1937 on the issue of mounting aggression, the US took no action – apart from joining Britain and France in making loans to China.
- However, from 1940, when Japan began to occupy parts of French Indo-china, the US began to impose economic sanctions on trade with Japan. In October 1940, these US restrictions were partial but, in July 1941, the US imposed a total ban on the sale of all vital materials to Japan, as well as freezing all Japanese assets in the US.
- Just five months after these US actions, Japan launched its attack on the US Pacific fleet stationed in Pearl Harbor.

4.1 How did the League of Nations respond to Japan's expansionism?

Before the onset of the Great Depression, the second half of the 1920s had witnessed a general improvement in international relations. However, in the early 1930s, it quickly emerged that the economic impact of the Depression on domestic conditions in several countries was leading to the increasing adoption of aggressively expansionist foreign policies. This caused problems for the League of Nations which, before 1936, was faced with two serious challenges – one was Japan's invasion of Manchuria in 1931. The other was Italy's invasion of Abyssinia in 1935 (see section 6.2, Invasion of Abyssinia).

Crisis over Manchuria

This was a difficult situation for the League in several ways: because both China and Japan were members of the League; and because both Britain and France – the most important members of the League in 1931 – both had colonies in Asia and, given the impact of the Depression on their domestic economies, were determined to safeguard their separate interests in the region. However, overall, the League's response to what was essentially its first real challenge since it had been formed in 1920 was a failure. Significantly, it was a failure which was not noted by just Japan alone – both Mussolini and Hitler saw the League's responses to Japan's invasion as indicating that neither Britain nor France were prepared to take serious joint action to prevent expansionist foreign policies.

International Responses to Japanese Expansionism

Although Japan claimed that their initial military actions in Manchuria had been to protect their investments and interests from attacks by 'bandits', it was clear that the Japanese were the aggressors in this situation. Furthermore, China quickly appealed to the League for help, and clearly expected the League to order Japan to halt their occupation and withdraw their forces.

SOURCE A

In 1931 the League of Nations faced its first serious challenge. On 18 September Japanese forces occupied Manchuria, which was theoretically part of China. China appealed to the League for redress. It was not an easy problem. The Japanese had a good case. The authority of the Chinese central government – nowhere strong – did not run in Manchuria, which had been for years in a state of lawless confusion. Japanese trading interests had suffered greatly. There were many precedents in China for independent action – the last being a British landing at Shanghai in 1926. Besides, the League had no means of action. No country, at the height of the economic crisis, welcomed the idea of cutting off its remaining fragment of international trade with Japan … What would be gained if the League of Nations condemned Japan? Merely a display of moral rectitude which, in so far as it had any effect, would set Japan against British trading interests.

Taylor, A. J. P. 1964. *The Origins of the Second World War*. Harmondsworth. Penguin Books. pp. 90–1.

However, several countries – including Britain – were partly sympathetic to Japan's actions in Manchuria, which were being presented to the world by Japan as merely an attempt to restore order. This was why the Japanese referred to their actions as the 'Manchurian Incident'. Consequently, the League was quick to respond to the suggestion made by Japan's government that a Commission of Enquiry be established to investigate the situation.

The Lytton Commission

On 8 December 1931, the League formed a commission headed by Britain's Lord Lytton. This included representatives from other League member states – France, Italy, and Germany – and from the US, even though it was not a member of the League of Nations. Over several months, the commission gathered information and did not present a report to the League until October 1932 – by which time, the Japanese army (in defiance of Japan's civilian government) had occupied even more of Manchuria and, in March 1932, had renamed the province 'Manchukuo'. In order not to offend Japan too much, the report – while accepting that Japan had legitimate economic interests and special rights in the region – stated that its military actions, though not outright aggression, had not been those of self-defence. However, the report also criticised China for the deterioration of relations between the two states, and accepted Japan's argument that China's internal unrest and instability had adversely affected Japan's economic interests in Manchuria. The report thus suggested that China and Japan should begin negotiations to settle any outstanding differences.

Fact: Britain had an extensive empire and significant trading interests in Asia and the Far East and, given the impact of the Great Depression, was reluctant to jeopardise these by alienating Japan – in fact, there were even fears that Japan might attack British colonies in the region. As the US was not a League member, Britain feared that economic sanctions might lead to loss of trade to the US while, at this stage, there was no sign that the US would join in military action to oppose Japanese aggression in the region. These fears and concerns were shared by France, the other main member of the League.

KEY CONCEPTS QUESTION

Causation: What were the main reasons for the reluctance of Britain and France to take serious action against Japanese aggression in 1931–32?

Fact: The only countries which did recognise Manchukuo (which translates as 'land of the Manchus') were Germany and Italy, both of which were still members of the League.

4 Japanese Expansion in East Asia, 1931–41

Fact: Matsuoka Yosuke, the leader of Japan's delegation to the League, pointed out that other countries in the League – including both Britain and France – had used military force against China in the recent past. The League's punishment of Japan was seen as evidence that the Western powers were merely discriminating against an Asian power. In particular, they argued that Japan had taken Manchuria from Russia and had put in considerable investments to improve its infrastructure and economy.

Fact: Stalin had just recently launched the first Five-Year Plan, and was aware that the USSR was not ready to face the armies of Imperial Japan. Thus the Soviet Union avoided a clash with Japan when its Kwantung Army advanced into northern Manchuria, which had long been a Russian sphere of influence. Instead, the USSR offered to sell the Chinese Eastern Railway – eventually, in March 1935, this was concluded and the Soviet Union withdrew from Manchuria.

> **QUESTION**
>
> What are the value and limitations of this source for historians studying Britain's foreign policy concerning Japanese expansionism in the early 1930s?
>
> *Remember: To answer questions like this, you will need to comment on aspects such as the origins and possible purpose of the source.*

The final conclusions of the report recommended that Japan should withdraw its troops and officially recognise Chinese sovereignty over Manchuria; it also explicitly stated that the League should 'not recognise' Manchukuo as an independent country, as it had only come into existence because of the actions of the Japanese army. In February 1933, the report was adopted by all members of the League at a meeting of the League's General Assembly by a vote of 42 to 1 – the one exception being Japan. When a motion was then passed which condemned Japan's recourse to force before all peaceful means of redress had been exhausted, the Japanese delegation walked out of the meeting, complaining that the condemnation of Japan's actions was unfair.

As a result, Japan refused any compromise and then officially withdrew from the League the following month.

The League's response and its significance

Japan's attitude presented real problems for the League, as this was the first time that an important and powerful member had refused to accept its decisions. The situation was complicated by the economic impact of the Depression – for example, Britain was reluctant to use force or to apply economic sanctions. France, too, could see no justification for taking action over a small country so far from Europe. Both these countries, in the economic context of the Great Depression, were fearful of antagonising Japan, in case this had a negative impact on their trade and their colonial interests in the region.

Furthermore, neither the US nor the Soviet Union – both with their own interests in the region and the two powers probably best placed to take action – were members of the League.

> **SOURCE B**
>
> I think I am myself enough of a pacifist to take the view that however we handle the matter [Manchuria], I do not intend my own country to get into trouble about it. There is one great difference between 1914 and now and it is this: in no circumstances will this government authorise this country to be party to this struggle.
>
> Extract from a speech made in the House of Commons, by British foreign minister Sir John Simon, in February 1933. Quoted in Boscoe, D. L. 2009. *Five to rule them all: the UN Security Council and the Making of the Modern World.* New York. Oxford University Press. p. 11.

In addition, at the time, the British and French governments did not see a dispute in Asia as being either particularly damaging to the League's authority as one in Europe would have been, or a possible threat to collective security in Europe itself.

As a result, the League took no effective action – although, in February 1933, it confirmed that the new state of Manchukuo should not be recognised by member states, no economic sanctions were imposed.

International Responses to Japanese Expansionism

THE DOORMAT.

Figure 4.1 A British cartoon, published in 1933, criticising the League's weak response to Japan's invasion of Manchuria

However, later events arguably showed that the Manchurian Incident was highly significant for collective security and world peace.

SOURCE C

The Chinese reconciled themselves to the loss of a province they had not controlled for some years; and in 1933 peace was restored between China and Japan. In later years the Manchurian affair assumed a mythical importance. It was treated as a milestone on the road to war, the first decisive 'betrayal' of the League, especially by the British government. In reality, the League, under British leadership, had done what the British thought it was designed to do: it had limited a conflict and brought it, however unsatisfactorily, to an end. Moreover, the Manchurian affair, far from weakening the coercive powers of the League, actually brought them into existence. It was thanks to this affair that the League – again on British prompting – set up machinery, hitherto lacking, to organize economic sanctions. This machinery, to everyone's misfortune, made possible the League action over Abyssinia in 1935.

Taylor, A. J. P. 1964. *The Origins of the Second World War*. Harmondsworth. Penguin Books. p. 92.

Fact: Some historians see the events of 1931 as the first real step in the series of diplomatic and military crises of the 1930s which eventually culminated in the Second World War. In fact, the Japanese invasion of Manchuria can be seen as the official start of that war – beginning in Asia and then spreading to Europe and then the rest of the world only eight years later.

4 Japanese Expansion in East Asia, 1931–41

Historical debate:
Not all historians see Japan's aggression in Manchuria in 1931–32 – and the League's relative inaction – as being that significant. A. J. P. Taylor, for instance, argued that the Manchurian crisis actually brought the League members together, and led them to draw up a more effective system for imposing economic sanctions. Though this, ironically, arguably led to the problems with Italy over its invasion of Abyssinia in 1935 which, eventually, saw Italy leave the League and join forces with Hitler's Nazi Germany. Most historians, however, have argued that the League's failure over Manchuria marked a decisive break with the idea of collective security which had been the basis of international diplomacy in the 1920s.

QUESTION
In what ways was the League's relative inaction over Manchuria a significant turning point in international relations in the 1930s?

It was thus a crucial turning point, which encouraged other countries – most notably Italy and Germany – to attempt to solve their own economic problems via the adoption and implementation of an aggressive and expansionist foreign policy. Such countries were quick to see how Japan had been able to secure new territory by clear aggression with little more than a verbal censure from the League of Nations.

Faced with a clear act of military aggression, the League had shown itself too weak to respond and, instead, to be ready to accept in practice the results of an aggressive foreign policy. It also showed that no state – not even one belonging to the League – could expect assistance from the League if attacked by an aggressive neighbour. These lessons were rapidly absorbed, and applied, by the 'have-not' nations.

SOURCE D

In February 1933, the League of Nations declared that the State of Manchukuo could not be recognised. Although no sanctions were imposed upon Japan, nor any other action taken, Japan, on March 27, 1933, withdrew from the League of Nations. Germany and Japan had been on opposite sides in the [First World] war; they now looked upon each other in a different mood. The moral authority of the League was shown to be devoid of any physical support at a time when its activity and strength were most needed.

Churchill, W. 1948. *The Gathering Storm*. London. Cassell and Co. p. 80.

More immediately, Japan's actions in Manchuria clearly challenged the balance of power in the Pacific – an area in which the US had been establishing its own economic interests and political influence for many decades.

Japan's invasion of China, 1937

One obvious consequence of the League's failure to take action over Manchuria was that it was almost immediately faced with evidence of Japan's expansionist aims as regards the mainland of China itself. The invasion and occupation of Manchuria had provided Japan with a sound geographical and strategic position from which to extend its influence and conquests into China. In fact, as has been seen above, Japan's actions against mainland China had begun as early as January 1932, with what became known as the first Shanghai Incident. As with Manchuria, China appealed to the League but to no avail. After a series of further 'incidents' from 1932 onwards, Japan had launched all-out war on China in July 1937. Once again, in September 1937, China turned to the League for assistance: but its 'response' was the same as over the Manchurian Incident in 1931. Although, in October, the League issued a statement giving China its 'spiritual support', no effective action was taken. Britain and France which – since Hitler had become chancellor of Germany in January 1933 – were facing increasing German attempts to undermine the post-war peace settlements of 1919–20 in Europe, were thus reluctant to challenge Japan.

4.2 What political developments occurred within China as a result of Japanese aggression?

Because of Jiang Jieshi's determination to fight a civil war in order to crush the communists in China, the Nationalist government was unable to oppose the Japanese incursion into Manchuria in 1931. Instead, it appealed to the League to stop this aggression. However, the League's willingness and ability to respond was restricted by the combined impact of the Depression, the emerging policy of appeasement, and the USA's refusal to get involved.

Even in 1937, when the Japanese launched a full-scale war against China, the League's response was merely a rather general condemnation of Japanese aggression. The Nationalist Chinese government's appeal for help was essentially ignored. Although the countries which had signed the Nine-Power Treaty (see section 4.3) met in a Conference in Brussels at the end of October 1937, there was no practical outcome. In October 1937, Roosevelt, the president of the US, called for Japan's aggression to be 'quarantined' – but took no action.

The only nation which did send some help to China at the start was Stalin's Soviet Union which, in September 1937, formed the **Sino–Soviet Non-Aggression Pact** with China. Soviet aid included the formation of a Soviet volunteer air force, the provision of military aid and over $250 million dollars of credit for the purchase of military supplies. Although this aid was relatively limited, it made the Soviet Union the biggest provider of foreign aid to China until 1940, when the US and the Western powers finally decided to help China in a serious way.

Within China, the impact of Japan's attack in 1937 – and especially the atrocities committed in Nanjing – led to a real determination to resist the Japanese army.

The Second United Front

Japan's increasing incursions into China's mainland in the period 1932–37 had resulted in Jiang being forced by his own generals, in December 1936, to form a Second United Front with the forces of the Chinese Communist Party to resist the Japanese. Even though Jiang's GMD forces did undertake some military operations against the Japanese after 1937, he was still determined to crush the communists – as a result, armed clashes between these two forces occasionally still broke out.

However, with Jiang's forces mostly concentrated in the south of China, the communists in the north were increasingly able to take control of rural areas. Their determination to fight the Japanese, and the economic and social reforms they implemented in the areas that they liberated, won them increasing political support. Eventually, as the Second World War came to a close, the civil war was resumed and, despite US backing, Jiang and his GMD were finally defeated in 1949.

Fact: One of the first of the 'have-not' countries to take these lessons on board was Mussolini's Fascist Italy. Italian nationalists, like those in Japan, wanted a 'New Order' in world affairs which would enable Italy to dominate its main regions of interest around the Mediterranean and Adriatic Seas – in particular, north Africa and the Balkans. Within one year of Japan's successful conquest of Manchuria, Mussolini began planning his invasion of Abyssinia.

QUESTION

What was the Nine-Power Treaty, and when was it signed?

Which countries attended the Nine-Power Treaty Conference in October 1937?

Sino–Soviet Non-Aggression Pact: The signing of the Anti-Comintern Pact between Japan and Nazi Germany in November 1936 had worried Stalin, who feared a two-front war. In part, the Sino-Soviet agreement of 1937 was a way of deflecting a possible two-front war against Nazi Germany and Japan (which had for decades had its eyes on Siberia) by allowing China to keep fighting. However, Soviet aid ended in April 1941, when the Soviet Union signed the Soviet–Japanese Neutrality Pact, which was designed to prevent the USSR having to fight a war against Japan and Nazi Germany at the same time.

4 Japanese Expansion in East Asia, 1931–41

Fact: Despite its continued deep hostility to communism, the US was increasingly frustrated by the fact that Jiang tended to keep the supplies he received for later use against the Communists' Red Army. Fighting had already broken out between GMD and CCP forces outside Beijing as early as 1938. In 1941 – while the war against Japan was still continuing – Jiang ordered a massive attack on the Red Army. He saw this action as just the first step in another extermination campaign.

Fact: Following the defeat of Nazi Germany in May 1945, the Soviet Union had, by August, gathered sufficient forces to declare war on Japan and enter the Pacific War, as had been agreed earlier with Britain and the US. On 8 August – two days after the US bombing of Hiroshima, and one day before the bombing of Nagasaki – the Soviet Red Army invaded Manchuria.

> **SOURCE E**
>
> The iconic status of Yan'an [Mao Zedong's headquarters after the Long March] as a beacon of radical resistance attracted large numbers of migrants, some 100,000 between 1937 and 1940... Many of them came in search of a new future for China, feeling that the Nationalists were already hopelessly compromised by the brutality of their government's behaviour before 1937... The initial years of the war saw significant expansion of the Communist Party and its allied forces. Between 1937 and 1941 the number of members rose from some 40,000 to 763,447, and from a total force of some 92,000 at the start, the combined Eighth Route Army and New Fourth Army rose to some 440,000 troops over the same period. Within the communist base areas, there were also local militias....
>
> Mitter, R. 2014 *China's War with Japan 1937–1945: The Struggle for Survival.* London. Penguin Books. pp. 189–93.

The Second Sino–Japanese War after Pearl Harbor

Almost immediately after the US had declared war on Japan in December 1941, US military supplies began to arrive in Jiang's wartime capital of Chongqing, via what was known as the Burma Road. Later, US airfields were built in southeast China which enabled US bombers to disrupt Japan's maritime trade and cut off most of its imports. In April 1944, Japanese forces launched a major offensive to capture these US airfields. Initially, this met with some success and, by the end of 1944, large parts of southeast China had been occupied. These advances resulted in cutting Chongqing's links with the coast. However, this marked the zenith of Japan's conquests in China: during 1945, Japanese forces were in retreat in the Pacific and in Burma; then, in August 1945, the dropping of nuclear bombs by the US on Hiroshima and Nagasaki ended the Second World War – and the Second Sino-Japanese War. By then, Japan still had over 1 million troops in China.

4.3 What was the international response to Japanese aggression?

Apart from the League, the various separate responses of different world powers to Japan's expansionism helped contribute to the outbreak of the global war known as the Second World War.

International diplomacy in the 1930s

The League of Nations was only one aspect of international relations during this period. Individual member states had also always pursued their own national interests – this was, in fact, one of the factors which had undermined the League of Nations almost from its inception.

Soviet foreign policy

Since 1931, when Japan invaded Manchuria, Stalin had begun to worry about the growing threat from Japan which, during Russia's Civil War 1918–20, had intervened and occupied parts of Siberia. It soon became clear that Japan was interested in expanding into Soviet territories beyond the Manchurian border. Stalin was particularly concerned that Jiang Jieshi – instead of resisting the Japanese invasion – preferred to attack the Chinese Communist's Red Army. This initially meant that large Japanese forces were not tied down by any Chinese counter-attack. Thus, in order to stay on friendly terms with Japan, he agreed to the sale of the Eastern Railway to Japan's new puppet state of Manchukuo.

However, his fears resurfaced during 1936–37 when first Japan, and then Italy, signed the Anti-Comintern Pact with Nazi Germany. Given Britain and France's continuing policy of appeasement of Nazi Germany's European challenges to the peace treaties of 1919–20, Stalin and his advisers feared that the Soviet Union might have to face a combined two-pronged attack: from Nazi Germany in the west and from Japan in the east. Thus, in August 1937, just one month after Japan had invaded mainland China, the Soviet Union signed a new treaty with Nationalist China which included the sending of military supplies to the GMD armies.

Tensions with Japan, however, continued to increase – and, from May to August 1939, several clashes between Japanese and Soviet forces took place along the border between Japanese Manchukuo and the communist state of Mongolia, which was allied to the Soviet Union. Japan had expected quick victories – in part, because it assumed that Stalin's purges of Soviet military leaders had seriously weakened the Red Army of the USSR. However, there was stiff Soviet resistance and, in August 1939, Japanese forces had suffered a crushing defeat at Khalkhin-Gol. The following month, Japan and the Soviet Union agreed a ceasefire.

The debate within Japan's government and military circles, about whether to 'Strike North' (against the Soviet Union) or 'Strike South' In the Pacific and southeast Asia) was eventually resolved in favour of the latter option. This was in no small part because of the determined Soviet military resistance along the border with Manchuria. Partly as a result of this resistance – and Japan's growing problems with the war in China – in April 1941, Japan and the Soviet Union signed the Japanese-Soviet Non-Aggression Pact. This included agreements by the Soviet Union and Japan, respectively, to recognise the territorial integrity of both Manchukuo and Mongolia. Even before Japan had launched its attack on Pearl Harbor, Soviet spies had discovered that the Japanese government had decided against expanding into Soviet territory and, instead, were going to expand in the Pacific and southeast Asia. Although Nazi Germany launched its invasion of the Soviet Union in June 1941, Japan decided against joining Germany in this attack – despite the fact that they had signed the Tripartite Pact in September 1940. Instead, Japan and the Soviet Union remained at peace throughout the Second World War until, in August 1945, the USSR disowned the Non-Aggression Pact of 1941, declared war on Japan and invaded Manchuria.

> **KEY CONCEPTS QUESTION**
> **Significance:** In what ways was Japan's defeat at the battle of Khalkhin-Gol in August 1939 an important turning point?

The Western democracies

In the 1930s, the foreign policies of the main European democracies were considerably restricted by the economic effects of the Great Depression. Countries such as Britain and France concentrated on solving their own economic crises, and

4 Japanese Expansion in East Asia, 1931–41

Figure 4.2 Photo of the signing of the Japanese–Soviet Non-Aggression Pact, in Moscow, April 1941

one common response was to cut government expenditure, including on armaments. Aggressor nations, such as Japan, Germany and Italy, were quick to appreciate that the economic and financial problems of the democracies made these countries less formidable as potential opponents. Britain and France in the 1930s, for instance, were arguably in a much weaker position to defend the international status quo than at any time since the end of the First World War. Countries such as Japan, Germany and Italy – which saw territorial expansion as a way of solving their own economic problems – were quick to attempt to exploit the resultant international power vacuum.

Thus, as the League became increasingly effective, the European democratic countries turned to direct diplomacy and, in particular, tried to involve the US – globally already the most powerful state – in limiting military aggression. Hence the calling of the Nine-Power Treaty Conference in October 1937, in an attempt to deal with Japan's invasion of China.

The Nine-Power Treaty Conference

In response to US president Roosevelt's 'Quarantine Speech' of October 1937 (see Source G below), Britain proposed that China's case before the League be transferred to a Nine-Power Treaty Conference. As this was connected to the Washington Naval Conference and its resultant agreements of 1922, this brought the US into the picture.

The Conference met in November 1937. However, Britain and France were already following the policy of appeasement and were reluctant to take action – especially when they realised that the US had no intention of taking meaningful action either. By the end of the month, when the Conference came to an end, no effective actions had been agreed to stop the Japanese aggression against China. It would not be until the outbreak of the Second World War that China would receive any significant aid from the Western powers. In the meantime, Japan was able to continue with its war against China. In fact, in July 1939, Britain even agreed to recognise Japan's conquests in China, following negotiations with foreign minister Arita Khatira.

The response of the US

The most important non-League member was the US and its response to Japan's military expansion was closely linked to what, for several decades, US policy makers had seen as US economic, trade and strategic interests in the region.

The US and Japan before 1931

Following the events of 1868, when the US had forced Japan to open up to US trade, concern in the US had mounted regarding the rapid industrialisation and modernisation which took place in Japan. These developments were seen as a threat to US interests and plans in the region. Consequently, in 1900, the US had joined other European nations in intervening in China during the Boxer Rebellion (see section 2.3); and had played an important part in mediating the end of the Russo–Japanese War of 1904–05, via the Treaty of Portsmouth, signed in New Hampshire in the US. One of the USA's main aims in this treaty was to limit Japan's territorial gains after the war.

Fact: Strangely, in view of the Anti-Comintern Pact, which Germany had signed with Japan in November 1936, Nazi Germany continued to provide aid to China until as late as 1938. This was a continuation of the Sino–German cooperation which had pre-dated Hitler's appointment as German chancellor in 1933. Most of the aid provided was to help Jiang Jieshi wage his 'extermination' campaigns against the forces of the Chinese Communist Party.

SOURCE F

… Americans must now begin to look outward. Command of the seas is the chief element in the power and prosperity of nations. It is imperative to take possession of such maritime bases as can be righteously obtained. Hawaii occupies a position of unique importance powerfully influencing the commercial and naval control of the Pacific.

Alfred Thayer Mahan. *Atlantic Monthly*. 1890.

Although Roosevelt ceased to be president after 1909, his ideas continued to be influential – in large part because the new president, William Howard Taft, was essentially his proposed candidate for the Republican Party's nomination. Taft's main contribution to US influence in the Pacific was 'Dollar Diplomacy' – using US financial power to ensure US economic domination in China and the Pacific, as well as Latin America. In 1911, the US joined a large European consortium to develop railway systems in China. US banks also tried, unsuccessfully, to buy the South Manchurian Railway Company, in an attempt to limit Japanese and Russian influence in China. Although Woodrow Wilson, who became Democratic president in 1912, officially renounced this policy of 'Dollar Diplomacy', this had little practical impact on the actual conduct of US foreign policy in both the Pacific and Latin America.

The USA's recognition of the new Nationalist republican government which had come to power in China, following the **'Double Tenth' Revolution**, angered Japan.

The 'Double Tenth' Revolution: This had taken place on 10 October 1911, and had overthrown the last emperor of China. The Nationalists, amongst other aims, were determined to end China's subservience to the foreign powers which had carved up China into economic spheres of influence, and was continuing to do so.

4

Japanese Expansion in East Asia, 1931–41

Fact: As was the case with Britain, the US had its own interests and aims regarding China and so was careful not to be too outspoken. In addition, several political leaders in the US saw Japan as a block against the spread of communism in the Far East which it feared would have serious implications for its own substantial and growing economic interests in the region.

> **QUESTION**
> Why did the US not take action to oppose Japan's invasion of Manchuria in 1931?

This was because it was hoping the continued lack of a stable and effective government in China would enable it to push forward its expansionist plans regarding that country. Despite these differences, and some moments of friction, US–Japanese relations were mostly stable. However, this began to change after the Depression took a hold in both countries. In Japan, militaristic regimes began to dominate Japan in the 1930s.

The US and the Manchurian Incident

The first real sign of declining relationships came with the Japanese invasion of Manchuria in 1931. From then on, the US – very much a Far Eastern power by 1931 – was increasingly worried about its interests in the region. Although not a member of the League, the US sent representatives to join the Lytton Commission, and had informed all signatories – including Japan – of the Washington Naval Agreements that it would not accept any territorial changes achieved by the use of force. The US pointed out that such expansionism would be against the Kellogg-Briand Pact which, along with sixty other countries, both Japan and the US had signed as recently as 1928. This agreement, initially signed by just the US and France in 1926 – after Germany had been allowed to join the League of Nations – stated that all signatories agreed to renounce the use of force as a way of achieving national objectives.

Though this US response – a much more vociferous criticism of Japan's actions in Manchuria than that made by the League – seemed supportive of the League's efforts, it was not backed by any action. In fact, the US, by 1931 seriously affected by the Great Depression, had no intention of limiting its trade with Japan. Thus it was of no help to China – and confirmed the British and French belief that any effective action against Japan was impractical.

The US and Japan's invasion of China

These concerns seemed confirmed in 1937, when Japan began its invasion of China, and then announced its New Order policy in Asia.

Unlike Britain and France, the US was not involved in the mounting tensions in Europe resulting from Hitler's increasingly aggressive foreign policy. Thus it seemed best placed to oppose Japanese aggression against China. At first, it seemed as though it would take real action: in October 1937, US president Roosevelt delivered his 'Quarantine Speech', which suggested that the US should help countries attacked by aggressive nations. China read this as meaning US help was imminent and morale in the country was boosted.

> **SOURCE G**
>
> Some fifteen years ago the hopes of mankind for a continuing era of international peace were raised to great heights when more than sixty nations solemnly pledged themselves not to resort to arms in furtherance of their national aims and policies. The high aspirations expressed in the Briand-Kellogg Peace Pact and the hopes for peace thus raised have of late given way to a haunting fear of calamity. The present reign of terror and international lawlessness began a few years ago …
>
> It seems to be unfortunately true that the epidemic of world lawlessness is spreading. When an epidemic of physical disease starts to spread, the community approves and joins in a quarantine of the patients in order to protect the health of the community against the spread of the disease …
>
> Extracts from Roosevelt's 'Quarantine Speech'. http://millercenter.org/president/speeches/speech-3310

International Responses to Japanese Expansionism

Figure 4.3 Roosevelt making his 'Quarantine Speech' in Chicago, 5 October 1937

Increased tensions between the US and Japan

The Nine-Power Treaty Conference which met from October to November 1937, did not result in any agreement to take effective action against Japanese aggression. Apart from the policy of appeasement being followed by Britain and France at this time, the US was still essentially following a policy of 'isolationism'. Nonetheless, in December 1937, the US joined Britain and France in making loans to China to enable it to purchase war supplies. However, in 1939, the US also negotiated trade agreements with Japan: these allowed Japan to purchase military trucks, machine tools for the construction of aircraft, and strategic materials such as oil, steel and scrap iron – even though such products were vital to Japan's armed forces. Despite the continued fighting in China, it was to be several more years before the US finally restricted these exports to Japan. In fact, these bans were not taken as a response to Japan's aggression in China, but because Japan had extended its expansionism into Indo-china and the Pacific.

Yet there was continued verbal condemnation of Japan's actions, and public attitudes in the US were generally sympathetic to the plight of China and its people. Very quickly, US policies towards Japan became much harder, while it moved at the same time to strengthen its ties with Jiang Jieshi and the Nationalist GMD government in China.

Fact: Initially, US sales of oil, steel and scrap metal to Japan were reduced – not banned. By October 1940, however, steel and scrap metal sales had been totally banned; though it was not until after July 1941 that oil was totally banned. It was the restricted exports of these vital oil supplies that eventually contributed to Japan's decision to invade parts of French Indo-china – and to the chain of events which eventually culminated in Japan's decision to launch the attack on Pearl Harbor.

4 Japanese Expansion in East Asia, 1931–41

Fact: The Soviet defence was led by General Zhukov, who later became the main leader of the Soviet Union's Red Army on the Eastern Front against Nazi Germany's invasion of 1941. In fact, Soviet spies discovered, before the attack on the US naval base of Pearl Harbor in Hawaii, that the 'Pacific' faction had won the debate. This enabled them to switch a large part of their troops stationed in Siberia to the Eastern front at crucial times.

Tensions were raised by Japan's growing links with the Fascist and Nazi governments of Italy and Germany.

Figure 4.4 A photograph of Chinese-American Cubs and Scouts in New York's 'Chinatown', protesting in 1938 against Japan's war on China

Initially, both Britain and the US hoped Japanese expansion would be directed against the Soviet Union. In fact, Japan's government was split into two factions – one favouring expansion at the expense of the USSR; and the other wanting to expand in Asia, which they saw as Japan's own 'backyard'. Eventually, the latter faction won out – in part, because of the unexpectedly-robust Soviet defence against Japanese incursions into Mongolia in 1939. The victory of the 'Pacific' faction was confirmed by the decision to expand at the expense of the colonial territories of Britain, France and the Netherlands.

US ban, July 1941

On 28 July, following Japan's decision to place large armed forces in southern Indo-china, the US announced a total ban on vital supplies – such as oil and iron – to Japan, and froze all Japanese assets in the USA. Roosevelt stated that these would not be restored until Japan had made peace with China.

Fact: As well as the US, Britain, Australia and the Dutch government in exile also imposed these bans in response to Japan's expansionism in Indo-china. These bans had a serious impact on Japan which, for instance, had to import 80% of its oil requirements – for both civilian and military purposes. These embargoes angered Japanese nationalists, and Japan's media portrayed these actions as the 'ABCD encirclement': the initials standing for 'American-British-Chinese-Dutch'.

However, the only other possible sources for Japan to access oil in the region were the British and Dutch colonies in Southeast Asia. The Netherlands had been defeated by Nazi Germany in May 1940, but Japan was not yet strong enough to take on a combined Anglo-American naval force. Fears that the US was actually building up its

International Responses to Japanese Expansionism

naval forces in the Pacific in order to block any further Japanese expansion in the region culminated in the surprise attack on Pearl Harbor on 7 December 1941. This was a Japanese attempt to ensure the US would not be able to prevent them from taking over the important natural resources the Japanese economy and war commitments so badly needed. The large Japanese force, which had been sent to Indo-china in July 1941, was now well placed for further expansion in the region. The first attacks on the Dutch

Figure 4.5 Japan's imperial conquests in Asia and the Pacific between 1941 and 1943

4

Japanese Expansion in East Asia, 1931–41

Theory of knowledge

History and truth:
According to US journalist and author Ambrose Bierce (1842–1914), *'History is an account, mostly false, of events mostly unimportant, which are brought about by rulers, mostly knaves, and soldiers, mostly fools.'* How far do you think his observations are valid in relation to Japan's expansionism, and the reactions to it, in the period 1931–41?

East Indies began in December 1941, just one day after the attack on Pearl Harbor. At the same time, Japan also launched attacks on the Philippines, and British-owned Hong Kong and Malaya.

Activities

1 Imagine you are a delegate at the League of Nations in 1931, and draft a speech setting out your views on whether the League should or should not take action against Japan for its invasion of Manchuria. Whether you argue for or against action, your reasons need to be based on detailed references to the recent past and present circumstances.

2 Draw a timeline – giving dates and brief details – of international reactions to Japanese expansionism in the period 1931–41.

3 Carry out some further research on the USA's responses and reactions to Japanese expansion from 1931–41. Do you think the US, rather than Japan, was most responsible for the eventual outbreak of war between them? Explain the reasons for your decision in a couple of paragraphs, making sure your points are supported by detailed references to events and historical interpretations.

End of chapter activities

Summary

You should now have a good understanding of how the League of Nations and individual countries responded to the expansionist foreign policies pursued by Japan in the 1930s.

You should also be able to explain the reasons for the various responses.

Finally, you should be able to understand how those responses – or lack of responses – contributed to Japan's decision to extend its expansionist policies in such a way that it ended up fighting a war against the US and Britain.

Summary activities

There has been much historical debate about why the League of Nations, and individual states, did little to oppose the increasingly expansionist foreign policies pursued by Japan in the 1930s.

Copy the diagram below and, under each heading, give brief details and, where relevant, brief summaries of the main historical viewpoints and arguments – including, where possible, names of specific historians.

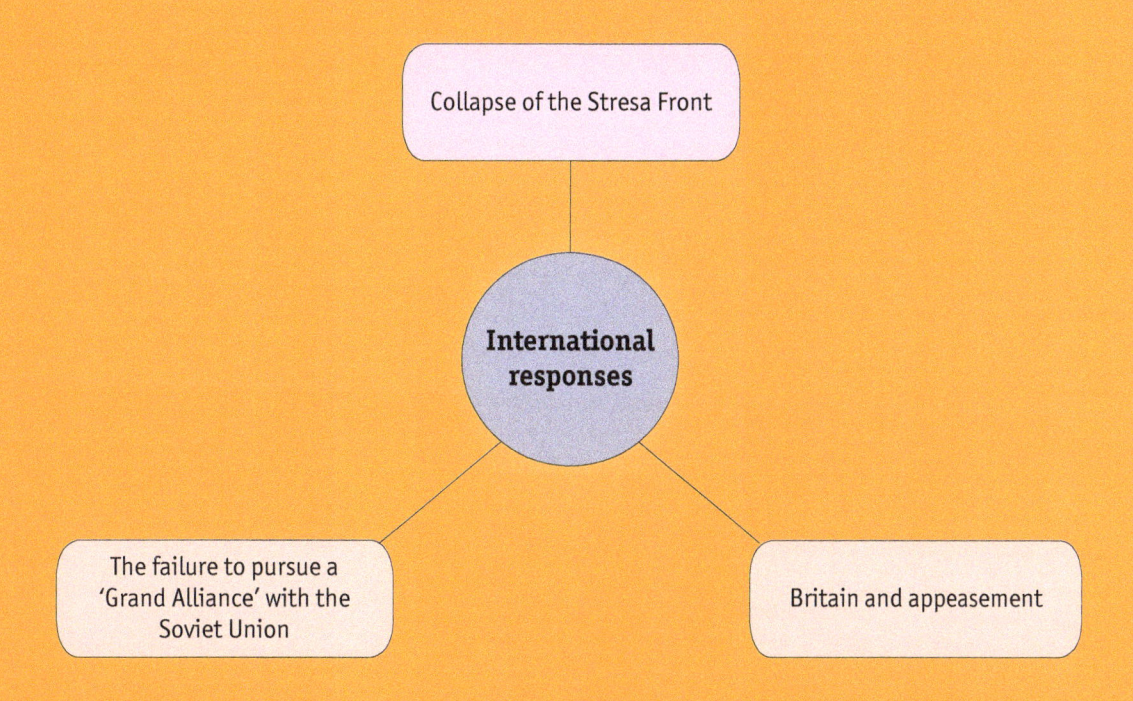

- Collapse of the Stresa Front
- International responses
- The failure to pursue a 'Grand Alliance' with the Soviet Union
- Britain and appeasement

4 Paper 1 exam practice

Question

SOURCE A

The Chinese reconciled themselves to the loss of a province they had not controlled for some years; and in 1933 peace was restored between China and Japan. In later years the Manchurian affair assumed a mythical importance. It was treated as a milestone on the road to war, the first decisive 'betrayal' of the League, especially by the British government. In reality, the League, under British leadership, had done what the British thought it was designed to do: it had limited a conflict and brought it, however unsatisfactorily, to an end. Moreover, the Manchurian affair, far from weakening the coercive powers of the League, actually brought them into existence. It was thanks to this affair that the League – again on British prompting – set up machinery, hitherto lacking, to organize economic sanctions. This machinery, to everyone's misfortune, made possible the League action over Abyssinia in 1935.

Taylor, A. J. P. 1964. *The Origins of the Second World War*. Harmondsworth. Penguin Books. p. 92.

SOURCE B

In February 1933, the League of Nations declared that the State of Manchukuo could not be recognised. Although no sanctions were imposed upon Japan, nor any other action taken, Japan, on March 27, 1933, withdrew from the League of Nations. Germany and Japan had been on opposite sides in the [First World] war; they now looked upon each other in a different mood. The moral authority of the League was shown to be devoid of any physical support at a time when its activity and strength were most needed.

Churchill, W. 1948. *The Gathering Storm*. London. Cassell and Co. p. 80.

Compare and contrast the views expressed in **Sources A** and **B** about the League of Nations' reactions to Japan's invasion of Manchuria. **[6 marks]**

Skill

Cross-referencing of two sources

Before you start

Cross-referencing questions require you to compare **and** contrast the information/content/nature of **two** sources.

Before you attempt this question, refer to Chapter 9 for advice on how to tackle these questions, and a simplified mark scheme.

Student answer

Sources A and B are slightly similar in their views about the League of Nations' reactions to Japan's invasion of Manchuria. Although Source A, which was written in 1964, doesn't explicitly state what actions the League took, it does imply that it did not take strong action. This is shown by the comment that it had 'unsatisfactorily' limited the potential problems thrown up by Japan's actions in Manchuria. The view that the League did very little is also mentioned in Source B, written in 1948. This source states more explicitly that the League took little action: the source does this by making it clear that 'no sanctions were imposed upon Japan, nor any other action taken'. Thus both sources give a similar view.

Examiner comments

There are clear/precise references to both sources, and a similarity/comparison is identified. Also, the sources are clearly linked, rather than being dealt with separately. The candidate has thus done enough to get into Band 2, and so be awarded 4 or 5 marks. However, as no differences/contrasts are made, this answer fails to get into Band 1.

Activity

Look again at the two sources, the simplified mark scheme, and the student answer above. Now try to write a paragraph or two to push the answer up into Band 1, and so obtain the full 6 marks.

Paper 2 practice questions

1. Evaluate the significance of the League of Nations' response to Japan's actions in Manchuria as regards the foreign policy of Nazi Germany and Fascist Italy.
2. 'The main reason for the inaction of the League of Nations over increasing Japanese expansionism in Asia was its lack of a military force.' To what extent do you agree with this statement?
3. Compare and contrast the reactions of two nations, each chosen from a different region, to Japanese expansionism after 1931.
4. Examine the consequences of US policies towards Japan in the period 1931–41.

Case Study 2: German and Italian Expansionism, 1933–40

5 Causes of German and Italian Expansion

TIMELINE

- **1861 Mar:** Kingdom of Italy established
- **1867 Apr:** North German Confederation formed
- **1870 Jul:** Italian unification completed
- **1871 Jan:** German unification completed
- **1879** the start of 'Scramble for Africa'
- **1884–99** Germany establishes colonies in Africa and the Pacific
- **1885** Italian colonies of Eritrea and Somaliland established in Africa
- **1896 Mar:** Italy defeated at battle of Adowa
- **1910 Dec:** Italian Nationalist Association formed
- **1911–12** Italo–Turkish war – Italy establishes colony of Italian East Africa
- **1914 Aug:** First World War begins
- **1915 May:** Treaty of London
- **1918 Jan:** Wilson's Fourteen Points
- **1919 Jun:** Treaty of Versailles
- **Sept:** Treaty of St. Germain; D'Annunzio seizes Fiume
- **1920 Jan:** League of Nations established
- **Feb:** Hitler launches Nazi Party
- **1921 Oct:** Mussolini forms National Fascist Party
- **1922 Oct:** March on Rome; Mussolini becomes prime minister
- **1923 Aug:** Corfu Incident
- **Nov:** Hitler's unsuccessful Beer Hall Putsch
- **1926 Sept:** Germany allowed to join League of Nations
- **1929 Oct;** Stresemann dies; Wall Street Crash
- **1933 Jan:** Hitler appointed chancellor
- **1934 Sept:** Schacht's 'New Plan'
- **1936 Sept:** Göring's Four-Year Plan
- **1935 Oct:** Italian invasion of Abyssinia
- **1937** Mussolini launches the *Romanita* exhibitions

KEY QUESTIONS

- What was the impact of Fascist and Nazi ideology on expansionist foreign policies in Italy and Germany?
- What was the impact of economic issues on expansionist foreign policies in Italy and Germany?
- How did conditions in Europe in the 1930s contribute to the collapse of collective security?

Overview

- In many ways, some of the roots of fascism and its nationalist ideology in both Italy and Germany are to be found in the 19th century when, for the first time, these two countries became unified states.

- In both countries, this unification – completed in Italy in 1870, and in Germany in 1871 – was achieved by a combination of political developments and internal and external military conflicts.

- Once in existence, ultra-nationalists in both these European countries campaigned for imperial expansion, in order to match the empires already established by Britain and France. By the end of the 19th century, both Italy and Germany had gained colonies in Africa and, in Germany's case, also in the Pacific.

- Because of the First World War, and then the subsequent peace treaties, nationalism further increased in both countries. Both Italy and Germany were disappointed and angered by the peace treaties. Partly because of these nationalist frustrations, fascist movements developed in several countries – especially in Italy and Germany.

- As early as 1922, Mussolini was able to become prime minister of Italy and establish his Fascist dictatorship.

- An important part of the ideology of both these early fascist parties was an extreme form of nationalism, which wanted to re-draw the European borders established by the peace treaties of 1919–20, and to expand their national territories.

- The Wall Street Crash in 1929, and the subsequent Great Depression, played an important part in the Nazi Party gaining power in Germany in 1933. The economic impact of the Depression on both Italy and especially Germany made territorial expansion even more attractive as it would give access to more raw materials.

- At the same time, the Depression seriously undermined the ability of the League of Nations to maintain peace in Europe. This made the growing nationalist and expansionist aims of Fascist Italy and Nazi Germany seem more achievable.

5.1 What was the impact of Fascist and Nazi ideology on expansionist foreign policies in Italy and Germany?

fascism: This is a term deriving from the Italian word *fascio* (plural *fasci*), meaning 'group' or 'band'. In 1893, in Sicily, radical groups of mostly socialist workers had formed *fasci* to organise demonstrations and strikes in protests against low wages and high rents. Mussolini adopted the term for his political movement in 1919. He later claimed that it referred to the *fasces* – the bundle of rods carried by *lictors* (bodyguards) in ancient Rome. (also see Source B below)

The interwar period between the end of the First World War and the start of the Second World War saw considerable economic and political turmoil, including revolution and attempted revolutions. One notable political development was the emergence and spread of **fascism** in Europe.

The first country to experience the rise to power of a fascist party in this period was Italy, where Benito Mussolini became prime minister in 1922.

Figure 5.1 Fascists Blackshirts demonstrating in Rome, 4 November 1922, after their triumphant 'March' on the city the previous month

Fascism also emerged in several other European states, including in Britain and France and, most notably, in Germany in 1933. Other states, such as Portugal and Spain, also ended up with semi-fascist governments during this period. However, fascist ideology was not the only ideological or political influence which eventually led to the expansionist policies pursued by Italy and Germany in the interwar years. Nationalism – which predated fascism – was another important factor.

Fascist ideology

One of the problems in assessing the relative importance of fascist ideology to explain the expansionist foreign policies pursued by Germany and Italy in the period after 1933 is that – unlike Marxism – fascism has no coherent or unified ideological

5 German and Italian Expansionism, 1933–40

root – no definite *Weltanschauung* or 'world view'. Despite such problems, historians have attempted to define the main features of fascism. According to the historian Alexander de Grand, the most coherent element in Mussolini's fascism was a sort of 'nationalist fascism', which favoured an 'aggressive foreign policy' in order to achieve territorial expansion. Other aspects of fascism which were important elements in foreign policy were its belief in 'violent action', 'racial supremacy', 'nationalism' and 'empire'. Historians such as R. Griffin and S. Payne have argued that one of the core aspects of fascist ideology is a populist form of 'ultra-nationalism'. In fact, during the late 19th century, many nationalists in Europe had already begun to move towards a form of extreme and reactionary nationalism, before Mussolini founded his Fascist Party in Italy.

Italian nationalism before 1933

Before Mussolini became prime minister of Italy, nationalism had been a strong political force in Italy since the 19th century. Italy, like many other countries in Europe – especially Germany – saw the rise of nationalism, in response to the French Revolution and the Napoleonic Wars.

Italian unification

Fact: One of the most important early Italian nationalists was Giuseppe Mazzini. Other nationalists who became important later on were Cavour and Garibaldi.

Until the 19th century, 'Italy' was an idea or aspiration, rather than a country, as it consisted of several different states – as late as 1847, the Austrian statesman von Metternich had described Italy as 'a geographical expression'. However, the experience of Napoleon's conquest of Italy, which brought many of these states together, inspired some Italians to work for Italian unification and independence; but Italian nationalists remained a small minority for several decades.

Risorgimento: This process of unification is known as the *Risorgimento*, or 'resurgence' or 're-birth' of Italy. After 1815, a literary and cultural revival had taken place in Italy. This nationalist movement also campaigned against Italian divisions and foreign domination, and called for political unification.

Despite such problems, changed circumstances from 1859 allowed Italian nationalists eventually to bring about the **Risorgimento** ('unification of Italy') in 1861. In that year, the kingdom of Italy was finally established, which brought the whole peninsular together in one state – with the exceptions of Rome and Venice. By 1870, both Venice and Rome had also been made part of Italy.

Italia irridenta and empire

The frontiers of the new Italy, however, still did not include all Italian-speakers – many of these lived in neighbouring territories which were under foreign rule. This gave rise to the idea of **Italia irridenta** ('unredeemed Italy'): that Italy could not be 'whole' or complete until all Italians lived in one state. These lands included the south Tyrol on the border with Austria-Hungary, and several areas on the Adriatic coast.

Italia irridenta: This term means 'unredeemed land' and refers to the Italian-inhabited areas ruled by Austria-Hungary in the northern Adriatic during the 19th and early 20th centuries. These were Trentino and Trieste, which contained large numbers of Italian speakers.

For many Italian nationalists, the goal of the new state of Italy should be to gain these lands – either by diplomacy or, if necessary, by war. After 1870, these nationalists believed that a strong foreign policy would both help unify Italians by creating a sense of national pride, and gain Italy international respect.

In particular, after 1879, when the 'Scramble for Africa' began, the new state of Italy was keen to share in this new phase of European colonial expansion. These views were eventually to form an important part of Italian fascism.

Causes of German and Italian Expansion

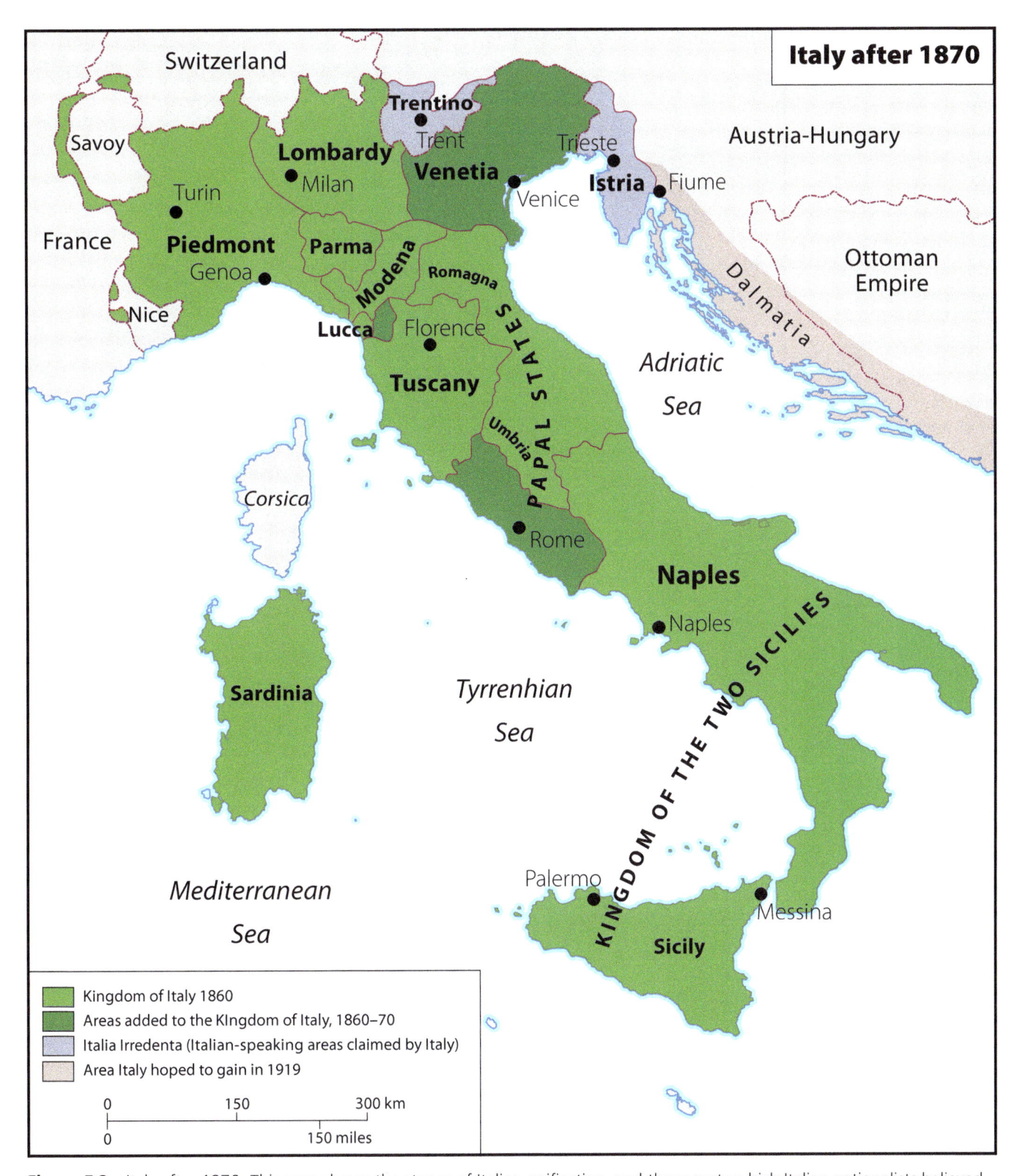

Figure 5.2 Italy after 1870. This map shows the stages of Italian unification, and those parts which Italian nationalists believed should also be part of Italy

5 German and Italian Expansionism, 1933–40

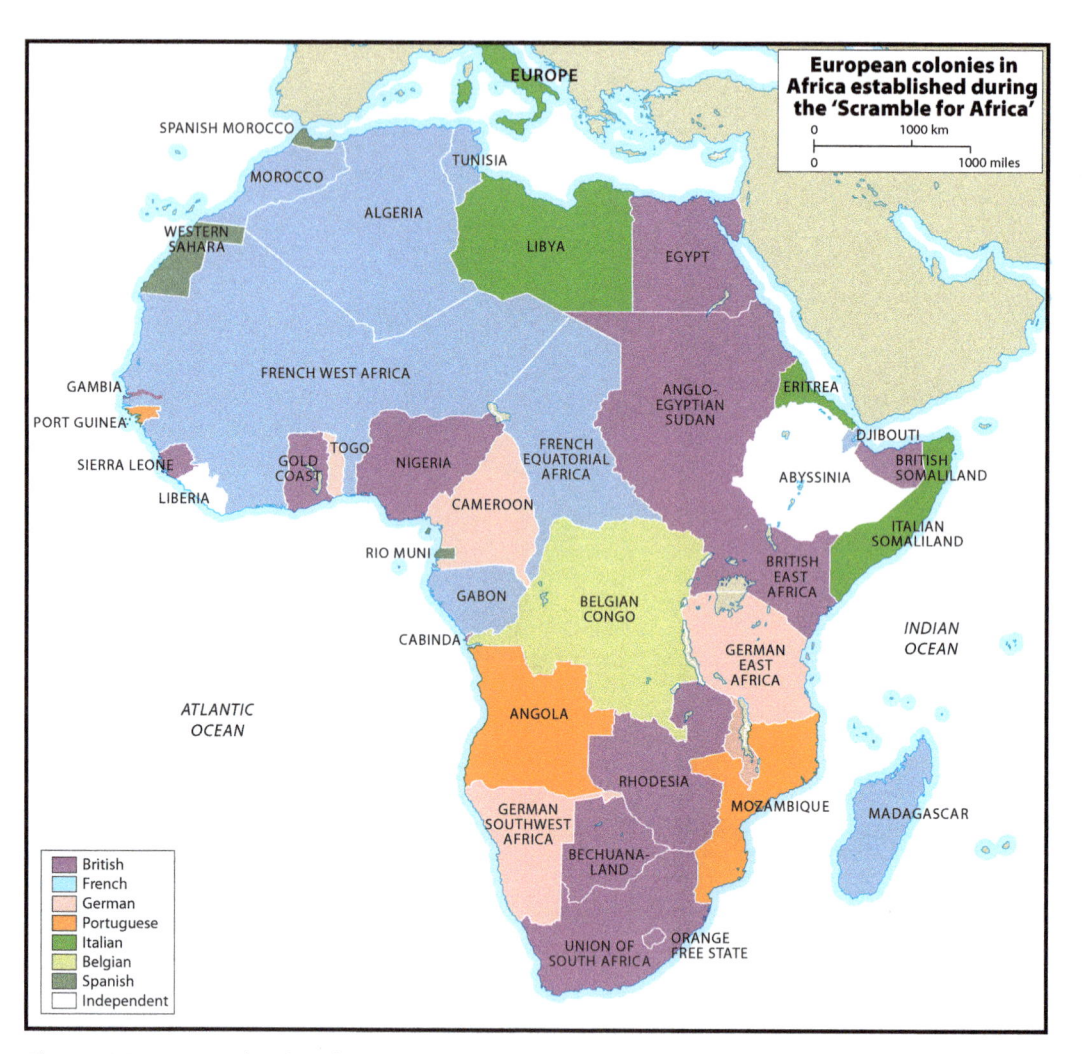

Figure 5.3 A map showing the colonies European powers had established during the 'Scramble for Africa'

Associazione Nazionalista Italiana **(ANI):** This was Italy's first 20th century nationalist party. It was formed in 1910 and had previously pushed for the conquest of Libya. After 1914, it supported war against Austria as a way of gaining the *'terra irredenta'*. Later, it became close to Mussolini's Fascist Party, and the two parties merged in 1923.

Fact: In 1879, Germany (only created in 1871) and Austria-Hungary had signed the Dual Alliance. This was intended mainly by Germany as a defensive alliance which would help avoid war, as it prevented France (following its defeat in 1871) from having Austria-Hungary as a potential ally. In 1882, Italy joined this alliance, making it the Triple Alliance. Turkey later joined this alliance in 1914 but, in 1915, Italy dropped out of the Triple Alliance. The other major alliance was the Triple Entente, made up of Britain, France and Russia.

Fact: Many Italians felt that officers had often sacrificed thousands of lives needlessly. In all, over 600,000 were killed, about 450,000 permanently disabled, and a further 500,000 seriously wounded.

In 1882, Italy established a foothold in Eritrea on the Red Sea coast and, in 1885, Italian forces began to push into Ethiopia – but were defeated by the Ethiopian army. Nonetheless, in 1885, Eritrea and Italian Somaliland were established as Italian colonies. In 1893 – with the encouragement of Britain – Italy tried again to expand at the expense of Ethiopia. In 1895, Italy occupied the province of Tigre in Abyssinia. However, after several military clashes, it suffered another defeat at the hands of the Ethiopians, at the battle of Adowa in 1896. This was seen by many Italians as a terrible national humiliation. Despite this setback, in 1911, Italy attacked Ottoman-ruled Tripolitania, in what became known as the Italo–Turkish War of 1911–12. Once conquered, Tripolitania – along with the adjoining provinces of Cyrenaica and Fezzan – was re-named Italian East Africa. In 1934, Italian East Africa became the Italian colony of Libya. Yet many nationalists, still angry at Italy's defeat in 1896, continued to press for a more aggressive imperial policy.

Causes of German and Italian Expansion

Impact of the First World War and the Peace Treaties 1914–19

In 1910, the extremely nationalist and imperialist Italian Nationalist Association **(ANI, *Associazione Nazionalista Italiana*)** had been formed. This became an important nationalist movement in Italy – many of these dissatisfied nationalists and frightened conservatives longed to return to a more glorious Italian past: one that would re-create the empire of Ancient Rome. As it became clear that a European war was imminent, many Italian nationalists saw participation in such a war as a way of gaining more colonies, and obtaining the *Italia irredenta* lands.

Before 1914, Italy had been part of the Triple Alliance but, when war broke out in 1914, the Italian government had not taken part and instead had decided to see which side would offer the best terms for Italy's participation. Negotiations with the Triple Alliance in the period 1914–1915 soon revealed that Austria would never concede Trentino or Trieste; while the Entente promised these, along with other Austrian territory in the south Tyrol, and Istria and northern Dalmatia on the Adriatic coast.

Instead, after the Treaty of London in May 1915 – in which Britain and France promised to support Italy's various territorial ambitions – Italy switched sides and fought on the side of the Triple Entente. Italian forces were involved in heavy fighting against Austria, and the Italian army was soon bogged down in a costly war of attrition.

In November 1917, the Italians suffered a terrible defeat at the hands of the Austrians at the battle of Caporetto – over 40,000 Italian soldiers were killed and about 300,000 were taken prisoner. The nationalists blamed the government for being inefficient and failing to supply the troops with enough equipment. Though a costly victory was won at Vittorio Veneto in October 1918, many Italians remembered the defeats and the high casualties.

Consequently, when the war ended in November 1918, many Italian nationalists expected to obtain the lands and colonies they had been promised. **Vittorio Orlando,** the Italian prime minister, went to the Paris Peace Conferences in January 1919, expecting to receive all that had been promised by the Treaty of London. Under pressure from the nationalists, he also demanded the port of Fiume, on the border of Istria, as it contained a large Italian-speaking population. Finally, Orlando wanted Italy to receive a share of the former German colonies in Africa.

Although Italy did eventually receive most of what it wanted, there were some important exceptions: there was to be nothing in Africa, and Britain and the United States refused to grant Italy Fiume and northern Dalmatia, arguing that these were vital for the new state of Yugoslavia.

Italy's long-term opponent, Austria-Hungary, had been defeated and no longer even existed, leaving Italy now clearly dominating the Adriatic.

Italian nationalism and the 'mutilated victory'

Italian nationalists were disgusted once the likely terms became clear, and accused the Liberal government of allowing Italy to be humiliated and cheated. The popular nationalist **Gabriele D'Annunzio** spoke for many Italians – especially war veterans – when he called it a 'mutilated victory'.

Vittorio Orlando (1860–1952)

He was appointed prime minister following the defeat at Caporetto, in 1917 and was still Italy's prime minister at the end of the First World War. Italy had expected to get control of the Adriatic coastline, but did not – he then resigned as prime minister. His failure to secure all of Italy's territorial claims at Versailles was used by Mussolini and the Fascists in their campaign to show how weak the Italian government was. Orlando initially supported Mussolini in 1922, but withdrew support in 1924.

Gabriele D'Annunzio (1863–1938)

He was a poet and writer; as an ultra-nationalist, he supported Italy's entry on the side of the Triple Entente when the First World War broke out. He joined up as a pilot, becoming something of a war hero after dropping propaganda leaflets over Vienna. He was an *irredentist*, and was angered when Fiume (now Rijeka in Croatia) was handed over to the new state of Yugoslavia after the war.

QUESTION

What do you understand by the term 'mutilated victory'? What areas were claimed by Italian nationalists after 1919?

5 German and Italian Expansionism, 1933–40

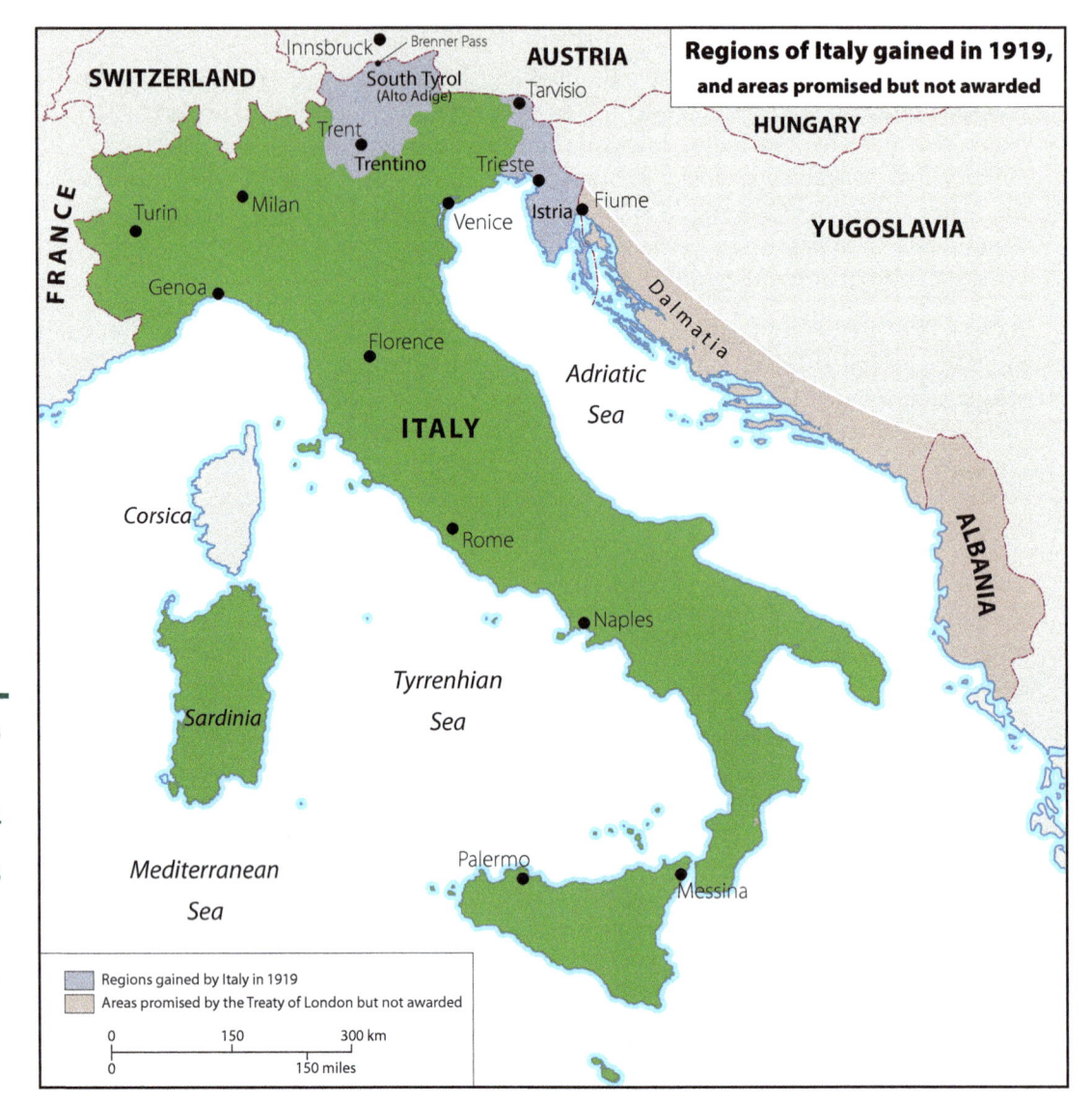

Figure 5.4 A map showing the regions Italy gained in 1919, and those areas promised by the Treaty of London but not awarded

Arditi: The term (which comes from the Italian verb 'ardire', which means 'to dare') translates as 'the daring ones'. These were the black-shirted commando (or 'storm') troops of the Italian army, whose officers hated the Liberal political system which, in their eyes, had betrayed their wartime sacrifices by not obtaining for Italy the land which had been promised, and by doing little to crush the revolutionary left. These troops were demobilised in 1920, but their name – and uniform – was used by D'Annunzio's supporters who took over Fiume in 1919.

ACTIVITY
Carry out some further research on the ways in which D'Annunzio and the Arditi influenced Mussolini as he began to build his fascist movement.

On 12 September 1919, D'Annunzio led 2,000 armed men to the city of Fiume, one of the areas not awarded to Italy by the peace treaties. D'Annunzio's force quickly took control and, in open defiance of the Liberal Italian government and the Allies, continued to rule the city for the next fifteen months. Though eventually forced to surrender the city in December 1920, his bold action made him a hero to Italian nationalists, and acted as an inspiration to Mussolini – in particular, he decided to adopt the theatrical trappings used by D'Annunzio, especially the black shirts of the **Arditi,** the ancient Roman salute, and the many parades and balcony speeches.

Italian fascism

Mussolini never even made any concerted effort to define the basic beliefs of his fascist movement until after he had become prime minister. However, in 1925,

Causes of German and Italian Expansion

Figure 5.5 Mussolini with D'Annunzio

Mussolini began moves for the drawing up of a clear statement of fascist doctrine. Under the leadership of the philosopher **Giovanni Gentile**, over 200 intellectuals met in Bologna – as a result of the meeting, they drew up the *Manifesto of Fascist Intellectuals*, which was a programme explaining the main ideological beliefs of fascism.

However, this attempt to bring together the diverse and often contradictory ideas of fascism was not particularly effective. A more concerted effort came in 1932 – ten years *after* Mussolini had become prime minister of Italy – when Gentile (with some help from Mussolini) wrote a very lengthy entry on fascism for the *Enciclopedia Italiana* in 1932, of which he was editor. The first part of this was then published separately as *The Doctrine of Fascism* in 1933, under Mussolini's name – however, as before, this was as much a statement of what fascism was *against* (essentially liberalism, socialism, democracy and pacifism) as it was what they stood *for* (action, the nation, authority and the state). In the section entitled 'Political and Social Doctrine of Fascism', Gentile explained that fascism was anti-communist, anti-socialist, and strongly opposed to the 'economic conception of history' and the centrality of 'class war' – both of which are fundamental to Marxism and communist ideology.

> **Giovanni Gentile (1875–1944)**
> He was known as the 'philosopher of fascism', and his philosophy of 'Actual Idealism' corresponded to the fascist liking for action. Gentile became Minister of Public Education under Mussolini in 1923. He was also an important member of the Fascist Grand Council, and remained a loyal supporter of Mussolini after the foundation of the Salo Republic in 1943. The following year, he was killed by anti-fascist partisans.

5 German and Italian Expansionism, 1933–40

> **SOURCE A**
>
> Against individualism, the Fascist conception is for the state… It is opposed to classical LIBERALISM, which… denied the state in the interests of the individual… for the Fascist, everything is in the state, and nothing human or spiritual exists, much less has value, outside the state. In this sense Fascism is totalitarian…
>
> Fascism is opposed to SOCIALISM, which confines the movement of history within the class struggle and ignores the unity of classes established in one economic and moral reality in the state…
>
> Fascism is opposed to DEMOCRACY, which equates the nation to the majority, lowering it to the level of that majority….
>
> Above all, Fascism…. believes neither in the possibility nor in the utility of perpetual peace. It thus repudiates [rejects] the doctrine of PACIFISM – born of a renunciation of the struggle and an act of cowardice in the face of sacrifice. War alone brings up to their highest tension all human energies and puts the stamp of nobility upon the peoples who have the courage to meet it…
>
> Extract from the *Enciclopedia Italiana*. Quoted in Hite, J. and Hinton, C. 1998. *Fascist Italy*. London. Hodder Education. p. 121.

'Social Darwinism': This was based on a profound misreading of Darwin's work by, amongst others, Herbert Spenser. It is particularly linked to simplistic and racist ideas about how to apply the biological concept of natural selection to society, politics and sociology. Spenser, for instance, believed that people and nations were like animals, in that it was 'natural' for them to struggle and fight in order to determine the survival of the fittest. These ideas had begun to emerge in the US and Europe in the 1870s, and were soon linked to the development of racial theories and eugenics. Fascism often used such ideas to justify imperial expansion at the expense of 'weaker' or 'inferior' peoples.

However, several other aspects of Italian fascist ideology were also to be found in the slightly later version of German Nazism. These were, firstly, a form of **'Social Darwinism'**, which was rooted in a belief in the necessity and value of forceful and violent struggle in order to ensure the 'survival of the fittest'. According to this aspect of fascist ideology, weaker groups and nations did not deserve to survive and should be eliminated in order to keep the strong 'healthy'. The other aspect ideological Italian and German fascism shared in common, which was linked to this idea of 'Social Darwinism', was the nationalist belief that all those who shared a common language, history and culture should be able to live together in a 'greater' or expanded nation, and that an aggressive foreign policy was a sign of strength and would enable the nation to become even stronger.

Fascism and nationalism before 1922

Shortly after the First World War had begun, Mussolini had set up his own newspaper, *Il Popolo d'Italia (The People of Italy)* in November 1914, to campaign against peace and for war, in the hope that a successful war would bring Italy new territories in Europe and Africa. The paper was financed by wealthy Italian companies, such as Fiat, which expected to gain lucrative war contracts, and also by the French government. Not surprisingly therefore, the paper was a strong advocate of intervention. Later, his paper was partly financed by Britain and Tsarist Russia.

In 1919, Mussolini set up a Fascio di Combattimento (battle group) in Milan and, in October 1921, he formed his National Fascist Party (Partito Nazionale Fascista - PNF).

From then on, in order to widen the appeal of his Fascist Party, Mussolini increasingly stressed fascism's commitment to strong government and, especially, to patriotism and imperial expansion. This form of militaristic nationalism was bound to lead to wars of conquest.

Causes of German and Italian Expansion

Figure 5.6 Fascist Blackshirts from a Fascio di Combattimento

Fact: Despite advocating intervention, Mussolini did not volunteer for the army but, in September 1915, he was conscripted. In 1917, he was invalided out of the army after an accident during a training exercise. He then resumed his role as editor of *Il Popolo*, blaming the Liberal government for military incompetence and calling for a dictator to take charge of the war effort. His *Manifesto to the Nation*, published in November 1917 after the defeat at Caporetto, called for a 'national union' to work for victory in the war.

The *Romanità* movement

Once Mussolini and the fascists had gained power in 1922, their first aim was to consolidate their power in Italy. However, to help them do this, Mussolini used an aggressive foreign policy almost from the beginning – this was the Corfu Incident of August 1923. This happened when an Italian general was murdered on Greek soil while making maps on behalf of the Conference of Ambassadors of a disputed area (see section 6.2, Emerging expansionist aims, 1922–33). Mussolini took advantage of this opportunity to demand that Greece pay 50 million lire as compensation and make a full apology. When Greece refused to pay (as they had not been responsible), Mussolini – ignoring criticism from the League of Nations – ordered Italian marines to invade the Greek island of Corfu. Although the Conference of Ambassadors eventually forced Italy to withdraw its troops, and the Greek government refused to apologise – although they did pay the 'fine' demanded by Mussolini – the incident made many Italians see Mussolini as a national hero.

Following this foreign policy success, Mussolini and the fascists increasingly tried to link their regime to the earlier greatness of Ancient Rome and its emperors. This became known as the *Romanità* ('Romanness') movement. Fascist writers, artists and scholars tried to portray fascism as a revival of, and a return to, Ancient Roman civilisation. From 1926, Mussolini was increasingly referred to as *Il Duce* (Latin for 'The Leader'), while fascist propaganda portrayed him as a new 'Caesar' who would restore Italian greatness by pursuit of an expansionist foreign policy. From 1937, a variety of *Mostra Augustea della Romanità* exhibitions and events were held to celebrate the 2,000th anniversary of the birth of the emperor Augustus. Over the entrance to the main exhibition, was a quote from Mussolini: *'Italians, you must ensure that the glories of the past are surpassed by the glories of the future.'*

5 German and Italian Expansionism, 1933–40

Theory of knowledge Activity

History: Emotion and actions
According to the philosopher Bertrand Russell (1872–1970), *'The opinions that are held with passion are always those for which no good ground exists, indeed the passion is the measure of the holder's lack of rational connection.'* Carry out some research on Italian fascist and nationalist ideology and propaganda. Then write a couple of paragraphs to show how Mussolini used emotion in order to build support for a new Italian empire.

SOURCE B

Rome is our point of departure and our point of reference. It is our symbol and, if you like, our myth. We dream of a Roman Italy, an Italy that is wise and strong, disciplined and impersonal. Much of the spirit of Ancient Rome is being born again in Fascism: the Lictorian fasces are Roman, our war machine is Roman, our pride and our courage are Roman too. Civis Romanus sum [I am a Roman citizen].

Part of a speech delivered by Mussolini in 1935, in Hite, J. and Hinton, C. 1998. *Fascist Italy*. London. Hodder. p. 106.

Figure 5.7 Mussolini revising the ancient glories of Rome – viewing a statue of Julius Caesar installed in the recently-evacuated forum

Fact: Mussolini's empire was to be based around the Mediterranean Sea, which he frequently referred to as *'Mare Nostrum'* (Latin for 'Our Sea'). The term had often been used by Italian nationalists during the 19th century – especially during the 'Scramble for Africa' in the 1880s. Mussolini took the term over and even talked of making the Mediterranean Sea an 'Italian lake'. Partly to ensure this, he made efforts to strengthen the Italian navy.

As part of this cult, Mussolini also had the fascist symbol incorporated into the national flag. Another aspect of this claimed linkage to Ancient Rome was the emphasis increasingly placed on the need to establish a second empire – 'the resurrection of the Empire'. This ideology was extended to the school curriculum: for example, infant school pupils had to repeat a prayer which included a wish for 'the resurrection of the Empire'. According to *Romanità*, the fascist 'New Man' was a modern version of the idealised Roman centurion, who would then help establish this new Italian empire. The entire *Romanità* project was a powerful source of both Italian and fascist nationalism.

Associated with this idea of a new 'Roman' empire was the concept of *spazio vitale* ('vital space') – this was the fascist idea that a strong state should expand beyond its natural boundaries to control areas vital to its interests. As far as Mussolini's fascist regime was concerned, Italy's *spazio vitale* was to include the whole Mediterranean area and northern and eastern Africa, from the Atlantic Ocean to the Indian Ocean.

Causes of German and Italian Expansion

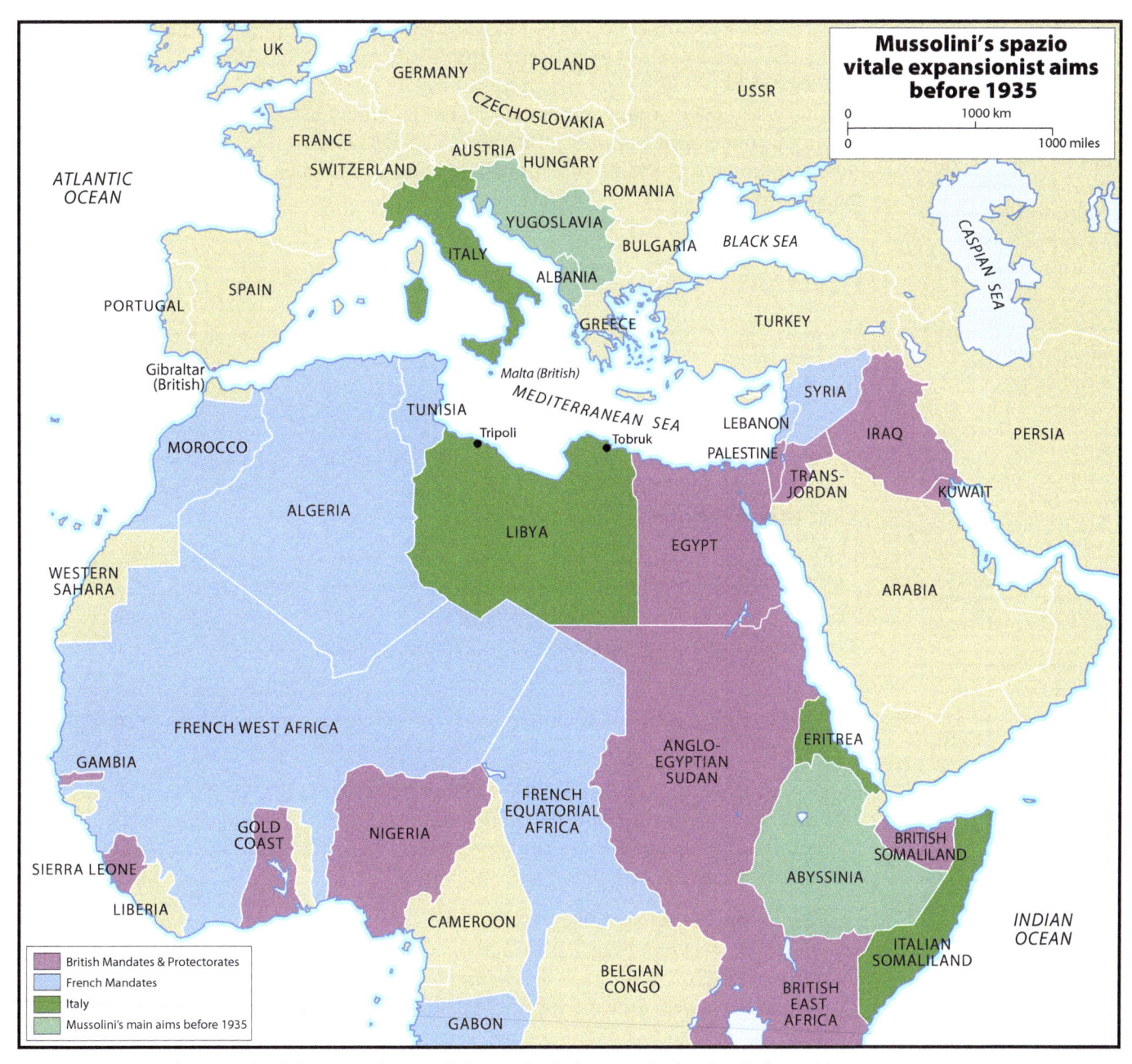

Figure 5.8 Map showing the full extent of Mussolini's *spazio vitale* expansionist aims before 1935

In Europe, Mussolini was determined to control south-eastern states such as Yugoslavia and Albania. Later, once the Second World War had begun, he added Greece and the Balkan states of Romania and Bulgaria, and even Hungary, to his 'wish list'. Whilst in Africa, control of the north and the east would help secure Italian dominance of the Mediterranean. The whole *spazio vitale* area was to be divided into two areas: *piccolo spazio* ('small space') was to be inhabited only by Italians; while *grande spazio* ('large space') would be inhabited by other nations under Italian control. Once established, this new 'imperial Italy' would spread culture and civilisation in the same way that Ancient Rome did.

5

German and Italian Expansionism, 1933–40

QUESTION
How significant was the propaganda and ideology of the *Romanità* movement in helping to support an expansionist foreign policy?

However, with the exception of the Corfu Incident, Mussolini avoided an aggressive foreign policy until after 1933. In part, this was because he was not in a strong enough military or political position to achieve his expansionist aims by force. In fact, the pressure exerted by Britain and France, acting together, in 1923 over Corfu had shown up the relative weakness of Italy at this stage. Nonetheless, fascist propaganda constantly stressed the value of nationalism, and continued its calls for an expanded Italian empire.

German nationalism before 1933

Germany, like Italy, did not come into existence as a unified state until the second half of the 19th century – in fact, it was not officially formed until 1871.

German unification

Before 1871, 'Germany' – like Italy – was just a collection of many separate states. In all, there were over 250 of them, linked only by language and by the fact that they were part of the **Holy Roman Empire**.

Holy Roman Empire: This was a collection of lands whose rulers – at least, in theory – owed allegiance to the Holy Roman Emperors. The latter were also the emperors of the Austrian (or Habsburg) Empire; although Austria was the most powerful of the German states, it also contained many non-German lands.

Some of the German states – such as Prussia, Saxony and Bavaria were relatively large, but most were small. These states were divided by religion (they were either Catholic or Protestant); in addition – and again just like Italy – the areas where the German language was spoken did not correspond to any one single country.

However, the French Revolution and Napoleon's conquest of large parts of the 'German' areas of the Holy Roman Empire resulted in the emergence of an **early form of German nationalism**.

early form of German nationalism: Most early forms of German nationalism were movements which concentrated on opposition to French rule and to the ideals of the French Revolution. They were also often anti-Semitic and anti-liberal. In addition, for many years national unity was associated with French rule, which had been more resented in Germany than in Italy – hence attachments to small local states remained strong.

For instance, Johann Fichte – a Berlin academic – wanted to see the creation of a German nation – in 1807–08, he published his *Addresses to the German Nation*. In particular, the student movements were clearly inspired by both the liberal and nationalist ideas of the early French Revolution.

Following Napoleon's defeat, the great powers – Britain, Russia, Austria and Prussia (along with France) met from 1814–15 at the Congress of Vienna to re-draw the map of Europe. This Congress accepted the existence of the smaller number of German states – and these were grouped together in a German Confederation (the Deutscher Bund), which was given a Diet (Assembly) – sometimes known as the Bundestag or Bundesversammlung – in which the various rulers of the different states could meet. However, the new German Confederation and its Bundestag were both supervised by Austria.

Fact: Although some of these ideas – such as liberalism and democratic rights – had later been abandoned by Napoleon, he had made some important territorial changes within the German lands. In particular, he had allowed larger states to take over smaller ones, while he also merged several states to form 39 larger units. This eventually made the creation of a single German nation much easier.

During the period 1815–19, following the defeat of Napoleon and the establishment of the German Confederation, student movements sprang up in many German university towns and cities. However, although these developments amongst university students were not part of a nationwide movement, the Austrian authorities moved to repress the student activists after 1815. In 1820, the Austrians pressured the German Bund into passing the Carlsbad Decrees: these established tighter controls on universities and tightened censorship. Nationalist or liberal professors were dismissed, and nationalist publications were either censored or banned altogether. As Metternich, the Austrian chancellor stated: '*A word spoken by Austria is an unbreakable law for Germany.*' Such repression of German nationalism continued through the 1830s, and German nationalists

Causes of German and Italian Expansion

were forced to meet clandestinely in private homes, or in clubs or societies which officially had nothing to do with nationalist politics.

Initially, even amongst German nationalists, there were divisions about what 'Germany' should be. Some favoured a 'Grossdeutschland' ('Big Germany') – this would include Austria and the southern states. Others supported the idea of a 'Kleindeutschland' ('Small Germany'), based on an enlarged north Germany. In addition, German nationalists were divided about the political formation such a Germany should have – some favoured a liberal and democratic system; others preferred the idea of a strong monarchical system.

Despite these problems, by 1848, several hundreds of thousands of Germans were involved in various historical, music or sports societies – many of their members played important parts in the unsuccessful revolutions of 1848.

In the end, German nationalism was carried forward by the actions of the German state of Prussia which, in 1834, was behind the formation of a free trade association between itself and several other smaller north German states. This trading association was known as the **Zollverein**, and involved 17 states – significantly, Austria was not part of it.

Eventually, virtually all German states belonged to it. However, whilst some people saw this as the beginnings of a united Germany, many states simply saw it as a purely economic agreement for mutual benefits, and remained opposed to the idea of any political union.

In fact, it was not until 1859 that a Nationalist Association (Nationalverein) was formed. Yet, unlike Italy, there were no obvious nationalist leaders, and German nationalism remained an unorganised collection of patriotic groups, or cultural and artistic developments, rather than developing into an effective nationalist political movement.

Eventually, the emergence of a new German nation was the result of Prussia using a combination of military and economic methods: what Bismarck (who became chancellor of Prussia in 1862) referred to as 'blood and iron'. In particular, Bismarck was determined to end the German Bund, which was still dominated by Austria; instead, he aimed for the creation of a North German Confederation which would be dominated by Prussia. After short successful wars against Denmark in 1864, and against Austria in 1866, the North German Confederation was created in 1867 – with Prussia clearly in charge. One important result of these successful short wars was that the army and militarism became increasingly important, and war was seen as an acceptable way of expanding territorially. By 1867, it was clear that a powerful German state would soon appear in Europe.

Prussia's wars in 1864–66 had not only effectively eclipsed Austria's influence within Germany – it had also undermined the position of France as the major continental power in Europe. The final stage of the creation of Germany was the Franco–Prussian War of 1870–71, which saw Prussian forces relatively quickly defeat those of France. In January 1871, five months before the Treaty of Frankfurt had formally ended the war in May 1871, the creation of the new German Empire had already been announced. The new Germany was the pre-existing North German Confederation which was then joined by the south German states. Significantly perhaps, in light of future developments, this announcement was made at a military ceremony in Versailles – it was

Fact: As Austrian authority collapsed during the early stages of these revolutions, many German states saw liberals and nationalists assume some government posts. In April 1848, these new political leaders met in Frankfurt to discuss the formation of a united Germany. In May, elections for a new national assembly were held. However, although they eventually agreed – after lengthy disputes between themselves – to offer the king of Prussia the throne of a 'Kleindeutschland' in March 1849, he refused to accept and, as the impetus of the revolutions faded, the Frankfurt Parliament was eventually dispersed by troops.

Zollverein: This translates as 'customs' (zoll) 'union' or 'association' (verein). It acted almost as a nation, making trade agreements and treaties with countries such as Holland, Britain and Belgium. Several contemporaries saw this economic agreement as a clear step towards the creation of a politically-united German nation. Certainly, the members of the Zollverein met together in an assembly to decide economic issues.

5 German and Italian Expansionism, 1933–40

Figure 5.9 German unification, 1815–71

clear that the new Germany, under Prussian leadership and control, was very much a militarised state.

German militarism and imperialism before 1914

The new state of Germany, though large, had few clear natural boundaries, thus one foreign policy concern from the start was how to secure its borders. In particular, France – though defeated in 1871 – was seen as a potential threat; consequently, Germany sought protection by a combination of diplomacy and the creation of a large modern army. In addition, during the 1880s, the new state eventually wished to find its place 'in the sun', by beginning to gain an empire overseas – for both economic and strategic reasons – to match those already possessed by Britain and France. However, these ambitions created tensions between these European states.

As regards Germany's armed forces, these continued to develop largely independently of the civilian government, and militaristic values became widespread. These were reinforced by frequent large military processions and parades, while parts of the court and government became increasingly militarised as regards attitudes and even dress. In addition, the German military – like all military forces – regularly drew up military war plans: mostly, these assumed that France would be the main opponent.

As the image of a 'great power' in late 19th century Europe included the possession of an empire, German nationalism after 1871 was initially focused on imperialistic expansion. After 1879, the main European powers – and the US – made big efforts to extend their control over those areas which still remained independent. In particular, the focus was on the continents of Africa and Asia. However, until 1884, Bismarck was relatively uninterested in such colonial expansion – in part, as he feared it might jeopardise the complicated web of alliance he had put together to reduce the threat of a revenge war by France. However, many Germans pushed for colonial expansion, and a Colonial Society was formed to press the economic and prestige reasons for obtaining colonies. Despite this, it wasn't until 1884 that Bismarck gave the go-ahead – this saw Germany gain several colonies in parts of Africa and the Pacific in the period 1884–99.

However, the economic gains for Germany rarely outweighed the financial and diplomatic costs and, by 1889, Bismarck had decided against further expansion. This brought him into conflict with the new German kaiser Wilhelm II, who was determined to expand abroad. As a result, in 1890, Bismarck was forced to resign, and the new kaiser increasingly took charge of military and foreign policy. As well as allowing Bismarck's alliance with Russia to collapse, Wilhelm II also greatly expanded the German navy, which increasingly created tensions with Britain. In 1914, less than 25 years after Bismarck's resignation, Germany – and Europe – was at war.

Impact of the First World War and the Peace Treaties 1914–19

Initially, there was much nationalist support for the war and, at first, the First World War went well both for Germany and for Austria – its main ally in the Triple Alliance. Germany's war plan – **the Schlieffen Plan** – which was designed to enable Germany to survive a two–front war, saw France quickly invaded via Belgium, and it soon looked as though Paris would fall to the German army.

However, the British Expeditionary Force joined with the French to prevent this, while Russia's army mobilised quicker than planned; and, by November 1914, a stalemate existed on the Western Front. New weapons and tactics, and several hugely-costly offensives failed to break it, and the First World War soon became a war of attrition. In April 1917, the US joined the Triple Entente and, although revolution in Russia meant German troops could be switched from the east to the west, Germany's last offensive in the spring of 1918 failed after early successes. Then, in August 1918, the Allies – now with fresh troops from the US – were able to launch a counter-offensive. With hunger, mutinies and revolution within Germany, in October 1918, the German General Staff handed power over to a civilian government, so that the army could avoid being directly blamed for any subsequent peace settlement. They then secretly advised this new German government that Germany would have to surrender – even though no enemy troops were actually on German territory. Thus, on the advice of Germany's top military leaders, Germany signed the armistice in November 1918.

However, the German government assumed that the peace treaty would be based on the Fourteen Points, issued by US president Woodrow Wilson in January 1918. These had called for a peace that was not punitive, and which would honour the principles of self-determination. Yet when the main allied leaders met in Paris in January 1919, it soon became clear that Germany was going to have to sign a harsh treaty. Ominously,

the Schlieffen Plan: The main idea of the Schlieffen Plan was based on the belief that, once war was declared, Russia (as it was relatively backward as regards economic and military preparedness) would take some time to mobilise – thus the idea was that Germany could quickly defeat France, as in 1870–71, and then be able to turn all its forces against Russia in the east. It was also based on the assumption that Britain would remain neutral in the event of a war between Germany and France.

5 German and Italian Expansionism, 1933–40

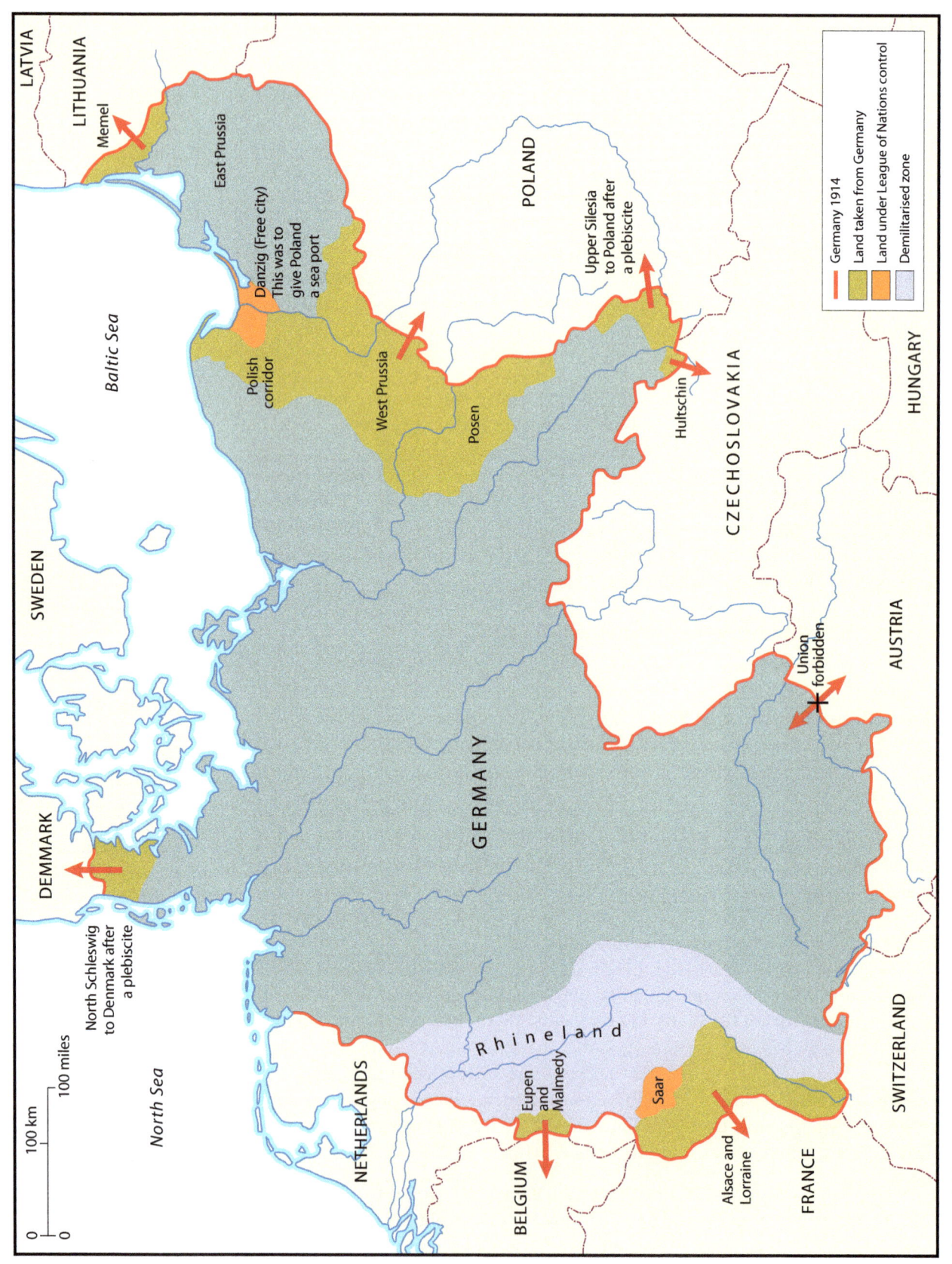

Figure 5.10 Germany's territorial losses in the Treaty of Versailles

no German representatives were present as the Allies began to draw up the Treaty of Versailles, which was the treaty intended to deal with Germany. Once the terms had been agreed between the Allies, the German representatives were called in simply to sign the treaty. The terms were seen as so harsh by them that, at first, they refused to sign – but were informed by the German military chiefs that they could not prevent an Allied invasion of Germany. So, very reluctantly, they signed.

The terms of the Treaty of Versailles were relatively harsh – but nowhere near as harsh as those imposed on Russia by Germany in the Treaty of Brest-Litovsk in March 1918. As well as restrictions on the size of its army and navy, Germany lost land to Poland, France, Belgium and Denmark. In all, Germany lost 10% of its lands in Europe, along with 12.5% of its population, 16% of its coalfields and 50% of its iron and steel industries. All its overseas colonies were taken away, while Anschluss (union) with Austria was expressly forbidden. In addition, it was forced to accept what became known as the 'War Guilt Clause', by which Germany accepted total responsibility for starting the war, and agreed to pay reparations (compensation) for all the damages suffered by the Allies (see section 5.2, Economic impact of the First World War and the Treaty of Versailles below). Finally, Germany was not allowed to join the newly-established League of Nations.

German nationalism and the 'diktat'

Right up to the signing of the armistice in November 1918, the German people had been told by the kaiser and his military-dominated government that Germany was actually winning the war. Hence many in Germany felt that the 'undefeated heroes' of the German army had been 'stabbed in the back' by enemies and traitors at home, whilst German soldiers – after heavy casualties – had finally been on the point of victory. Thus those who had signed the armistice were seen by German nationalists as the 'November criminals' (*Novemberverbrecher*).

Fact: For German nationalists, these 'enemies and traitors' were variously a mixture of liberals, democrats, socialists, communists and Jews. The 'stab-in-the-back' myth (*Dolchstosslegende*) was first put forward by Hindenburg and Ludendorff – despite the fact that they knew the German Army had informed the new government that they would have to agree to an armistice. This myth proved to be a strong one, and was later used to good effect by Hitler and the emerging Nazi Party in the 1920s. As it was the new democratic government of the Weimar Republic which had signed the armistice and peace treaty, many German nationalists never really supported the democratic changes to Germany's constitution – and hence were not worried when Hitler and the Nazis argued for its overthrow.

Figure 5.11 A 1924 right-wing German political cartoon showing the new government's politicians – the so-called 'November criminals' – stabbing the German army in the back, by signing the armistice and then the Treaty of Versailles. The caption reads: 'Germans, remember!'

5 German and Italian Expansionism, 1933–40

Fact: Although seen as unfair by the German people, in reality, Germany did not lose that much territory – and what it did lose was far less than what it had taken from Russia in the Treaty of Brest-Litovsk in 1918. In addition, the German economy revived quickly in the second half of the 1920s; while the amount of reparations was progressively reduced after 1919. Finally, throughout the 1920s, Germany was able to avoid complying with many of the military restrictions imposed by the Treaty of Versailles.

Then, once the conditions of the Treaty of Versailles were made public, there was much nationalist resentment at what were seen as grossly unfair terms.

For many Germans, this treaty was particularly resented as it seemed to be punishing the German people, when they had little influence over the kaiser and his military commanders, or the policies they had pursued before 1914. The fact that the treaty had been drawn up and imposed without any German representation led many Germans – not just nationalists – to see it as a diktat, or 'dictated peace'. It was in this post-war atmosphere that German Nazism was born.

Figure 5.12 A protest in Munich against the decisions of the Treaty of Versailles on 1 June 1919. In all, over 30,000 Germans protested in Munich alone

German Nazism

German Nazism – like Italian Fascism – developed as a direct result of the First World War. Unlike Mussolini, Hitler (an Austrian, not a German) seemed to have had no real interest in politics before 1914; but as the war came to an end, he began to develop an increasingly extreme form of German nationalism. Like many, Hitler was deeply affected by the Treaty of Versailles, and he soon determined that this treaty should be overturned. In 1924, just four years after Hitler had formed his Nazi Party, his political views and aims were set forth in a book he wrote whilst in prison, Mein Kampf.

Fact: Hitler's early admiration of Mussolini's fascism is shown by the fact that he adopted the Roman salute, the idea of uniforms for the Nazi Party's paramilitary forces, along with other aspects of Mussolini's propaganda techniques.

As well as sharing with Mussolini's Fascist Party hatred of democracy, liberalism and all left-wing political parties, he also expounded on foreign policy. Here, too, were great similarities with Italian Fascism: including the idea of *Lebensraum* ('Living Space'), which was very similar to Mussolini's idea of *spazio vitale*. However, unlike Italian Fascism, the Nazis' nationalist ideology did not aim for the establishment of a colonial empire – instead, the focus was on gaining *Lebensraum* and resources by expanding in eastern Europe. As well as regaining land lost to Poland in 1919, this policy was particularly aimed against the Soviet Union: in addition to destroying 'communism', such expansion would gain the greater German Reich sufficient food and raw materials to make it self-sufficient. Thus, like Italian Fascism, Nazi ideology led in the direction of an aggressively expansionist foreign policy – and, ultimately, to the prospect of war and conquest. In order to achieve this, Nazi ideology and policies – again like Mussolini's – included the idea of increasing the nation's birthrate, in order to ensure sufficient soldiers for such wars.

Figure 5.13 Mussolini and Hitler reviewing troops in Munich in 1937

Nazism and German nationalism after 1918

In Bavaria, following the violent suppression of a short-lived socialist revolution during 1918–19, an extreme right-wing nationalist administration had come to power. It was in this atmosphere that Hitler first joined the German Workers' Party (*Deutsche Arbeiterpartei* or DAP). Despite its name, usually associated with left-wing movements, it was an extreme nationalist party. It was had been formed in March 1919 by Anton Drexler, who was also its leader. Once a member, Hitler soon emerged as an effective speaker and, in February 1920, he persuaded its members to change the party's name to the National Socialist German Workers' Party (*Nationalsozialistische Deutsche Arbeiterpartei* or NSDAP). He also got the re-named party to accept a new 25-point party programme. This was essentially a right-wing nationalist, corporatist and anti-Semitic programme.

Significantly for German foreign policy after 1933, it called for the overturning of the provisions of the Treaty of Versailles, and for all German-speakers to be united in a greater German Reich. Soon, the party was known as the Nazi Party. Then, in November 1923, Hitler attempted to imitate Mussolini's successful 'March on Rome', which had taken place the previous year. However, Hitler's 'March on Berlin' failed to get out of Munich – and, as a result, is known as the Beer Hall Putsch. Although Hitler

> **KEY CONCEPTS QUESTION**
>
> **Significance:** What were the most significant similarities between these two types of fascism as regards foreign policy?

5

German and Italian Expansionism, 1933–40

was briefly imprisoned for this violent attempt to overthrow the German government, he used his time in prison to write his book, *Mein Kampf* ('My Struggle'). In it, he expounded all his ideas – including those on German unity and nationalism, and on what kind of foreign policy Germany should follow.

KEY CONCEPTS QUESTION

Change and continuity: To what extent was fascist ultra-nationalism in both Italy and Germany simply a continuation of 19th century forms of nationalism?

5.2 What was the impact of economic issues on expansionist foreign policies in Italy and Germany?

By 1933, both Italy and Germany were experiencing various economic problems. The most important of these related to the economic impacts of the First World War and then the **Great Depression**.

Great Depression: This was the depression which followed the Wall Street Crash in October 1929 (the collapse of the US stock exchange). All major countries, with the exception of the USSR, were badly affected during the 1930s: decline in world trade and production, along with high unemployment and poverty. Another European country badly affected by the Depression was Germany.

During the 1930s, an expansionist foreign policy increasingly seemed to offer a quick way of obtaining extra resources in order to offset domestic economic problems.

The Italian economy 1900–33

The period 1900–33 saw Italy experience various economic problems – while the main ones were connected to the First World War and then the Depression, earlier economic issues were also important, as were the various impacts of fascist economic policies.

Economic divisions before 1914

In the early 20th century, significant economic divisions existed in Italy. The south, compared to northern and central Italy, was very poor and backward. The amount of land suitable for farming in the south was restricted by geography and climate, while most of the available lands were part of large estates (known as *latifundia*) owned by a small minority of wealthy landowners. Hence the vast majority of the population were extremely poor. In northern and central Italy, agriculture was more developed, with a much greater use of modern farming methods and machinery. However, even here, productivity was much lower than in the countries of northern Europe.

The biggest economic difference between north and south, however, was in relation to industry.

Fact: Immediately after 1870, industrial development in Italy was relatively limited. In the north, there were some iron and steel concerns, and a few ship-building firms. However, development was hindered by the lack of coal and iron-ore, while the traditional silk industry of the south was soon wiped out by the more efficient silk manufacturers in the north. Later, hydro-electric power from dams built in the Alps was used in the north, and soon provided the basis for a rapid industrialisation, beginning in the 1880s.

In 1899, the Fiat car company was established and, by 1913, was exporting over 4,000 cars a year. Towns and cities in the north grew rapidly, and led to the creation of a large industrial working class, as well as to the rise of a powerful class of rich industrialists and bankers, and a sizeable lower middle class. While industry thus expanded in the north, there was no real investment in the south.

Economic impact of the First World War

The First World War had a tremendous effect on the relatively weak Italian economy. In order to finance its involvement in the war, the Liberal government had borrowed heavily from Britain and the US – as a result, the national debt had risen from 16 billion lire to 85 billion. Even this proved inadequate, so the government printed more banknotes, resulting in rapid inflation, with prices increasing by over 400% in the period 1915–18. This inflation destroyed much of the middle classes' savings, reduced the rent incomes of many landowners, and resulted in the real wages of many workers dropping by over 25%. At the end of the war, the situation was made much worse by high unemployment, as the war industries closed and over 2.5 million soldiers were demobilised.

The war also deepened the economic divisions between north and south Italy. Those industries linked to war production (especially steel, chemicals, motor vehicles, rubber and woollen industries) did extremely well, as they were guaranteed big state contracts – when inflation began to hit, industrialists simply passed on the increases to the government.

Fact: Companies such as Pirelli (tyres) and Montecatini (chemicals) made huge profits, while Fiat continued to expand and, by 1918, was the largest motor manufacturer in Europe. However, the end of the war meant the loss of lucrative state contracts, as the government cut back expenditure in order to cope with mounting debts.

The south, still predominantly agricultural, did not share in this prosperity; farming was badly affected by the large numbers of peasants and farm labourers conscripted for the war. However, during the last years of the war, in an attempt to limit the attraction of socialism and the Russian **Bolsheviks**, the government had promised a programme of land reform after the war.

Bolsheviks: These were the more revolutionary element of the Russian Social Democratic Labour Party (a Marxist party). Led by Lenin – and later joined by Trotsky – they took power in Russia in November 1917. The Bolsheviks later changed their name to the Russian Communist Party, and worked hard to aid and encourage socialist revolutions in other countries – especially in more advanced capitalist countries such as Germany.

The effects of fascist economic policy, 1922–31

Apart from the economic effects of the First World War, the Italian economy also suffered from some aspects of fascist economic policy. Mussolini had no real understanding of, or interest in, economics. However, he realised the importance of a strong economy to consolidate his regime, and to lay the foundations for an aggressive and expansionist foreign policy. Thus, in many respects, Mussolini's main concern was to make Italy a rich and great power.

To achieve this, Mussolini believed it was necessary to make Italy economically self-sufficient in food and in raw materials for industry. This would require not only overcoming problems of poverty and improving agriculture at home, but also conquering a large empire to supply Italy with raw materials.

To achieve the economic greatness he desired, Mussolini decided to launch a series of initiatives or campaigns he called 'battles'. The first of these battles was announced in 1924 and was directed at trying to overcome the long-term poverty which existed in Southern Italy. In 1925, a much more serious campaign – 'the Battle for Grain' – began, in response to a poor harvest and a consequent increase in grain imports. The aim was to get Italian farmers to grow more cereals (especially wheat) in order to reduce Italy's dependence on foreign imports.

SOURCE C

Wheat was the vital commodity that could feed an army, and Italy did not grow enough of it. In the early 1920s about 2.5 million tonnes a year, nearly one-third of the requirement, had to be imported, at a cost of almost 3 billion lire. This was about one-fifth by value of all imports. Italy already had to import coal and oil; and could not import basic foodstuff as well.

Clark, M. 2005. *Mussolini*. London. Pearson. p. 130.

5 German and Italian Expansionism, 1933–40

autarchy: (sometimes spelled: 'autarky') this means 'self-sufficiency', and usually applies to countries or regimes which try to exist without having to import particular foods, fuels, raw materials or industrial goods. It can also refer to the attempt – for instance, as happened in Fascist Italy and Nazi Germany – to be totally self-sufficient in all important areas. Invariably, such attempts had limited success.

Fact: In October 1935, Italy launched an invasion of Abyssinia (now called Ethiopia), which was sandwiched between the Italian colonies of Eritrea and Somaliland. Mussolini sent 500,000 troops who used tanks, bombers and poison gas against people often only armed with spears. Britain and France were reluctant to impose sanctions as, at this time, Mussolini was still seen as a useful ally against Hitler's ambitions – the previous year, he had joined them in the Stresa Front to oppose Hitler's attempted takeover of Austria. The sanctions did not ban oil or use of the Suez Canal – and by May 1936, the invasion had succeeded.

Figure 5.14 Mussolini encouraging harvesters at Aprilla during the 'Battle for Grain'

The following year, 1926, saw the start of the 'Battle for Land' – a further attempt to increase the amount of available farming land. Marshes and swamps were drained, in particular, the Pontine Marshes near Rome. This created many small farms, while the actual work, financed from public funds, created jobs for the unemployed.

On 18 August 1926, the 'Battle for the Lira' started when the value of the lira dropped. In order to restore its value abroad (to help stop price rises) and to increase, as well as to maintain, Italian prestige, it was revalued. This allowed Italy to continue importing coal and iron for armaments and shipbuilding.

However, most of Mussolini's economic 'battles' were far from successful, often because they were not consistently fought. No new villages – promised by the 'Battle over the Southern Problem' – were built. The 'Battle for Grain', although it succeeded in almost doubling cereal production by 1939 (making Italy self-sufficient in wheat), also involved misallocation of resources and resulted in Italy having to import olive oil, while fruit and wine exports dropped, as did the numbers of cattle and sheep. The 'Battle for Land' saw only one area effectively reclaimed (the Pontine Marshes) – as it was near Rome, Mussolini saw this as a way of impressing visitors and tourists.

The 'Battle for the Lira', which involved artificially overvaluing the lira, also resulted in declining exports – and, thus an increase in unemployment – as Italian goods became more expensive. Car exports, in particular, were badly hit. It also began a recession in Italy which was made worse by the Depression.

Thus, most of Mussolini's 'battles' which were intended to achieve **autarchy** caused at least as many problems as they solved; this tendency was increased by the effects of the Depression.

Italy and the Great Depression

For the Italian economy, the worst years of the Depression were from 1931–37. Before the Depression, Mussolini had not interfered with private enterprise and had, in particular, favoured large companies and heavy industry. However, once the Depression began to take effect, Mussolini began to favour some state intervention – at first, by encouraging job-sharing schemes. By 1933, unemployment had risen to over 2 million, while millions more (especially in the rural south) suffered from under-employment. Over 30% of labouring jobs in agriculture were lost, and many women were forced to give up their jobs to unemployed men. By 1930, Mussolini had to drop earlier claims that his regime had improved the living standards of working-class Italians.

Historical debate:
One of the many areas which continues to generate debate amongst historians relates to the effects of the fascist regime's economic policy in terms of it being a 'modernising dictatorship'. A. J. Gregor, amongst others, controversially claimed that Italian Fascism was similar to Stalin's regime in the USSR, in that it attempted to carry out the rapid industrialisation of a backward economy. Others, while not going so far, consider that fascism did play some part in 'modernising' Italy's economy. However, many historians see Mussolini's fascism as having failed to modernise because of its deference to 'traditional' economic interests.

QUESTION
Carry out some further research of your own on the topic 'a modernising dictatorship'.

SOURCE D

We must rid our minds of the idea that what we have called the days of prosperity may return. We are probably moving toward a period when humanity will exist on a lower standard of living.

Part of a speech made by Mussolini in 1936. In Robson, M. 1992. *Italy: Liberalism and Fascism 1870–1945*. London. Hodder & Stoughton. p. 101.

In 1931, in an attempt to deal with these problems, Mussolini's government decided to use public money to help prevent the collapse of banks and industries hit by the Depression. Thus, in 1933, the Institute of Industrial Reconstruction (Instituto per la Recostruzione Industriale - IRI) was set up. Initially, it took over various unprofitable industries on behalf of the state. By 1939, the IRI had become a massive state company, controlling many industries, including most of the iron and steel industries, merchant shipping, the electrical industry and even the telephone system.

In particular, the effects of the Depression led Mussolini to adopt increasingly protectionist measures, and to increase the push towards fascist autarchy. This tendency became even stronger after 1935, when many member-countries of the League of Nations imposed some economic sanctions on Italy following its invasion of Abyssinia.

Once Mussolini began to involve Italy in more military adventures and wars, the push for autarchy – and the problems it caused – increased accordingly. Nonetheless, there were some moderate achievements: by 1940, industrial production had increased by

5 German and Italian Expansionism, 1933–40

9%; as a result, industry overtook agriculture as the largest proportion of GNP for the first time in Italy's history. In addition, between 1928 and 1939, imports of raw materials and industrial goods dropped significantly. Overall, however, the end result of fascist economic policy was not a significant modernisation of the economy, or even increased levels of productivity, and Italy was much slower in recovering from the Depression than most other European states. Once Italy became involved in the Second World War, these economic and industrial weaknesses became increasingly apparent.

The German economy 1900–33

The German economy before 1914

Many of the German states had industrialised quite quickly during the second half of the 19th century – in particular, some of these German states developed strong coal and iron industries, along with a rapidly-expanding railway network. Later, they were quick to move into the newer chemical and electrical industries. Once Germany had been officially created in 1871, the economic benefits which had resulted from the expansion of the Zollverein were increased, as all remaining internal tariffs were abolished. Then, in 1879, Bismarck introduced a new external tariff system on imported goods. This was to protect, in particular, German farmers from Russian food imports and German factory owners from British industrial goods. As a consequence, there was further rapid economic growth, giving the new Germany one of the world's fastest-growing industrial bases. Within Europe, Germany had the fastest growing economy – and this economic growth and prosperity – especially after 1890 – enabled Germany to build a large modern army, and to build an increasingly-strong navy.

Historical debate: Although the economist J. M. Keynes argued that the reparations created real problems for the German economy, historians such as D. Peukert (1991) have pointed out that the payments – about 2,000 million marks a year – represented only 2% of Germany's total national output in the 1920s. Furthermore, during the 1920s, the total amount of reparations was reduced by negotiation with the Allies.

Fact: The invasion of the Ruhr in 1923 came about as France and Belgium claimed Germany had failed to make the coal deliveries it was supposed to under the terms of the reparations agreement. It was this military action which had directly led to Hitler's attempt to take power in 1923. At first, the German government had encouraged Germans to engage in passive resistance to the occupation. But, when the resulting economic problems – which included hyper-inflation – led the government to end resistance, German nationalists had been outraged.

SOURCE E

The German population soared from 49 to 60 million between 1890 and 1914, and the economy grew faster than that of any other country in Europe. In 1914, Germany's steel output was higher than that of Britain, France and Russia combined and coal production had risen to second position behind Britain. The prominence of science and technology in the school curriculum gave Germany a notable lead in new, 'high-tech' industries. Germany's industrial strength was used to increase its military strength.

McDonough, F. 1997. *The Origins of the First and Second World Wars*. Cambridge. Cambridge University Press. p. 3.

However, the rapid emergence of the new Germany as one of Europe's leading industrial and military powers was one of the factors which led to the outbreak of the First World War in 1914.

Economic impact of the First World War and the Treaty of Versailles

The First World War had a largely negative impact on Germany's economy – as it did on the economies of the other European participants. The stalemate which quickly developed on the Western Front put a great strain on Germany's economy – while many industries switched over entirely to war production, Germany's national debt was massively increased: from 5,000 million marks to 144,000 million marks

Causes of German and Italian Expansion

by the end of the war. In addition, Germany lost industrial customers to countries such as the US and Japan; while, as the war dragged on, world trade in general declined. In particular, Europe's export market had virtually collapsed, and inflation rose – in Germany, by 1918, prices were 500% higher than they had been in 1914. Furthermore, industrial production in Germany had dropped to about two-fifths of its pre-war level.

Although the modern industrialised German economy meant that, at first, Germany coped with the demands of 'total war' better than less-developed economies (such as Russia's) did, in the end, the strains of a two-front war proved too much, even for the German economy. As food shortages became increasingly serious, economic problems, strikes, political unrest and, eventually, revolution began to emerge in Germany. It was in this economic context that the Allies imposed the Treaty of Versailles on the defeated Germany.

The Treaty of Versailles, as well as depriving Germany of many of its important industrial areas (see section 5.2, Economic impact of the First World War and the Treaty of Versailles), also imposed reparations (compensation) as part of the 'war guilt' clause – the figure was finally set by the Reparations Committee at £6.6 billion in May 1921. Although this initially caused economic problems in 1922 – which resulted in France and Belgium invading the Ruhr in 1923, after Germany had asked for a 4-year postponement in making its second payment – the treaty did not actually destroy either the German economy or Germany as a great power. Even as early as 1919, Germany was still potentially the most powerful of the states on the European mainland: the Russian and Austrian empires had collapsed, while France was more seriously weakened by the war than Germany.

After the economic crisis of 1923, however, Germany made a quick recovery under the leadership of **Gustav Stresemann** who, from 1923–29, acted as chancellor and then foreign secretary. Under him, a new currency – the *Rentenmark* – was immediately introduced to stabilise the currency. Stresemann then began to negotiate for a reduction in the reparations bill. Although the figure set in 1921 remained, the annual repayments were reduced and the time-scale extended. In addition, the US agreed to make a substantial loan to Germany to help its economy recover: the **Dawes Plan** of 1924 initially lent Germany 800 million marks.

In return, Germany had to agree to introduce a new currency – the *Reichsmark* – which (unlike the *Rentenmark*) was to be based on Germany's gold reserves. Although German nationalists resented the continued reparations payments, the German economy boomed during the second half of the 1920s: as a result, this period became known as the 'Golden Years'. Industrial output which, even before 1924, had already reached pre-war levels, greatly increased after the Dawes Plan; and exports rose by over 40%. Further loans from the US and increased foreign investment were used to further increase industrial production and modernise Germany's infrastructure and housing stock.

To most Germans, it seemed that Germany's economic problems were well and truly over, and that its economy would continue to expand. In this atmosphere, extreme nationalist groups – which were already beginning to push for territorial expansion – found they had little electoral support, and were increasingly marginalised. Especially as Stresemann, as well as overseeing economic growth, was also successfully – by negotiation with the Allies – improving Germany's diplomatic position in Europe. The Nazi Party, for instance, experienced what is often referred to as their 'Lean Years' between 1924 and 1929. In December 1924, they only won 14 seats in elections to the Reichstag; while, in 1928, this dropped to 12 seats.

Gustav Stresemann (1878–1929)

He became the most significant German statesman of the Weimar Republic. He worked with France to improve relations between Germany and the Allies in the period 1923–29. However, although a firm nationalist, he was also a conciliator who believed that it was necessary to cooperate with the Allies in order to 'revise' the Treaty of Versailles. His long-term aims were to get all Allied troops removed from Germany; to re-adjust Germany's eastern borders with Czechoslovakia and Poland; to end reparations completely; to make Austria part of a 'Greater Germany'; and even to get back Alsace-Lorraine and Eupen-Malmedy. However, he did not plan to use force to achieve these aims.

5

German and Italian Expansionism, 1933–40

Germany and the Great Depression

Dawes Plan: The US, which had loaned massive amounts to Britain and France during the First World War, was keen to see Germany make its reparations repayments. This would enable France to repay its US debts. In fact, though the US later criticised France for its insistence on heavy reparations, it refused a French suggestion in 1919 to cancel its US debts. As a consequence, the French felt they had to insist on compensation from Germany. In August 1929, the 'Young Plan' even reduced the reparations figure by about 75%, further reduced the annual payments, and extended the repayments period to 59 years.

However, despite the rapid growth of the German economy after 1924, there were some signs that the 'Golden Years' might soon come to an end. In part, this was because much of the recovery was dependent on foreign (especially US) loans. In 1928 alone, this amounted to over 5 billion marks. Furthermore, the bulk of the German banking system was based on short-term loans to German industries, which would not be repaid if those firms went bankrupt. One early sign of a possible slowdown came as early as 1926, when Germany's balance of trade moved into the red. In addition, unemployment remained a problem – though the figure of 2 million unemployed in 1926 had dropped to 1.4 million by 1928, this indicated a potential weakness in the German economy.

In early October Stresemann died, then, later in the month, the Wall Street Crash took place in the US. Within a short space of time, Germany's economy was shattered. It was the impact of the economic problems which gave Hitler and the Nazis their political opportunity – and they used it well. Within less than four years, Hitler was chancellor of Germany and, at long last, in a position to push forward the Nazis' expansionist foreign policy aims.

The Wall Street Crash put an end to US loans and, very soon, the US began demanding early repayment of those loans already received. This – combined with the impact of the Great Depression which followed the Wall Street Crash – quickly put an end to the relative prosperity most Germans had enjoyed in the years 1924–29. Soon, German

Fact: According to some later research, the real – but unofficial – unemployment figure by 1932 was over 8 million.

Figure 5.15 Unemployed queuing at the job centre in Hannover, 1930

Causes of German and Italian Expansion

industrial firms began to decline, and Germany was unable to pay for essential raw material and food imports. The number of bankruptcies increased significantly – as did unemployment, which increased from 1.4 million to 2 million by the end of the year. As firms continued to collapse, unemployment soared: to 3 million by 1930, to 4 million in 1931, and to over 6 million by 1932.

Millions of other industrial workers, though they retained their jobs, had their hours reduced by short-time working.

Banks continued to collapse, while industrial production dropped by 50%, and unemployment rose to over 30%. This severe economic crisis led to the collapse of a series of coalition governments and thus a sort of political paralysis. In this situation, governments increasingly relied on ruling by presidential decree, as allowed by Article 48 of the Weimar Constitution. With hindsight, it is easy to see this as the beginning of the

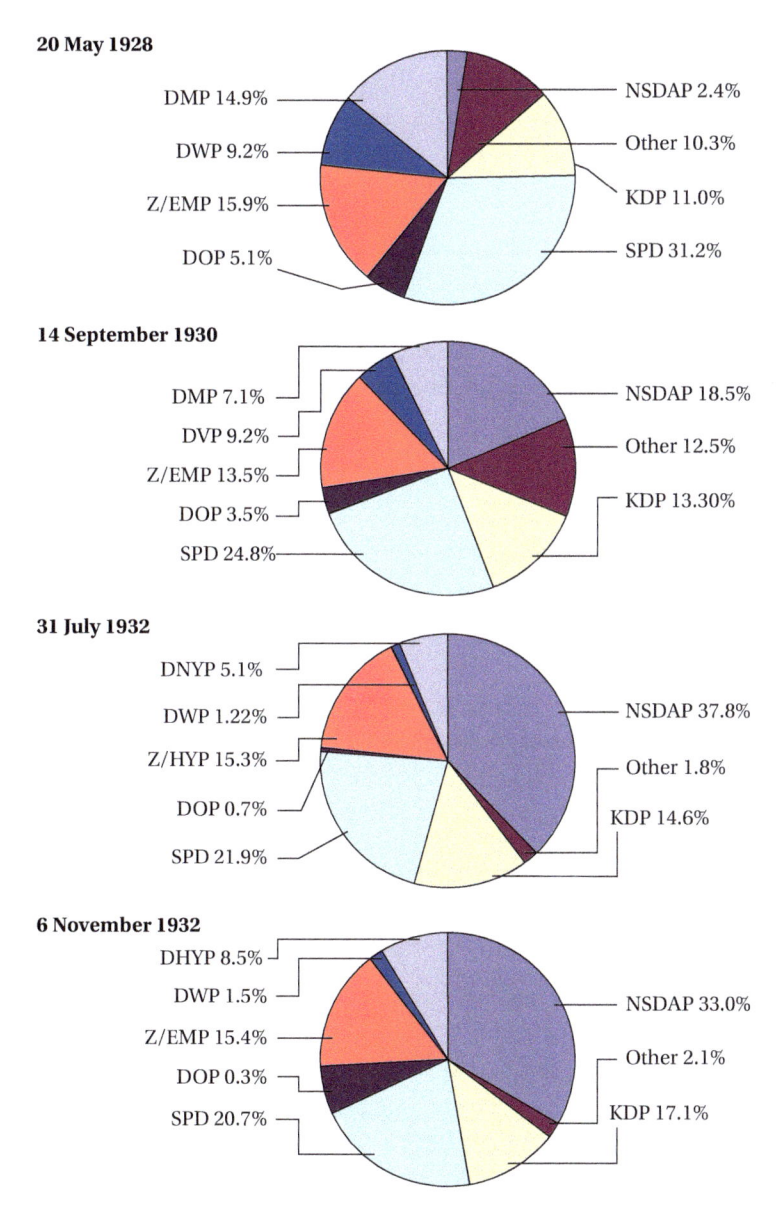

20 May 1928
- DMP 14.9%
- DWP 9.2%
- Z/EMP 15.9%
- DOP 5.1%
- NSDAP 2.4%
- Other 10.3%
- KDP 11.0%
- SPD 31.2%

14 September 1930
- DMP 7.1%
- DVP 9.2%
- Z/EMP 13.5%
- DOP 3.5%
- SPD 24.8%
- NSDAP 18.5%
- Other 12.5%
- KDP 13.30%

31 July 1932
- DNYP 5.1%
- DWP 1.22%
- Z/HYP 15.3%
- DOP 0.7%
- SPD 21.9%
- NSDAP 37.8%
- Other 1.8%
- KDP 14.6%

6 November 1932
- DHYP 8.5%
- DWP 1.5%
- Z/EMP 15.4%
- DOP 0.3%
- SPD 20.7%
- NSDAP 33.0%
- Other 2.1%
- KDP 17.1%

Figure 5.16 The Nazis' (NSDAP's) growing electoral breakthrough from 1928–32, as percentages of seats gained in the Reichstag

Fact: Very often, the rise of the Nazis to power is linked to the proportional system of voting established by the Weimar Constitution. This is seen as having allowed small extremist parties to gain political representation and influence beyond their real levels of support. However, it should be noted that, under the first-past-the vote system (used in countries such as Britain and the US), the July 1932 result would have enabled the Nazis to form a minority government.

5

German and Italian Expansionism, 1933–40

end of Weimar democracy. However, this economic and political crisis saw the Nazi vote rapidly increase in the various elections between 1929 and 1932. In 1930, the number of seats won by the Nazis rose rapidly, from 12 to 107; in July 1932, their seats increased to 230, making them the largest party in the Reichstag.

As they won more and more seats, some conservative and nationalist politicians began to sound out the possibility of some political deal with the Nazis.

However, in the November 1932 elections, the Nazi Party's votes and thus seats declined (from 230 seats to 196), while the performance of the German Communist Party (KPD) continued to improve. It was this political situation which formed the context for the deal offered to Hitler by von Papen, a former leading member of the conservative **German Centre Party** (*Deutsche Zentrumspartei*), and accepted by president Hindenburg. The offer was, in the end, that Hitler could be the chancellor of a coalition government put together by von Papen, who assumed that, as vice-chancellor, he could control Hitler as it seemed to him – and the German elites in general – as though the Nazis had passed their peak (though they were still the largest single party in the Reichstag). Thus, on 30 January 1933, Hitler became chancellor of Germany. By March 1933, he had established a purely Nazi government.

Effects of Nazi economic policy

When Hitler became chancellor of Germany in January 1933, although the economic problems resulting from the Great Depression were still in existence, the worst effects were already over – this was because of the actions taken by the various coalition governments between 1929 and 1932, and because world trade finally began to recover in early 1933. In fact, Hitler was not that interested in economics – for him, the three main aims after 1933 were to:

- restart the economy and solve unemployment via government expenditure on public work schemes
- establish German autarky (economic self-sufficiency and isolation from the international economic system
- create a *Wehrwirtschaft* ('war economy') so that Germany could fight and win a 'total' war in the future.

As early as February 1933, Hitler was talking about creating a 'military' economy which would allow territorial expansion. On the surface, Hitler's economic policy seemed to be successful – for instance, between 1933 and 1935, unemployment dropped from 6 million to 1.7 million, and continued to decline further. However, it should be noted that the decline in unemployment was also the result of following earlier programmes for recovery begun by the last Weimar governments, in addition to the Nazi government's public work schemes; increased expenditure on armaments; the introduction of conscription, after 1935; and the establishment of the German Labour Front.

Furthermore, as became increasingly apparent, Hitler's economic and military policies were creating new problems for Germany. The often uncoordinated Nazi plans, along with some of the policies followed by **Hjalmar Schacht** as president of the Reichsbank, had, as early as the summer of 1934, resulted in inflation and a serious balance of payments deficit in foreign trade. Hitler appointed Schacht as minister of economics to deal with these problems and, in September 1934, Schacht produced his 'New Plan'. As a result of various measures, the German economy soon began to show signs of recovery and, by the end of 1935, Germany had achieved a trade surplus, while industrial production was up by almost 50% compared to 1933.

German Centre Party: The *Deutsche Zentrumspartei* was usually just referred to as the Zentrum – ZP; sometimes, it was also known as the Catholic Centre Party. This party became increasingly authoritarian, right-wing and nationalist after 1929, and attempted several political deals with Hitler and his Nazi Party before 1933. In June 1932, von Papen resigned from the ZP – to forestall his expulsion from the party for having accepted the position of chancellor from Hindenburg (at the time, Bruning of the ZP was the chancellor).

Fact: The decline in unemployment was also increasingly achieved by the removal of certain groups (such as left-wing political prisoners and, later, Jews). These groups were placed in concentration camps and removed from the official statistics, while their jobs were taken by the unemployed. The Nazis also had strong gender prejudices. Consequently, some married women were removed from their jobs, so these could be given to unemployed men.

'mefo' bills: These were secret government bonds which Schacht had printed, to conceal the true expenditure on armaments.

Four-Year Plan: The plan aimed to control all imports and exports; increase agricultural production; make Germany self-sufficient in all important raw materials (such as metals, oil, petrol, rubber and textiles); and retrain sections of workers in key industries.

Causes of German and Italian Expansion

However, as Schacht was aware, these improvements were relatively limited and essentially short-term. In particular, his use of **'mefo' bills** was inflationary at a time when Germany still needed to import raw material for Hitler's re-armament programme. This was particularly worrying, as the cost of these products was increasing while Germany's reserves of gold and foreign currency were declining. In 1936, a new economic crisis arose over the state of the balance of payments, and Schacht argued that this problem could only be overcome by reducing spending on re-armament, and instead increasing exports so as to gain Germany more reserves of foreign currency. However, these suggestions were counter to the Nazis' plans – from 1936, Hitler had decided on a more aggressive foreign policy and so insisted on an even faster expansion of Germany's military strength. In addition, Germany's armed forces also opposed Schacht's suggestions.

In September 1936, Hitler responded to the crisis by placing Hermann Göring in charge of the **Four-Year Plan** – this was designed to make Germany's economy and military forces ready to fight a war in four years' time. In theory, Göring's plan was to operate alongside Schacht's plan; but, in practice, Schacht found his position and policies increasingly undermined by Göring's encroachments on the activities of his ministry. Furthermore, his warnings about the looming balance of payments problem were simply ignored. Eventually, in November 1937, Schacht resigned as minister of economics, and his place was taken by Walther Funk. However, Göring continued to decide the main economic policies.

From then on, Hitler gave greater priority to his plans for military expansion, and massive amounts of state money were poured into research and development, and into armaments production. In all, during 1936–40, this amounted to almost 50% of all industrial investment in the German economy. While the Four-Year Plan achieved some successes – such as big increases in aluminium production, and helping reduce unemployment down to only 300,000 by the end of 1938 – the Nazi 'economic miracle' was more myth than reality in many areas of the economy. Although total German industrial production increased by just over 100% between 1933 and 1938, the aim of being self-sufficient in raw materials was not met – this was particularly true for oil and rubber. In all, over 30% of Germany's important raw materials and 20% of its food still came from abroad. Even the massive re-armament failed to meet Hitler's plans – this was despite military spending increasing from 1.9 billion RM in 1933 to 32.3 billion RM in 1938. Thus, by 1939, Germany was not yet in a position to fight any major long-lasting war.

Nonetheless, it appears that Germany's economic situation in 1939 was such that a war was needed to prevent the German economy from collapsing. In particular, the 'mefo' bills issued earlier by Schacht were due for repayment in 1939 – if paid, it would have wrecked the German economy. The outbreak of war, in September 1939, prevented this as Hitler was able to write them off. In addition, war was also needed – if the living standards of German people were to be maintained – in order to plunder resources from weaker states. This was because, as Schacht had pointed out, the high costs of rearmament had created huge problems for exports, gold reserves, foreign currency earnings, and the supply of skilled labour to industries not linked to military production. According to Göring, there were only two choices in 1939: abandon the rearmament programme, or carry out several local 'lightning' wars in order to obtain the resources the German economy needed but could not afford to import if rearmament continued. Göring deliberately stressed the importance of *Blitzkrieg*, as he knew the German economy was not yet able to sustain any prolonged total war. In effect, it seemed that, by 1939, Hitler's economic policies since 1933 had made war almost inevitable if the Nazis wanted to retain what popular support they had.

Hjalmar Schacht (1877–1970)

He was a conservative banker and powerful financier, with close ties to Germany's industrialists and bankers. Although not a Nazi, he was strongly opposed to Germany's reparation obligations. Hitler made him head of the Reichsbank in 1933, a position he continued to hold until 1939. From 1934–37, he was also minister of economics. He was forced to resign from the latter post, as he opposed Nazi plans for German re-armament because he feared they would lead to inflation and economic collapse.

Historical debate:

Both B. H. Klein and A. Milward argued that Hitler did not intend to fight a major war – the plan was for a series of short 'local' wars in eastern Europe, using *Blitzkrieg* methods. This would enable Germany to obtain the raw materials it needed. W. Sauer argues that Hitler deliberately spent more on weapons and on keeping food prices low, in order to create a 'plunder economy' that would require a major war to keep the German people well fed, *without* having to cut military spending. However, historians such as R. J. Overy have argued that Hitler's aim was always world power and that he never saw Germany being ready by 1940 to fight a 'total' war with 1943 was a more realistic goal – in that sense, the Four-Year Plan was not a failure.

5

German and Italian Expansionism, 1933–40

Fact: Although Nazi Germany had early successes it began to suffer setbacks in the Soviet Union during 1941–42. The longer the war went on, the more the earlier weaknesses of the German economy became apparent. German war production was unable to match that of the Soviet Union – in part, this was because the German economy was unable to cope with the demands of Nazi policies.

Historical debate: Although historians such as R. Henig see the absence of the US and its policy of isolationism as fatally undermining the League from its very beginning, this is challenged by others – such as R. J. Overy – who see Britain and France as being strong enough in the 1920s to uphold the treaties. However, during the 1930s, Britain and France found it increasingly difficult to cooperate in the face of growing aggression from such countries as Japan, Italy and Germany.

5.3 How did conditions in Europe in the 1930s contribute to the collapse of collective security?

As well as nationalist and fascist ideology, and economic factors, within Italy and Germany contributing to the increasing adoption of aggressive and expansionist foreign policies, the general European situation in the interwar years made such policy moves – in both Europe and in the rest of the world – seem possible. This was the result of a combination of political and economic factors, many of which resulted directly from the First World War. All these factors combined, in the 1930s, to create significant diplomatic shifts which eventually led to the collapse of collective security and, eventually, to the outbreak of war.

Weaknesses of the League

The League of Nations, established in January 1920 after the First World War, was supposed to prevent aggression and war. Its most important functions were:

- to guarantee the territory of states via collective security
- to prevent conflicts
- to settle disputes peacefully
- to act as an agency for disarmament.

Although its objectives owed much to US president Woodrow Wilson's 14 Points, the US – by 1919, already the world's most powerful nation – did not join. Thus for much of its existence, it was essentially seen as a European club of First World War victors. Furthermore, the League had several specific weaknesses: in addition to membership – or, rather, non-membership issues, it also had other problems which undermined its chances of successfully implementing its aims. Especially after the start of the Great Depression, these became increasingly obvious and significant during the 1930s.

Non-membership

From its beginning, three of the great powers of the world were not members of the League. Until September 1926, Germany was not allowed to join. Even after Germany became a permanent Council member in 1926, the League was seen as a 'victors club'. Fear of communism meant that Soviet Russia was also not allowed to join – in fact, the Russian government condemned the League as a capitalist club dominated by imperialist powers. Especially significant was the refusal of the US to join the League.

Aggression and collective security

Wilson had seen the main purpose of the League as being to guarantee – by collective action – the territorial integrity and political independence of all members against external aggression. Several states (including Britain) had tried unsuccessfully to get Wilson to drop this, as they had no desire to become the 'policemen of the world'.

Causes of German and Italian Expansion

THE GAP IN THE BRIDGE.

Figure 5.17 A cartoon published in the British magazine, Punch, commenting on the refusal of the US to join the League of Nations

SOURCE F

The persistence of internationalist idealism in the 1920s masked important weaknesses in the international order. In the first place, there was a certain moral ambiguity about the British and French position. While they preached the virtues of self-determination and democracy, they strenuously denied granting either to the subject peoples of their empires. Although liberal enough at home, both states could be thoroughly illiberal in the colonies when they were dealing with nationalist forces hostile to European imperialism. When Britain adhered to the Kellogg–Briand Pact, it was only on the condition that it could still resort to force in its own empire. When the League tried to outlaw aerial bombing in 1931, Britain refused to abandon it as an instrument of colonial control … The moral authority of the League suffered from what was perceived to be the hypocrisy and self-serving of the 'satiated' powers. This situation made it difficult for Britain and France to resist the claims of other states in the 1930s that wanted to build an empire, or to ignore the strident demands for self-determination from the national minorities created by the peace settlement.

Overy, R. J. 1994. *The Inter-War Crisis 1919–1939*. London. Longman. pp. 74–5.

QUESTION

How, according to **Source F**, did the actions and attitudes of Britain and France undermine attempts to prevent aggression in the 1930s?

5 German and Italian Expansionism, 1933–40

Fact: These diplomatic meetings and agreements included the Locarno Treaty of 1925, which saw Germany, France and Belgium promising not to use force to change their borders with each other. Germany also promised to accept the de-militarisation of the Rhineland. Britain and Italy then agreed to act as guarantors of these agreements. Significantly, however, this agreement gave no guarantees concerning German acceptance of its eastern frontiers. Nonetheless, the Locarno Treaty played a big part in Germany being allowed to join the League the following year. In 1928, the Kellogg-Briand Pact saw 15 countries – including Germany – promise to renounce the use of force for national objectives. However, no enforcement machinery was created, while attempts to get this promise incorporated into the League of Nations' Covenant failed.

The ability of the League to take common action to uphold collective security was further undermined by the decision of the main powers to establish – at the same time that the League was founded – a Conference of Ambassadors, consisting of Britain, France, Italy and Japan. This was specifically set up to supervise the peace treaties of 1919–20, and any possible revision of the borders drawn by those treaties. This body met at regular intervals in Paris, and often resulted in confusions of responsibility with the League of Nations, with many important decisions frequently being made independently of the League. In fact, most of the diplomatic meetings and agreements after 1919 were the result of work either by the Conference of Ambassadors, or by direct diplomacy between states, rather than the League. In part, this was because France, which felt insecure as a result of the League's weaknesses, insisted that enforcement of treaties should therefore be undertaken by the Conference of Ambassadors and not left to the League.

SOURCE G

The Locarno Pact was greeted with exuberant relief as the dawning of a new world order.... But amidst all the jubilation, no one noticed that the statesman had sidestepped the real issues: Locarno had not so much pacified Europe as it had defined the next battlefield.

The reassurance felt by the democracies at Germany's formal recognition of its Western frontiers showed the extent of the demoralization and the confusion that had been caused by the [mix] of old and new views on international affairs. For within that recognition was implicit that the Treaty of Versailles, which had ended a victorious war, had been unable to command compliance with the victors' peace terms, and that Germany had acquired the option of observing only those provisions which it chose to reaffirm. In this sense, Stresemann's unwillingness to recognise Germany's Eastern frontiers was ominous; while Great Britain's refusal to guarantee even the arbitration treaties gave international sanction to two classes of frontier in Europe – those accepted by Germany and guaranteed by other powers, and those neither accepted by Germany nor guaranteed by the other powers.

Kissinger, H. 1995. *Diplomacy.* New York. Touchstone. p. 274.

The League's procedures to prevent aggression also had several practical problems. Firstly, member states were to submit any dispute to the Council; however, Council decisions had to be unanimous – as the Council was dominated by Britain and France, and as these two countries had quite different views about the role of the League, unanimous agreement proved difficult to reach. Secondly, if a member failed to comply with League procedures, economic sanctions (such as trade boycotts and the banning of financial relations with an aggressor), could be imposed. However, many members were hesitant about becoming involved in trade boycotts, in case non-member states (such as the US or the Soviet Union) simply took over the trade. If economic sanctions failed, the Council could recommend military sanctions, using troops provided by member states. France had wished the League to have its own armed forces, so that it could undertake direct military intervention – but Britain, among others, had opposed this. In 1923, a Draft Treaty of Mutual Assistance, suggested by France to give the League powers to take rapid military action in the event of unprovoked aggression, had been blocked – again by Britain.

Causes of German and Italian Expansion

However, in January 1924, Ramsay MacDonald had become the new Labour prime minister of Britain. Also in 1924, France tried again with the Geneva Protocol, which aimed to commit all members to undertake collective military action. MacDonald supported the Geneva Protocol, and had said that Labour's foreign policy would be based on the League's Covenant – his nickname was 'Mac the peacemaker'. He thus put the Geneva Protocols forward in September 1924, but then lost the October 1924 election. The new Conservative government did not support the scheme, and blocked it in March 1925. Thus, in practice, if a country refused to abide by the rules of the League, or left, there was little the League could do.

Disarmament

Disarmament also proved extremely contentious – the existence of communist Russia, and the power vacuum in central and eastern Europe, meant that many states, such as Poland and Czechoslovakia, were reluctant to disarm. More importantly, France was extremely concerned about disarming, given Britain's refusal to give the League real military powers, and the refusal by both Britain and the US to promise any military support. Though Britain was willing to reduce its level of weapons, the non-membership of the US meant disarmament talks often by-passed the League. However, though Britain did urge the League to set up a commission to draw up a disarmament convention, a Preparatory Disarmament Commission was not set up at Geneva until 1926.

Increasing failure

While the League had several successes in the 1920s, it was significant that most of the disputes did not involve major states. Greater problems emerged in the 1930s, with the impact of the Depression and the rise of more aggressive and nationalistic regimes. Apart from largely ineffective attempts to deal with Japanese and Italian aggression in the first half of the 1930s, the League also consistently failed to take action against increasing infringements of the peace treaties by Nazi Germany from 1935 onwards. By then, it was clear to many that the League was increasingly irrelevant. This was shown clearly in October 1936, when civil war broke out in Spain. Despite the German and Italian military help openly given to Franco against the elected Popular Front government, the response of Britain and France was to form an ineffective Non-Intervention Committee. Even when their merchant ships were attacked, Britain and France took no action.

The Great Depression

As well as badly affecting both Italy and Germany, the Great Depression also caused significant problems for other European countries. In particular, both France and Britain suffered problems – this was significant, as they were the most important members of the League in the 1930s.

General impact in Europe

The Great Depression, which had developed very quickly following the 1929 Wall Street Crash in the US, soon impacted on the countries of Europe in the 1930s. Many of these countries – whether victors or losers in the First World War – were often still coping with the effects of the war: lost markets, war debts, overproduction, unemployment and/ or reparations. As the US resorted to protectionist tariffs to safeguard its own economy, other countries quickly followed suit. By 1931, tariff rates in Europe as a whole had more than doubled, compared to the tariffs in existence just before the Wall Street Crash.

> **ACTIVITY**
> Carry out some additional research on the various factors contributing to the weakness of the League. Then draw up a table listing these factors – ranked in order of importance, and giving brief details about each. Finally, write a short paragraph justifying what you consider to be the most significant factor.

Fact: The one European country not adversely affected by the Great Depression was the Soviet Union which had moved from a capitalist-owned to an essentially socially-owned economy. While the Great Depression led to serious declines in industrial production, and the attendant high unemployment, which caused serious problems in the rest of Europe (and the world), there was tremendous industrial development in the USSR (according to some estimates, industrial production almost tripled) – and no unemployment. In fact, as the Depression deepened, several US firms – including the Ford company – actually invested in the Soviet Union: this was despite the continuing US hostility to communism.

5 German and Italian Expansionism, 1933–40

Fact: For many countries in Europe, the end of the war had initially resulted in increased unemployment as soldiers were demobilised, and war-related production was ended. According to historians such as E. Hobsbawm, unemployment had remained high in most European countries in the 1920s. Even during the 'boom' of the second-half of the 1920s, unemployment rates varied between 10% – 20% in many countries.

As a result, world trade declined dramatically; while the withdrawal and repayment of US loans caused financial crises for many European states. In 1933, the League of Nations organised a World Economic Conference in London, which it was hoped could agree ways to end the economic and financial crisis. But the US made it clear it would not be party to any international agreements – thus the countries of Europe were clearly on their own. This made it increasingly difficult in the 1930s for European states to take joint diplomatic action when each country was desperately trying to solve their own economic problems.

SOURCE H

The role of the Great Depression in encouraging international instability must be considered when evaluating the causes of the Second World War… The most damaging consequences of the depression were felt in Germany. It was in the midst of the depression that Adolf Hitler's Nazi Party rose to become the largest party in Germany, which greatly aided Hitler's accession to office in 1933. It is very important to recognise the significance of the Great Depression on the unstable international relations of the 1930s. The optimism for peace in the 1920s gave way to the self-preservation of the 'hungry' 1930s. The depression plunged the free market into a major crisis. Most countries adopted protectionism and turned inwards to deal with social and economic problems. Democratic government was also challenged by new dynamic totalitarian regimes, with state-run economies, ruled by charismatic dictators such as Stalin, Hitler, Mussolini and Franco. In comparison, democratic leaders looked dull and ineffective.

McDonough, F. 2001. *Conflict, Communism and Fascism: Europe 1890–1945*. Cambridge. Cambridge University Press. pp. 105–6.

A political result of all these economic and social problems was that several countries began to move to the right – although Germany was the most obvious example, many countries saw the emergence of fascist and semi-fascist movements which often put considerable pressure on their respective governments. This was especially significant in France in the 1930s.

Britain

Fact: The Labour prime minister in 1929 was Ramsay MacDonald. From January to November 1924, he had been prime minister of the first-ever Labour government elected in Britain. This had also been a minority government, dependent on the votes of other parties in the House of Commons in order to get its policies made law.

MacDonald had begun as a radical, was a pacifist during the First World War, and strongly supported the League of Nations. However, after 1929, he began to move to the right – when he decided to cut unemployment benefit in 1931, and to head a coalition National Government (in which the Conservatives were by far the biggest group), he was expelled from the Labour Party, which saw him as a traitor.

In Britain, the impact of the Great Depression resulted in a rapid increase in unemployment: by as early as 1931, the unemployment rate rose to almost 25%. Although the minority Labour government, which had come to power two years earlier, in June 1929, initially attempted to deal with these problems by public works and increasing unemployment benefits, these were ended in the summer of 1931 as a result of a banking crisis. The government and the Bank of England attempted to raise money in the US, but a condition of the loans was that government expenditure should be drastically cut.

MacDonald accepted these US conditions, but this led to a revolt within the Labour Party so, instead of resigning, he decided – after consultations with the king and the leaders of the Conservatives and Liberals – to form a coalition government with the Conservative and Liberal Parties, in order to push through the cuts. He remained prime minister of this National Government until June 1935, when he resigned because of serious health problems. He was replaced as prime minister by the Conservative leader, Stanley Baldwin.

Causes of German and Italian Expansion

This National Government – as well as cutting unemployment benefits – also took Britain off **the gold standard** in 1931, and placed high tariffs on foreign imports in 1932. Although the economy began to pick up after 1932, unemployment remained high through most of the 1930s. One consequence of this was that the National Government continued to cut public expenditure. In 1932, Neville Chamberlain, as Chancellor of the Exchequer, drew up the lowest arms estimates for the entire period 1919–39. In the main, British governments after 1929 wished to avoid any risk of involvement in any conflict in Europe, as they were more concerned about protecting the British Empire – Japan's growth was seen as a serious threat.

France

In part because it was relatively less industrialised than Britain – and remained on the gold standard for longer – the impact of the Great Depression did not really hit France until about 1931–32. However, when it did hit, it was more severe and more long-lasting.

As in Britain, the impact of the Depression led to coalition governments in France; however, these proved much more unstable than the National Government in Britain. In 1933 alone, France had five different coalitions, in part, because the various parties could not agree on what actions to take to deal with the economic crisis. It was not until about 1938 that industrial production returned to the level of 1929. In addition, there was a financial crisis in 1936–37 – mainly because wealthy investors decided to send their money abroad, because of the policies of a **Popular Front** government elected in May 1936.

As a result of the financial crisis, Leon Blum – the prime minister and leader of the Socialist Party – was forced to resign in June 1937, and the Popular Front government collapsed. However, the unemployment and general hardship experienced by many French people in the 1930s was particularly important politically, as the country split along left/right lines. Because of these deep political divisions, it proved difficult for France to follow a strong and consistent foreign policy in the 1930s.

European divisions

The economic problems experienced by the main powers in Europe increasingly impacted on their foreign and defence policies. In particular, many governments were reluctant to increase expenditure on armaments at a time of economic crisis. In addition, there was even reluctance to apply economic sanctions against any country pursuing an aggressive and expansionist foreign policy – the fear was that other countries would simply step in, thus losing important markets to competitors. In addition, it soon became clear during the late 1920s and the 1930s that Britain and France – the two most powerful members of the League – had different priorities and concerns.

Britain was having to deal with rising nationalism in its empire – especially in Egypt and India. Thus Britain wanted political and economic stability in Europe, so it could concentrate on protecting its empire. Successive British governments believed the best way of ensuring German acceptance of the main terms of the Treaty of Versailles was to agree to some revision of the terms. France, however, in the absence of any firm Anglo-American military commitment, saw even the slightest changes as increasing Germany's strength. Even after Locarno in 1925, France remained concerned about security – and

the gold standard: This refers to the practice of linking a country's currency to its gold deposits, the international value of gold, and guaranteeing to fix its currency exchange rates in line with other countries also on the gold standard. This monetary policy had been common practice in most countries before the First World War and, after the war, most countries returned to it. Establishing a currency's value to a fixed value in gold was seen as a way of providing international economic and trading stability and security. However, during the Depression, many countries decided to abandon this practice. By coming off the gold standard, currencies could be 'devalued' – this meant the price of exports could fall and thus become more 'competitive' in global markets, and hopefully resulting in increased exports. However, as several countries did this, there was little lasting advantage for any of them.

Popular Front: This was a coalition of the Socialist, Radical and Communist Parties, formed in large part because of left-wing concerns about the rise of increasingly violent fascist groups in France. Leon Blum, the prime minister, presided over a range of progressive policies. These included attempts to raise productivity and boost incomes, as a way of increasing demand and so ending the worst effects of the Depression. For instance, a 40-hour working week was introduced, and several parts of the economy were nationalised: including the Bank of France and the railways. However, such policies were strongly opposed by industrialists and bankers.

5 German and Italian Expansionism, 1933–40

thus opposed to any serious disarmament – given Britain's continued refusal to promise serious military assistance in the event of German aggression. These fears multiplied in the period 1926–29 when German statesmen (including Stresemann) repeatedly indicated their desire to revise the Treaty of Versailles.

As a result of Britain's reluctance to give any military guarantees, French governments turned more and more to negotiating military pacts with countries on Germany's eastern borders. Czechoslovakia and Poland, in particular, owed their existence, or re-birth, to the defeat of Germany and the break-up of the Austro-Hungarian and Russian empires. These states were not in favour of any increase in Germany's strength and, also, like France, did not favour revisions of the peace treaties. As early as 1921, Czechoslovakia, Romania and Yugoslavia had formed the 'Little Entente'.

Unlike France, Britain was in favour of revisions in the east, especially as Britain felt a stronger Germany would be more able to resist the spread of communist revolutions than the small weak and often divided states of Eastern Europe. However, France felt that alliance with the successor states would provide some sort of check on Germany. Consequently, a series of treaties of mutual assistance were signed by France with these states: Poland (1921), Czechoslovakia (1924), Romania (1926) and Yugoslavia (1927). During the 1930s, as the number of crises grew,

Figure 5.18 Hitler and Franco, during their meeting at Hendaye on 23 October 1940

France sought to strengthen itself by some kind of alliance with the Soviet Union – who joined the League in 1934 – which would put additional pressure on Germany from the east. France moved quickly to negotiate a mutual assistance pact with the Soviet Union, which included a joint promise to protect Czechoslovakia from German aggression. Britain, however, disapproved of these links with Communist Russia – thus these two main members of the League continued to pursue separate diplomatic policies in the 1930s.

However, although Britain and France did work together during the Spanish Civil War – via the Non-Intervention Committee – Britain had earlier put pressure on France not to sell any kind of military supplies to Spain's legitimate and democratically-elected government. France had initially wished to help the republican government in Spain, as it did not want to see another semi-fascist government in power on its southern borders.

The collapse of collective security

The various economic and political problems experienced by countries such as Britain and France in the 1930s – as well as those experienced by Italy and Germany – eventually led to diplomatic shifts. These diplomatic re alignments eventually led to the end of collective security. Increasingly, British governments in the second half of the 1930s adopted a policy of appeasement in relation to the increasingly aggressive and expansionist foreign policies of Fascist Italy and Nazi Germany. This, in turn, made the outbreak of war more likely.

Collective security and appeasement

The League of Nations had been formed to stop the use of military aggression as a way of solving problems by negotiations and, if these failed, by the application of sanctions. One aspect of collective security in the interwar years was the attempt to uphold the peace treaties of 1919–20. In general, during the 1920s, Britain was prepared to work with France to ensure that the borders established by the peace treaties in Western Europe were retained. Italy, too, – despite its disappointments over its gains under the peace treaties – tended to work alongside Britain and France. At first, this continued even after 1922, when Mussolini began to create his fascist dictatorship in Italy. Countries like Britain, France and Italy attempted to uphold collective security. This was shown in 1934, when Fascist Italy joined with Britain and France to block Nazi Germany's first attempt to achieve Anschluss with Austria. In fact, Italy – along with Britain and France – had then formed the Stresa Front in 1935.

However, Germany in particular saw the League as little more than a 'club of victors', whose main role was to enforce what German governments – and many German people – saw as the unfair terms of the peace treaties. In 1935, when the League had rather half-heartedly opposed Italy's invasion of Abyssinia, Hitler had moved quickly. By offering support to Mussolini, he began the process of shifting Italy away from Britain and France and, instead, towards closer diplomatic relations with Nazi Germany.

This incipient shift in diplomatic relations was furthered by growing disagreements between Britain and France: Britain objected to French moves in 1934–35 to form an alliance with the Soviet Union, while France was frustrated by Britain's signing of the Anglo–German Naval Treaty in 1935, and by its refusal to oppose Hitler's decision to re-occupy the Rhineland in March 1936. These differences were, with hindsight, important factors in the collapse of collective security. In part, this was because from

5 German and Italian Expansionism, 1933–40

1937, the British prime minister Neville Chamberlain increasingly followed the policy of appeasement (see Chapter 7 for more details). This was based on attempting to avoid another war by negotiating with Nazi Germany on peaceful changes to those parts of the Treaty of Versailles to which Hitler objected. Although French governments were less sympathetic, they felt compelled to go along with this diplomatic approach, in order to retain friendly relations with Britain.

At the same time, Nazi Germany and Fascist Italy moved closer together – and also began to form agreements with Imperial Japan. This last development, in turn, put increased pressure on both Britain and France, as both countries had colonies in Asia. By 1939, as a result of these shifts in international diplomatic alignments and agreements, most of the main combatants of the Second World War were already joined together – to a greater or lesser extent – in the two opposed alliances which would face each other in what turned out to be the most destructive war in history.

Activities

1 Carry out some further research on the impact of the peace treaties of 1919–20 on nationalism and fascist ideology in both Italy and Germany. Then write a couple of paragraphs to explain why these treaties were so significant.

2 Imagine you are either an Italian or a German nationalist in 1920, and then write a letter to a newspaper setting out your arguments for territorial expansion.

3 List the main effects of the Great Depression on both Italy and Germany. Then write a couple of paragraphs to show how these effects increased the desire for territorial expansion in both these states.

End of chapter activities

Summary

You should now have a reasonable understanding of how various factors – especially fascist ideology and economic problems – within Italy and Germany contributed to the increased desire for territorial expansion in the 1930s.

You should also be able to comment on how the economic and diplomatic situation in Europe during this period contributed to the belief in Fascist Italy and Nazi Germany that an expansion foreign policy would not face any serious opposition from the League of Nations or from countries such as Britain and France.

Summary activity

Copy the diagram below and, using the information in this chapter and from any other available sources, make brief notes under the headings and sub-headings shown. Remember to include information on historical debate/interpretations, including names of historians.

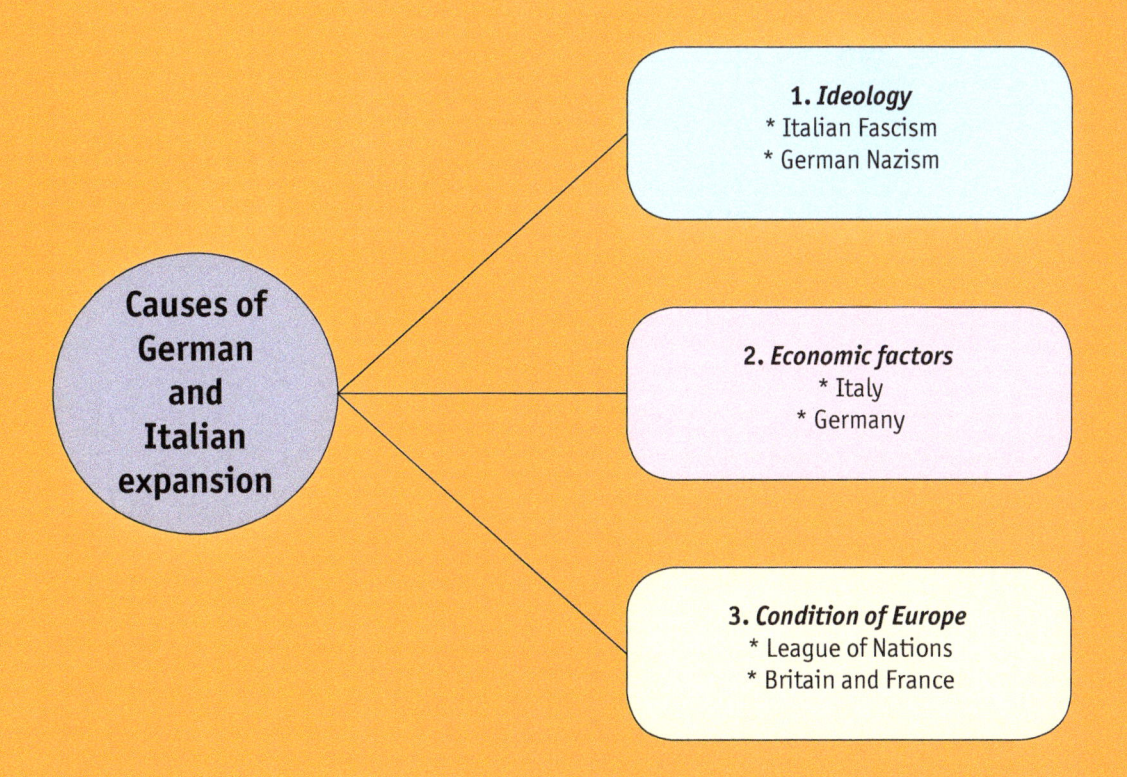

Causes of German and Italian expansion

1. *Ideology*
   * Italian Fascism
   * German Nazism

2. *Economic factors*
   * Italy
   * Germany

3. *Condition of Europe*
   * League of Nations
   * Britain and France

5 Paper 1 exam practice

Question

SOURCE A

Figure 5.19 A cartoon published in the British magazine, Punch, commenting on the refusal of the US to join the League of Nations

What message is conveyed by **Source A**? [2 marks]

Skill

Comprehension of a source

Before you start

Comprehension questions are the most straightforward questions you will face in Paper 1. This type of comprehension question simply requires you to understand the message of a source *and* make one or two relevant points that relate to the particular question. Before you attempt this question, refer to Chapter 9 for advice on how to tackle comprehension questions, and a simplified mark scheme.

Student answer

The message of Source A is that the League of Nations is weakened by the fact that the US decided not to join – the US is shown sitting down and not taking part.

Examiner comments

The candidate has provided **one** relevant point about the message intended by the source. This is enough to gain one mark. However, as no other aspect of the message of the source has been identified, this candidate fails to get the other mark available.

Activity

Look again at the source, and the student answer above. Now try to identify **one** other specific aspect of the source's message, and try to make an overall comment about the source's message. This will enable you to obtain the other mark available for this question.

Paper 2 practice questions

1. Compare and contrast the aims and influence of nationalist ideology in Italy and Germany before 1900.
2. Examine the role of fascist ideology in the development of an aggressively expansionist foreign policy in **either** Italy **or** Germany before 1939.
3. Evaluate the influence of the Great Depression on the adoption of an expansionist foreign policy in **either** Italy **or** Germany in the period 1929–39.
4. 'The policy of appeasement was the main reason for the collapse of collective security in the period 1929–39.' To what extent do you agree with this statement?

6 Germany's and Italy's Actions

TIMELINE

1924 Feb: Pact of Rome between Italy and Yugoslavia

1932 Feb: World Disarmament Conference begins

1933 Jan: Hitler appointed chancellor of Germany

Oct: Germany leaves Disarmament Conference and League of Nations

Nov: Germany begins re-armament

1934 Jan: World Disarmament Conference ends in failure; Nazi Germany makes Pact with Poland

Jul: Hitler attempts *Anschluss* with Austria

Sep: Soviet Union joins League of Nations

1935 Mar: Hitler announces German rearmament and reintroduces conscription

Apr: Stresa Front formed

Oct: Italy invades Abyssinia

1936 Mar: German Re-occupation of the Rhineland

Jul: Germany and Italy's intervention in Spanish Civil War

Oct: Rome–Berlin Axis (Germany and Italy)

Nov: Comintern Pact (Germany and Japan)

1937 Oct: Italy signs Anti-Comintern Pact (Rome–Berlin–Tokyo Axis)

Dec: Italy leaves the League of Nations

1938 Mar: *Anschluss* between Germany and Austria

Sept: Munich Conference

1939 Mar: Hitler invades rest of Czechoslovakia

Apr: Italy annexes Albania

May: Pact of Steel (Germany and Italy)

Aug: Nazi-Soviet Non-Aggression (Molotov-Ribbentrop) Pact

KEY QUESTIONS
- How did Germany challenge the post-war settlements, 1933–38?
- What were the main aspects of Italy's foreign policy, 1935–39?
- How did Germany expand, 1938–39?

Overview

- After the Corfu Incident in 1923, Fascist Italy pursued a peaceful foreign policy and, for a time, was prepared to cooperate with Britain and France.

- However, Hitler's appointment as chancellor in Germany in January 1933 soon began to change European diplomacy. This was because Hitler was determined to challenge the terms of the Treaty of Versailles.

- Once his internal position was secured in 1934, Hitler began to take the first steps in what became an increasingly aggressive foreign policy which, ultimately, would lead to the outbreak of the Second World War.

- Initially, Hitler turned his attention to Austria – in July 1934, he attempted to effect *Anschluss* (union) with Austria. This was expressly forbidden by the peace treaties and, despite their shared fascist ideology, Mussolini took steps to block this.

- In April 1935, Mussolini – still not sure about Hitler's intentions – joined Britain and France in the Stresa Front which was intended to contain Nazi Germany's ambitions.

- However, after Italy's invasion of Abyssinia in October 1935, Fascist Italy began to move away from Britain and France and the Stresa Front collapsed.

- Hitler then moved quickly to improve relations with Fascist Italy. At the same time, in March 1936, Hitler took advantage of the Abyssinian Crisis to re-occupy the Rhineland. Although this was against the Treaty of Versailles, neither Britain nor France opposed it.

- After the re-occupation of the Rhineland, Hitler's foreign policy became increasingly expansionist. During the Spanish Civil War, both Germany and Italy intervened on the side of the right-wing nationalist rebels and, in October, Hitler and Mussolini signed the Rome–Berlin Axis.

Germany's and Italy's Actions

- Further German expansion took place in 1938 – first, Anschluss with Austria (this time, there was no opposition from Italy) and then, in September 1938, the Munich Conference gave Hitler the Czech Sudetenland.
- In the spring of 1939, Nazi Germany invaded the rest of Czechoslovakia, while Fascist Italy occupied Albania. Nazi Germany and Fascist Italy moved closer together in May with the signing of the Pact of Steel.
- Finally, after the signing of a Non-Aggression Pact with the Soviet Union in August 1939, Hitler turned his expansionist aims on Poland.

6.1 How did Germany challenge the post-war settlements, 1933–38?

Before 1933, although several governments of Weimar Germany had tried to alter (or 'revise') some of the aspects of the peace settlements of 1919–20, this had always been done through peaceful diplomatic negotiations. However, the rise of Hitler and the Nazis to power in Germany in 1933 had a tremendous and increasingly negative impact on international affairs in this period. Although Hitler was mostly concerned with establishing internal control within Germany until 1934, once he had consolidated his domestic power base, he soon moved to a more aggressive foreign policy.

The World Disarmament Conference, 1932

Though the crisis over Manchuria (see section 4.1, Crisis over Manchuria) led to continued instability in the Asian and Pacific regions, this was not necessarily hugely significant for later developments in Europe. Nonetheless, the first important indication of problems to come in Europe came towards the end of the World Disarmament Conference in Geneva. This had been organised by the League of Nations in an attempt to secure agreed limits on army, naval and airforce weapons. It was initially attended by 61 nations, and five non-members – including both the USA and the USSR. France again unsuccessfully attempted to give the League its own army. A British proposal to limit offensive weapons such as tanks, bombs, submarines and chemical weapons obtained a 41-vote majority, but Germany and the Soviet Union refused to agree.

More immediately important was the fact that Germany insisted on 'equality of treatment' – arguing that either all nations should disarm to the German level set by the Treaty of Versailles, or that Germany should be allowed to re-arm up to the levels of other major powers. In fact, Germany had never fully complied with the disarmament restrictions of Versailles, and had begun some limited re-armament via the **Treaties of Rapallo and Berlin** which had been signed with Soviet Russia. As early as 1932, *before* Hitler had become Chancellor, German delegates walked out of the Conference, and said they would not return until they had been granted 'equality of treatment' – though the Conference continued without them.

Hitler's early foreign policy, 1933–35

Initially Hitler's foreign policy was essentially cautious and 'revisionist' – and, in many respects, the foreign policy aims he followed at first showed considerable continuity with those of previous German statesmen – including those of Gustav Stresemann.

Treaties of Rapallo and Berlin: The Treaties of Rapallo and Berlin were between Weimar Germany and Soviet Russia, and had been signed in 1922 and 1926 respectively. In return for technical aid, Soviet Russia allowed Weimar Germany to obtain weapons it was banned from having by the Treaty of Versailles. Thus, several years before Hitler came to power, Germany had been secretly developing banned weapons and beginning a limited rearmament. The 1926 Treaty of Berlin had been signed by Gustav Stresemann, the German statesman best known for his key roles in lessening tensions in Europe during the 1920s.

QUESTION

What did German delegates at the World Disarmament Conference mean by 'equality of treatment'?

6 German and Italian Expansionism, 1933–40

[Handwritten margin note: failing to keep Hitler restrained, and re-arming, may have let a monster free.]

Figure 6.1 This 1933 British cartoon refers to the failure of the Disarmament Conference

> **QUESTION**
> What is the message of this cartoon? How does the cartoonist get this message across?

Fact: Although Weimar politicians continued to follow Stresemann's cautious and moderate foreign policy approach after his death in 1929, there were signs from 1931 that Germany was beginning to consider a more unilateral attempt to revise the terms of the Versailles Treaty. Like Hitler, most Germans continued to see the treaty as a *diktat* (dictated) or 'slave' treaty.

Fact: Though Germany's departure from the League of Nations was a setback for the League and international relations in general, a new member – the Soviet Union – joined in September 1934. The Soviet Union, increasingly disturbed by Hitler's rise to power, had begun to fear Nazi Germany's intentions.

Thus, despite the aggressive rhetoric of *Mein Kampf* and Nazi election propaganda in the 1920s, German foreign policy did not at first undergo any dramatic changes in 1933. This continuity with 'Weimar diplomacy' in the early years of Nazi rule was due to a number of reasons: the German economy was still suffering from the Depression, Hitler's political position was not yet fully secure, and Germany's armed forces were too weak. Consequently, on becoming chancellor in January 1933, Hitler allowed the previous foreign minister – the conservative nationalist Constantin von Neurath – to remain in post. This was partly to reassure Germany's neighbours that there would be no dramatic changes to foreign policy under Hitler. However, the main reason was because Hitler's chief aim in 1933 was to establish Nazi control of Germany. Thus Hitler tried to maintain good relations with Britain and Italy – though he also tried to isolate France and weaken its influence. Nonetheless, as early as February 1933, Hitler told German army officers of his intention to expand Germany's military strength to make it the most powerful force in Europe by 1938. After that had been achieved, Germany would seek Lebensraum in the east – especially at the expense of the Soviet Union.

Withdrawal from the Disarmament Conference and the League, 1933

At the Disarmament Conference, Hitler stressed the German desire for peace, and repeated the earlier request for 'equality of treatment'. Britain supported the idea of both Germany and France having an army of 200,000, and urged France to agree. However, French insistence on a German guarantee that the Versailles limitations would be respected for the next four years led Hitler, in October 1933, to announce Germany's withdrawal from the Disarmament Conference. In the same month, Hitler also announced Germany's withdrawal from the League of Nations.

Although the Conference continued until January 1934, it ended in failure. France's refusal to compromise was seen as unreasonable, while Hitler won sympathy from some British politicians for his 'reasonable' approach.

Pact with Poland

France was further isolated in January 1934, when Hitler signed a ten-year non-aggression pact with Poland.

This temporarily eased general European concerns over Germany's intentions, but it also prevented closer Polish ties with France, and brought Poland under greater German influence. Britain welcomed this development, but France remained suspicious and increasingly pursued its security independently of Britain. Although the pact angered many officials in the German foreign ministry – as well as Nazi activists – in the international arena Hitler again appeared to be a reasonable statesman; while France's position had been undermined.

Fact: The non-aggression pact with Poland was signed despite the fact that all Weimar governments had objected to the loss of Upper Silesia, Danzig and the Polish Corridor. This pact undermined the earlier defensive system of alliances France had made with Poland and some other eastern European states. This system had been designed to put pressure on Germany's eastern frontier and so deter a future invasion of France.

SOURCE A

While Britain was therefore pressing for an arms limitation agreement with Germany and trying to pressurize France into making substantial concessions, France was preoccupied with the construction of an east European agreement along the lines of the Locarno treaty of 1925 which would include Germany … However, if Germany's agreement could not be secured, [Britain] feared the construction of a bloc of states encircling Germany. They warned that such encirclement might drive Hitler to some desperate act of aggression. Without British co-operation on measures of security, the French would not agree to further concessions on arms limitation. On 14 October 1933, Germany withdrew from the Disarmament Conference, denouncing it as a sham, and Hitler announced Germany's intention of withdrawing from the League. He would, however, consider returning when Germany's grievances were recognized and serious proposals put forward to meet them. There was worse news to come. In January 1934 Poland, fearing that treaty revision would be concluded at her expense in some agreement between France and Germany, became the first country to conclude a non-aggression pact with Germany. It would run in the first instance for ten years. Clearly, German rearmament was having its effect on the political calculations of east European leaders.

Henig, R. 1985. *The Origins of the Second World War 1933–1939*. London. Routledge. pp. 17–18.

First attempt at *Anschluss* with Austria, 1934

Hitler's first recognisably aggressive expansionist foreign policy action was an attempt, in July 1934, to bring about *Anschluss* with Austria.

This attempt (which resulted in the murder of the Austrian prime minister) alienated some of those in Britain who had developed sympathy for Germany's desire to revise parts of the Treaty of Versailles. In addition – despite their common fascist political beliefs – Mussolini opposed this union and moved 40,000 Italian troops to the Italian border with Austria in order to deter any German invasion. Hitler decided to back down as, at this stage, the German army was not ready for a serious military conflict. Although

Fact: In fact, the first attempt by Germany to achieve Anschluss with Austria after the First World War was in March 1931, when Bruning tried to create a customs union with Austria. This scheme was quickly blocked by the Allies.

6 German and Italian Expansionism, 1933–40

this was a disappointing – and humiliating – failure, Hitler continued to have *Anschluss* as one of his central foreign policy aims.

Re-armament and conscription

Hitler further alienated Britain and Italy in March 1935, when he announced that, contrary to the military restrictions of Versailles, Germany again had an airforce (*Luftwaffe*) and that, as Germany was no longer bound by the military terms of Versailles, it would re-introduce conscription and begin open German re-armament.

The immediate result of Hitler's announcements were not what Hitler wanted. In particular, Britain, France and Italy formed the Stresa Front in April 1935, to oppose further German actions in Europe. Significantly, this was not done via the League, which took no action itself against these clear breaches of the peace settlements. However, Hitler immediately began steps to weaken the Stresa Front. He made speeches stating how Germany wanted peace and re-armament. The effect was to further widen the gulf between British and French policies – Britain was impressed by these statements, while France remained unconvinced. As a result, in May 1935, France negotiated a mutual assistance pact with the Soviet Union, which included a joint promise to protect Czechoslovakia from German aggression.

Britain, however, disapproved of these links with communist Russia and objected to France's hardline stance in relation to Germany. Consequently, in June 1935, Britain signed the **Anglo-German Naval Treaty**, in an attempt to limit Hitler's planned naval expansion. Yet again, this resulted in France being further isolated. It also helped undermine the Stresa Front, as neither France nor Fascist Italy were consulted beforehand.

Fact: According to the 1919 Treaty of Versailles, the German army was to be limited to 100,000. However, in July 1932, von Papen had already begun German re-armament, when he authorised – in breach of the Treaty of Versailles – secret increases in the army and weapons produced. Almost as soon as he had become chancellor, Hitler had begun expanding the army and by mid-1934, it was already 240,000 strong. In fact, Hitler had been encouraged to make these unilateral moves by the return of the important Saarland in January 1935. This area – with significant coal and iron resources – had been ruled since 1920 by Britain and France under a League of Nations' mandate; but, in 1935, the people there had voted in a plebiscite to return to Germany.

Fact: The pact with the Soviet Union followed an unsuccessful French proposal to the Soviet Union to form an Eastern Pact, which would be made up of France, the Soviet Union, Czechoslovakia, Poland, Finland and the three Baltic States. This would be a mutual-aid treaty, designed to protect its members from possible aggression by Nazi Germany, and to guarantee the Locarno Treaties of 1925. However, for a number of reasons – including Britain's insistence that Germany should be allowed to join – this was never ratified.

Anglo-German Naval Treaty: In this new treaty, Britain accepted that Germany could expand its navy beyond the limit imposed in 1919 – provided it was never more than 35% of the size of Britain's.

Figure 6.2 The cartoon appeared on 19 July 1934, in the Daily Express, a British newspaper. The cartoon refers to the 'Eastern Locarno' alliance, proposed by the singer (France) to the Soviet Union

146

Growing German expansionism, 1936–38

Italy's decision to invade Abyssinia in October 1935 (see section 6.2, Invasion of Abyssinia) produced further – and more serious – strains between the members of the Stresa Front. Hitler was quick to take advantage of these growing tensions. During the period 1936–38, he decided to forge ahead with his plans for unilateral revision of the Treaty of Versailles. His first serious step was over the Rhineland in March 1936.

Re-occupation of the Rhineland, 1936

In response to the invasion of Abyssinia by Italy in October 1935, Britain and France had, somewhat reluctantly, applied some limited economic sanctions against Italy. Hitler acted quickly to let Mussolini know that he supported his action. As a consequence, the Stresa Front collapsed and, in January 1936, Mussolini let Hitler know that he no longer had any objections to Austria coming under German control should there be any future attempt at *Anschluss*, and Mussolini even hinted that he would not support any League of Nation actions should Hitler re-occupy the Rhineland.

Hitler decided to move quickly to re-occupy the Rhineland, in order to take advantage of the Abyssinian Crisis. On 7 March 1936, Hitler ordered German troops to enter the Rhineland which, according to the Treaty of Versailles, and the Treaty of Locarno, was to remain a de-militarised zone. Hitler took this step even though he knew the German army was still not strong enough to fight Britain or France. In fact, both the German foreign ministry and the German army's high command were opposed to such a risky action. In the end, Hitler had to agree that German troops could withdraw at the first sign of opposition from the Allies. Although only 22,000 troops were sent in, Hitler calculated that there would be no resistance from France or Britain – and he was proved correct, as Britain persuaded France to take no action. This success weakened Hitler's critics, and strengthened his resolve to take increasingly more aggressive expansionist actions in the immediate future.

The Spanish Civil War

After his successful re-occupation of the Rhineland, Hitler continued his efforts to get an alliance with Mussolini. In July 1936, a civil war broke out in Spain between its democratically elected Popular Front government and nationalists backed by the army. The following month, Hitler and Mussolini decided to help the nationalists with troops and weapons. Hitler, in particular, saw this as a useful opportunity to test German military equipment and *Blitzkrieg* tactics (which combined tank units and planes) in action.

This was especially important for the Luftwaffe, which gained valuable experience from the **Condor Legion's** bombing missions, whilst the importance of anti-tank and anti-aircraft guns was also established. In return for this German military assistance, Hitler got Franco to provide raw materials which greatly aided German re-armament.

Hitler also saw joint German-Italian intervention in Spain's civil war as a way of binding fascist Italy closer to Nazi Germany. Within a short while, their military cooperation in Spain resulted, in October 1936, in both countries signing the Rome-Berlin Axis, which confirmed Italy's move away from Britain and France. Then, in

> **ACTIVITY**
> Using the internet, and any extra resources available to you, find out more about the Franco-Soviet agreements of May 1935. List their main points and then their strengths and weaknesses.

Condor Legion's: The Condor Legion was a unit of the German air force – supported by armoured units of the German army – which 'volunteered' to fight on the side of Franco during the Spanish Civil War. Hitler sent the Condor Legion to Franco on condition it would be under German control. In particular, it used the Civil War as an opportunity to develop the terror bombing of civilians – mostly in the Catalonian and Basque areas of Spain. It also provided an opportunity to test Germany's new weapons.

Anti-Comintern Pact: 'Comintern' was an abbreviation for 'Communist International', which was the body set up by the Bolsheviks in 1919 to help the spread of revolution across the world. The Anti-Comintern Pact was designed to combat and destroy communism and the Soviet Union. It also made Britain and France uncertain about the fate of their Asian colonies. In April 1939, Franco – who had been victorious in the Spanish Civil War – also joined the Anti-Comintern Pact, though he refused to enter the Second World War until 1940.

6 German and Italian Expansionism, 1933–40

Fact: France, in particular, was keen not to alienate Mussolini with economic sanctions, as it feared – correctly, as it turned out – that the imposition of sanctions might drive Mussolini to seek an alliance with Nazi Germany. In that eventuality, France would then have fascist states on its northern and south-eastern borders. Significantly, the sanctions did not include oil, which was essential for modern warfare.

Fact: Hitler justified re-occupying the Rhineland by claiming that the Mutual Assistance Pact which had been signed between France and the Soviet Union in 1935 posed a threat to Germany, so German troops should be allowed to take up positions on Germany's frontiers.

Joachim von Ribbentrop (1893–1946)

He was a committed Nazi, and was German Foreign Minister from 1938–45. According to FBI files, he was the lover of Wallis Simpson who, at the time, was also King Edward VIII's mistress, and who later married him. Whatever the truth of these suspicions, the pro-Nazi views of Edward – and Wallis Simpson – led to Edward's being appointed as Governor of the Bahamas after war broke out. In part, this was because the British government feared he might pass military secrets to Nazi Germany and that, in the event of Britain being invaded, would be prepared to act as a puppet ruler.

Figure 6.3 The ruins of part of Guernica, a town in northern Spain, which was bombed by German planes of the 'volunteer' Condor Legion during the Spanish Civil War, on 26 April 1937

November 1936, Hitler signed the **Anti-Comintern Pact** with Japan – this was mainly directed against the Soviet Union, which was a long-term target for Hitler's desire for Lebensraum. In October 1937, Fascist Italy also joined the Anti-Comintern Pact. Italy's membership of this brought three aggressively expansionist countries together in what was known as the Rome-Berlin-Tokyo Axis – which is why, during the Second World War, these three countries were referred to as the 'Axis Powers'.

The Four-Year Plan

Despite the successful re-occupation of the Rhineland, Germany still faced certain political and economic problems which had to be overcome before any serious war could be fought. In particular, the traditional elites in the Foreign Ministry and the army wanted to pursue a more conservative way of creating a stronger Germany. In addition, Germany experienced a fresh economic crisis in 1936 – this showed that the German economy was not yet able to fight any sustained war. One response to this was the Four-Year Plan which, under the direction of Göring, was designed to get Germany ready, economically and militarily, to fight a war.

However, leading Nazis were divided over the diplomatic course to follow: some wanted to reach a closer understanding with Britain, while the foreign minister, **von Ribbentrop**, wanted Germany to join forces with Italy and Japan.

Hitler preferred the British option (mainly in the hope of achieving the destruction of the Soviet Union); but, with little sign that Britain was interested in a close relationship with Nazi Germany, he had decided – at least for the present – to align Germany with Italy.

The Hossbach Memorandum, 1937

By the end of 1936, Nazi Germany had succeeded in tearing up most of the Treaty of Versailles which related to Germany and its western borders without suffering any military consequences. As a result, Hitler now felt able to turn his attentions to his long-term aim of winning *Lebensraum* in the east. Thus far, he had achieved his territorial ambitions without having to go to war. During 1937, Hitler became encouraged by developments which increasingly suggested that Germany's position was becoming stronger – although he was disappointed that no Anglo-German alliance seemed likely. By 1937, the economic crisis of 1936 was mainly over, and Göring's Four-Year Plan seemed to be producing positive results.

On 5 November 1937, Hitler called a meeting with Neurath, von Blomberg (war minister) and the three commanders-in-chief of the armed forces. Historians are divided on the significance of this meeting, and on what claims to be a record of what was said. One of those present was Colonel Hossbach, Hitler's adjutant; although he took no notes during the meeting, he made a summary of the main points the following day – this has become known as the Hossbach Memorandum. According to Hossbach, Hitler told the attendees to get Germany ready for conquests in east Europe, to be completed by 1943–45 – while Germany was still militarily superior to Britain. The Hossbach Memorandum included plans to seize Austria and Czechoslovakia – even if it provoked war with Britain and France. Later in November, Schacht, the economic minister, who opposed rapid re-armament, resigned.

Hitler was further encouraged to pursue his expansionist ambitions in November 1937, when Lord Halifax arrived from Britain to say that Neville Chamberlain's government would support legitimate revisions of Germany's borders with Austria and Czechoslovakia, provided this was done peacefully.

Hitler's increasing control of foreign policy

Regardless of the debates surrounding the Hossbach Memorandum, Hitler's foreign policy became increasingly more adventurous after 1937. He made several personnel changes in an attempt to ensure greater personal control of the Foreign Ministry and the army. In January 1938, the moderate war minister von Blomberg and von Fritsch, the commander-in-chief of the army, were both dismissed, with Hitler himself taking over the post of minister for war and declaring himself to be the supreme commander of all the armed forces. He also created a new personal high command for the armed forces, under General Keitel, a known supporter of Nazi plans for German expansion; while Göring was made a field marshal. Other leading positions were also filled by convinced Nazis; while, later, Ribbentrop replaced Neurath as foreign minister. With his personal power secured, Hitler decided his next step in the territorial expansion of Germany should be at the expense of Austria.

Anschluss with Austria, March 1938

Anschluss with Austria remained Hitler's objective, despite his failure in 1934. In July 1936, he had persuaded the Austrian government to agree to accept German

> **KEY CONCEPTS ACTIVITY**
>
> **Change, continuity and perspectives:** Historians are divided over whether German foreign policy after 1933 was merely a more aggressive continuation of previous policies of expansion, or whether it was a distinctive change arising from Hitler's personal priorities. Most historians – G. Eley (1980) and F. Fischer (1986) amongst others – stress the continuity in general principles. Others argue that after Stresemann died, German foreign policy moved from peaceful collaboration to a more unilateral and expansionist stance. On the basis of what you have studied in this section, draw up a chart with two columns, headed 'Change' and 'Continuity', and enter brief details of examples of change and continuity in German foreign policy in the period 1933–36. Then, when you have completed the other sections on Germany's expansion, complete the chart for the years 1936–39.

6

German and Italian Expansionism, 1933–40

Historical debate:
Historians such as A. J. P. Taylor have questioned the reliability of the Hossbach Memorandum, and whether 1937 was, in fact, a turning point in Hitler's foreign policy. Some historians have seen this meeting more as a way of justifying his re-armament programme to doubting conservatives than as a definite plan for an intended war of expansion.

> **QUESTION**
> What is the message of this cartoon? How does the cartoonist get the message across?

supervision of its foreign policy in return for German promises to guarantee Austria's sovereignty. However, he used the Austrian Nazi Party to create a crisis in Austria. Then, in February 1938, the Austrian chancellor called a referendum on Austrian independence. When it looked as if the vote might reject union with Germany, Hitler insisted that a new Austrian government be formed, dominated by Austrian Nazis – this new coalition government then requested German troops to enter Austria, to help deal with disorder (which was mostly orchestrated by them!). On 12 March 1938, German troops crossed into Austria and *Anschluss* was finally achieved – in clear breach of the Treaty of Versailles. France (which technically had no government owing to elections) later denounced this action, but did not threaten any military response; while Britain maintained its policy of appeasement. Thus Hitler had, yet again, been totally successful in pursuing an expansionist foreign policy without a shot being fired.

Figure 6.4 Reactions to Germany's anschluss with Austria, 1938

SOURCE B

In 1936 when Hitler ordered German troops into the demilitarized Rhineland there was little international protest, … Few in Germany bothered to read Mein Kampf to discover Hitler's real motives and his obsession with territorial expansion. Nazi propaganda portrayed Hitler as a man of peace pursuing justifiable revisions of the humiliating Versailles Treaty.

The treaty that led to the Rome-Berlin Axis in November 1936 had changed the balance of power in Europe, and Austria, in particular, was left isolated as a result. Previously, Austria had depended on an alliance with Britain, France and Italy to secure her independence in the face of German demands. With Italy now on Germany's side, the balance of power in central Europe had shifted dramatically. …. As a result of the Rome-Berlin Axis, Hitler was now in a stronger position… The German invasion of Austria [on 12 March 1938] was Hitler's first move outside German territory in defiance of the Treaty of Versailles…. The Anschluss of Austria not only revealed the extent of Hitler's imperial ambitions, it also dealt a strategic blow at Czechoslovakia which could now be attacked from the south as well as from the west and north.

Welch, D. 1998. *Hitler*. London. UCL Press. pp. 58–9.

6.2 What were the main aspects of Italy's foreign policy, 1935–39?

Before 1935, Mussolini had wanted to make Italy a great power, based on the Mediterranean, with a large African empire – to gain what was called *'spazio vitale'* (living space). His ideas and actions were explicitly based on the idea of re-creating the empire of Ancient Rome. His foreign policy can be seen as having three distinct periods: 1922–35, when it was mainly peaceful; 1935–39, when it was more aggressive and Italy became increasingly allied to Nazi Germany; and 1940–45, when he took Italy into the Second World War.

Fascist diplomacy, 1922–35

Initially, Mussolini was not in a position to achieve his aims by force. The newly-created state of Yugoslavia seemed a potential block to Italian ambitions along the Adriatic; while, more importantly, Britain and France controlled strategically important areas in the Mediterranean and in Africa and the Middle East.

Emerging expansionist aims, 1922–33

His early use of force in the **Corfu Incident** in 1923, while it increased his support in Italy, also showed the relative weakness of Italy in the face of concerted Franco-British opposition – he was criticized by the League of Nations, and the Conference of Ambassadors forced him to withdraw. Consequently, for the next eleven years, Mussolini – often acting on the advice of traditional career diplomats – mainly stuck to peaceful diplomacy and a passive foreign policy. In February 1924, he persuaded Yugoslavia to sign the Pact of Rome which accepted Italian occupation of Fiume – this had been a city which Italy had expected to be awarded in the peace treaties of 1919–20. In May 1925, he signed the Locarno Pact; at the same time, Italian interests in Albania were pursued initially by economic penetration. In 1926, talks with Britain and France resulted in parts of Kenya and Egypt being given, respectively, to the Italian colonies of Somaliland and Libya.

Yet Mussolini was also using non-diplomatic methods to increase Italy's influence in Europe. He gave financial backing to an Albanian chieftain who eventually, in 1929, seized power and proclaimed himself King Zog; a Treaty of Friendship with Italy soon followed. He also increased secret support of extreme nationalists in Germany, Bulgaria, Austria and Yugoslavia.

Nonetheless, in 1928, he signed the Kellogg-Briand Pact which outlawed war – despite his dislike of France's forming the 'Little Entente' in 1927 with Yugoslavia, Czechoslovakia and Romania. This was because it seemed to block future Italian expansion in the Balkans – while France's position in North Africa also raised problems for expansion there.

From 1929, Mussolini's foreign policy began to change – he called for the 1919–20 peace treaties to be revised, and plotted with Hungary to overthrow the King of Yugoslavia. At an international peace conference in London, he demanded – unsuccessfully – that the Italian navy should be allowed to be as big as those possessed by Britain and France.

In many ways, the period 1931–34 was a turning point in Italian foreign policy and actions. In 1931, Mussolini noted the ineffectiveness of the League of Nations over Japanese aggression in Manchuria. Then, in 1933, details of Italian arms deliveries to the *Heimwehr* (a right-wing paramilitary group in Austria), and to the *Ustase* (a Croat

Fact: The strategically important areas controlled by Britain and France were Cyprus, Malta, Gibraltar and Corsica in the Mediterranean; and the Suez Canal, Egypt, Palestine, Morocco, Algeria and Tunisia in Africa and the Middle East.

Corfu Incident: In August 1923, an Italian general was murdered on Greek soil while making maps, for the Conference of Ambassadors, of a disputed area. Mussolini demanded a full apology from Greece, as well as 50 million lire compensation. When Greece refused (as they'd not been responsible), Mussolini sent troops to invade Corfu.

Fact: Mussolini used a combination of diplomacy and unilateral action to force Yugoslavia to sign the Pact of Rome. At the time, France – which was Yugoslavia's main ally – was too distracted by its occupation of the Ruhr to intervene. Fiume had been a target for Italian nationalists ever since 1919.

6 German and Italian Expansionism, 1933–40

terrorist group, based in Hungary, which wanted independence from Yugoslavia) came to light. These revelations disturbed Britain and France, and caused the powers of the Little Entente to strengthen their ties.

Nazi Germany and the Stresa Front, 1933–35

In 1933, Hitler became chancellor of Germany. However, although Hitler was a fellow fascist, Mussolini distrusted Hitler's plans for expansion; as a result, he attempted to play off Britain and France against Germany. He was particularly concerned about the Alto Adige area in north Italy (which contained many German-speakers), and saw Austria as an Italian – not a German – sphere of influence. He thus proposed a Four-Power Pact of Italy, Germany, Britain and France and, as early as September 1933, signed a non-aggression pact with the USSR. In 1934, he attempted to establish closer relations with Austria and Hungary.

So, when Hitler attempted to take over Austria in July 1934, Mussolini prevented this by placing Italian troops on the Austro–Italian border. In January 1935, he made an accord with France; when Hitler attacked the disarmament clauses of the Treaty of Versailles, and then introduced conscription, he formed the Stresa Front with Britain and France in April 1935, in order to block the threat of German expansion. Mussolini also calculated that, by siding with Britain and France against Germany, a more favourable attitude to his planned invasion of Abyssinia might be forthcoming.

Aggression and fascist 'crusades', 1935–37

Italy's first expansionist war was intended to recreate a modern version of the old Roman empire, centred on the Mediterranean and Adriatic Seas and on Africa. It began on 3 October 1935, when 500,000 Italian troops invaded Abyssinia – which was one of only two African states still retaining their independence. This Italian action was the first serious act of aggression by a major European power since 1920. The invasion took place at a time when allied foreign policy was already undermined by the impact of the Anglo-German Naval Treaty on relations between the members of the Stresa Front.

Invasion of Abyssinia

Mussolini had been making serious plans for the invasion of Abyssinia since 1932, and was determined to add Abyssinia to Italy's two existing colonies in East Africa: Eritrea and Somaliland. The pretext for the invasion was an Abyssinian-Italian Somaliland 'border' conflict which had taken place in December 1934 at the Wal-Wal oasis which actually lay well within Abyssinian territory. Italy had previously built a fort there, in breach of the Italo–Ethiopian Treaty of 1928. As a result of a skirmish, over 100 Abyssinian troops and 50 Italian and Somali troops were killed. Despite the involvement of the League, Mussolini then pushed ahead with his invasion plans. Italian forces in Italy's colonies of Eritrea and Somaliland were built up, and over the next nine months, as tensions increased, it was clear an invasion was imminent.

The Italian invasion finally began on 3 October. The invading forces had some early successes, as the Abyssinians were often only armed with spears, while the Italians had tanks and bombers – and used poison gas and mass executions to end resistance. Nonetheless, the Italian invasion soon began to slow down – partly as the result of determined resistance by Abyssinian forces, but mainly because of poor communications and the inadequacies of many Italian units. However, it was very much a one-sided war and, by its end, over 400,000 Abyssinians had been killed. Mussolini's calculations that Britain and France would not seriously object seemed confirmed when they drew up

---

Fact: While most Europeans at this time used the term 'Abyssinia', its real name was Ethiopia. Mussolini had had vague ambitions to invade Ethiopia from as early as 1923 – despite supporting Abyssinian membership of the League of Nations in that year, and signing a treaty of friendship with Abyssinia in 1928. As early as 1929, Italy had attempted to expand into disputed border areas on the fringes of the Italian colonies of Eritrea and Somaliland.

Theory of knowledge

History, empathy and emotion:
The historian James Joll (1918–94) once wrote: *'The aim of the historian, like that of the artist, is to enlarge our picture of the world, to give us a new way of looking at things.'* Yet is it possible for historians to 'empathise' with violent and racist regimes, such as Mussolini's Fascist Italy, without making moral and value judgements? If the personal views of historians affect what they write, does this make History less valid as an academic discipline than, for instance, the natural sciences?

the Hoare–Laval Pact, to offer Italy two-thirds of Abyssinia. However, this deal collapsed as a result of hostile public opinion; instead, the League of Nations imposed tougher sanctions than those which had been agreed earlier.

Figure 6.5 A cartoon published in the British newspaper *The Evening Standard* in 1935, commenting on Italy's brutal invasion of Abyssinia

SOURCE C

The problem of Italian-Abyssinian relations has very recently shifted from a diplomatic plane to one which can be solved by force only. The object is nothing more or less than the complete destruction of the Abyssinian army and the total conquest of Abyssinia, in no other way can we build the Empire.

The speedier our action the less likely the danger of diplomatic complications. In the Japanese fashion there will be no need whatever officially for a declaration of war and in any case we must always emphasise the purely defensive character of operations. No one in Europe would raise any difficulties provided the prosecution of operations resulted rapidly in an accomplished fact. It would suffice to declare to England and France that their interests would be recognised.

Memorandum from Marshal Badoglio, Chief of General Staff to Mussolini, December 1934. Quoted in Hite, J. and Hinton, C. 1998. *Fascist Italy*. London. Hodder. p. 214.

Fact: The limited sanctions imposed by the League specifically excluded vital war supplies. In addition, Britain did not close the Suez Canal to Italian ships; while Germany totally ignored all sanctions.

6 German and Italian Expansionism, 1933–40

Fact: Up until the League imposed sanctions, Hitler had been supporting Abyssinia. He changed this policy when Britain and France began to oppose Italy's invasion, as he saw this as a way of adding to the tensions which soon led to the collapse of the Stresa Front.

In fact, the League's half-hearted protests had little effect. Consequently, by May 1936, Italian forces had captured the capital, Addis Ababa. Abyssinia was then merged with the other Italian colonies to form Italian East Africa. Thus, Mussolini's first steps in carving out a new Roman Empire had been successful. Yet, the conquest brought little benefit to Italy – Abyssinia had poor agricultural land and not much in the way of raw materials. Furthermore, the invasion had alienated Britain and France – and made Italy increasingly dependent on Nazi Germany.

ACTIVITY

Find out more about the various results of Mussolini's invasion of Abyssinia. Then construct a list, putting these results in order of significance as regards shaping Mussolini's foreign policy after 1935.

SOURCE D

On 5 May 1936 Mussolini proclaimed victory to a huge crowd in piazza Venezia… he also proclaimed Victor Emmanuel III as the new Emperor of Ethiopia… It was a great personal triumph. He had won over the French in January 1935,… He had remained in the League despite sanctions… He had defeated not only the Ethiopians but also the might – or rather the peevish petulance – of the British Empire… However, Ethiopia proved a troublesome colony… Most of the western zones had not been conquered and guerrilla war continued there for years. In July Mussolini authorised … a terror policy of reprisals against rebels… But the cost was huge. Ethiopia provided no loot, indeed swallowed up Italian resources. By 1937–38 about 12.5 per cent of the total state budget was being spent in East Africa alone,… Ethiopia bled Italy dry… The other consequences were diplomatic…, and even more serious. When the Hoare-Laval scheme collapsed in December 1935, the 'Stresa front' against Germany collapsed with it.

Clark, M. 2005. *Mussolini*. Harlow. Pearson. pp. 198–204.

Britain and France's inability to approve his invasion of Abyssinia led Mussolini to move away from the Allies and closer to Germany. As early as January 1936, Mussolini let Hitler know that he no longer had any objections to a German *Anschluss* with Austria – in part, this was because Italy was now less able to prevent any takeover, because of the rift which had opened between Italy and its former allies, Britain and France. He also hinted that he would not support any League of Nation actions against Germany should Hitler re-occupy the Rhineland. Then, on 6 March 1936, he followed Hitler's lead and withdrew Italy from the League of Nations, and began to move closer to Nazi Germany. With the loss of Italy as an ally, Britain and France were forced to rely on each other.

The Spanish Civil War

This shift to a pro-German policy was confirmed in July 1936 when – almost immediately after the end of the Abyssinian war, and before Italy had recovered from its losses – he agreed to join Hitler in intervening in the Spanish Civil War, to help General Franco overthrow the democratically-elected Popular Front government. As Franco was supported by the Pope and the Catholic Church, Mussolini found it relatively easy to persuade Italians of the rightness of intervention, which was portrayed as yet another 'crusade' – this time, against communism.

Fact: Mussolini was angered and embarrassed by the fact that left-wing Italian political exiles, fighting as International Brigade volunteers for the Popular Front government, played a big part in the defeat of Italian troops at the battle of Guadalajara in March 1937.

Soon, Fascist Italy had sent over 70,000 troops – in fact, Mussolini made much more of a commitment to help the right-wing nationalist forces in Spain than Hitler did. The overall cost of Italy's intervention was over 10 billion lire. Italy provided over 600 planes and nearly 1,000 tanks, as well as over 90 warships. Some 6,000 Italian soldiers were killed in Spain. However, as with Abyssinia, this military adventure brought very few tangible results – apart from the islands of Mallorca and Menorca. It also had a largely negative impact on Italy's military capacity for several years.

Alliance with Nazi Germany

Mussolini noted the great reluctance of Britain and France to risk war over Germany and Italy's intervention in the Spanish Civil War.

Not surprisingly, Mussolini's Spanish intervention led to a widening of the breach between his former Stresa Front allies. Making the most of this rift, Hitler held out the prospect of an alliance with Nazi Germany. The result was that, in October 1936, Italy and Germany signed the Rome-Berlin Axis agreement. This marked a significant turning point in Italy's foreign policy: Mussolini and Hitler confirmed their joint opposition to communism, and also agreed to divide Europe into spheres of influence, with Italy to have the Mediterranean and the Balkans. The two fascist dictators moved even closer in December 1937, when Mussolini joined Germany and Japan in their Anti-Comintern Pact (formed originally in November 1936), which was intended to oppose communism and the Soviet Union.

Italy and the road to war, 1938–39

In March 1938, this new fascist alliance enabled Hitler to carry out *Anschluss* with Austria, in defiance of the Treaty of Versailles. Unlike in 1934, Mussolini just stood aside – even though Hitler had not given him the advance notice he had earlier promised for any such invasion.

Fact: Britain and France – who had formed the Non-Intervention Committee – even refused to act when British and French merchant ships were destroyed by Italian bombers and submarines. This lack of action was another consequence of the policy of appeasement.

Figure 6.6 Mussolini allowing Hitler to achieve *Anschluss* with Austria in 1938, despite this being against the Treaties of Versailles and St Germain, and having had opposed Hitler's earlier attempt in 1934

6 German and Italian Expansionism, 1933–40

Yet in April 1938, despite moving closer to Nazi Germany, Mussolini also signed a pact of friendship with Britain, and throughout 1938 resisted strong pressure from Hitler to sign a firm military alliance. In September 1938, he tried to act in the Munich Conference as a peacemaker between Germany and Britain and France; but he also ordered the Italian navy to prepare for war against Britain in the Mediterranean. In part, this was because the Munich Conference had finally convinced Mussolini that Britain and France would never take any firm action to curb German expansion. This belief was confirmed by the lack of response following Hitler's takeover of the rest of Czechoslovakia in March 1939, following his occupation of the Sudetenland the previous year.

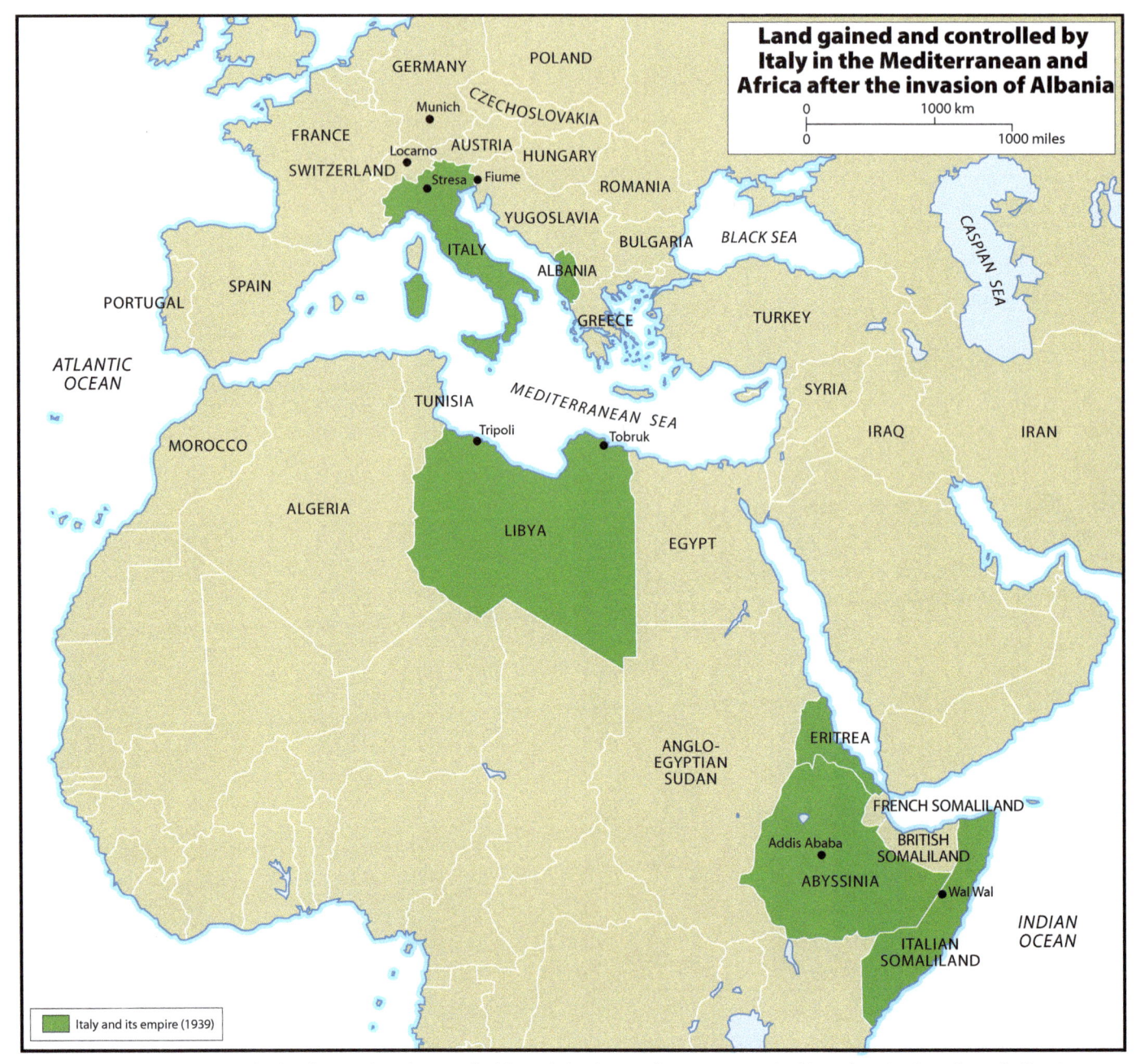

Figure 6.7 Map showing the land gained and controlled by Italy in the Mediterranean and Africa after the invasion of Albania

Invasion of Albania, April 1939

In April 1939, believing it was time to act, Mussolini decided to annex Albania and turn it into an Italian protectorate. Italian nationalists had long been interested in Albania and before the First World War, Italy had joined with Austria–Hungary to form the independent state of Albania. As soon as Italy had switched sides in the war in 1915, Italian troops had occupied the southern part of Albania. However, because of a determined Albanian resistance, and its own internal political problems following the end of the war in 1918, Italy had been forced to withdraw its forces in 1920. Despite this, Italian nationalists saw Albania as strategically important as it would allow Italy to control access to the Adriatic Sea and, because of its geographic position, would also make extending Italian influence into the Balkans much easier.

Mussolini, once appointed as prime minister in 1922, moved quickly to pursue Italian interests in Albania. At first, this was done by economic penetration, which began in earnest from 1925. In 1926 and 1927, Italy signed treaties with Albania which established a defensive alliance between the two states. Meanwhile, the Albanian government and economy were increasingly subsidised by loans from Italy; while the Albanian army was trained by Italian instructors, and Italians were encouraged to settle.

Figure 6.8 Italian troops entering the Albanian city of Durres, 7 April 1939. According to the Italians, only 25 Italian soldiers had been killed capturing this town, which was defended by less than 400 Albanians. However, the capture of Durres took several hours and, according to Albanian sources, over 400 Italians had been killed during the battle

6

German and Italian Expansionism, 1933–40

However, in 1931, King Zog I of Albania refused to renew the 1926 treaty with Italy – and, in 1934, signed trade agreements with both Yugoslavia and Greece. This annoyed Mussolini who, after Hitler had launched his invasion of Czechoslovakia without informing him first, decided to take his own independent action. On 25 March 1939, Italy issued an ultimatum to the Albanian government, offering money in exchange for accepting an Italian occupation of the country. This was refused, and the invasion began 7 April. By 12 April, the king had been deposed and Albania was declared an Italian possession.

Italy's invasion force had soon numbered over 100,000 troops, and was supported by 600 aircraft and naval units. As Italian military instructors had previously disabled many artillery pieces, and had ensured there was limited ammunition, the Albanian resistance was compromised from the start. Yet, ominously for Mussolini's self-image, Italian troops even had difficulty in conquering this small state – this would be replicated on many fronts in the Second World War which was only five months away.

> **QUESTION**
> How did Mussolini's invasion of Albania in 1939 suggest that Italy might not perform well in the Second World War?

The Pact of Steel, May 1939

In May 1939, Mussolini and Hitler finally signed a formal military alliance – the 'Pact of Steel'. This committed Italy to fight on Germany's side, should war break out. Yet Mussolini warned Hitler that Italy needed at least three years of peace, in which to recover sufficiently from the effects of the Abyssinian and Spanish wars, before getting involved in another conflict. Consequently, in September 1939, when the Second World War broke out, Italy did not join in – it would not be until May 1940 that Mussolini finally decided to join forces with his fellow fascist.

Fact: As with the Anschluss with Austria in 1938, Hitler's decision to invade Poland took Mussolini by surprise.

Sudetenland: The German-speakers who lived in the Sudetenland were former citizens of the Austrian empire – they had never been part of Germany.

6.3 How did Germany expand, 1938–39?

Not surprisingly, Hitler and his supporters had been greatly encouraged by the success of the Anschluss with Austria in March 1938. Hitler's attentions now turned to Czechoslovakia – though, at first, he restricted his focus to the 3.5 million German-speakers living in Czechoslovakia's border region of the **Sudetenland**.

Crisis over Czechoslovakia, 1938

Figure 6.9 Edvard Benes (1884–1948)

He was an active supporter of the League of Nations, and was a member of its Council from 1923–27. He was also a strong supporter of the enforcement of the peace treaties of 1919–20. He was president from 1935 to 1938. Although not a communist, he believed Stalin's Soviet Union would be a useful check on possible threats from Nazi Germany.

As well as breaching Versailles, the *Anschluss* with Austria also strengthened Nazi Germany's ability to threaten Czechoslovakia. Its president, **Edvard Benes**, was facing increasing problems with the Sudeten German-speakers. Hitler decided to use the pro-Nazi Sudeten German Party to stir up violence, in order to have another excuse for military action. In May 1938, the Czech government claimed that Hitler was planning to invade. Convinced that Britain and France would not risk a war over Czechoslovakia, Hitler seemed at this point to have decided on Czechoslovakia's complete destruction. However, he denied this was his aim; so Chamberlain, Britain's Conservative prime minister, sent Lord Runciman to mediate between the Czech government and the Sudeten Germans. Runciman concluded that the Sudeten Germans were an oppressed minority and that they should be allowed to become part of Germany.

The crisis continued to deteriorate towards possible war – especially as Czechoslovakia had had a defence treaty with France since 1924; while France and the USSR had both signed an undertaking to protect Czech independence in May 1935. In addition,

Figure 6.10 The front page of the British newspaper the *Daily Sketch*, 1 October 1938

6

German and Italian Expansionism, 1933–40

the Czechs had an efficient, though small, army and seemed prepared to resist. Consequently – as with the Rhineland in 1936 – Hitler's military advisers warned that the Four-Year Plan had not yet made Germany ready for a European war.

However, in September 1938, Chamberlain decided to negotiate with Hitler in person. On 15 September, they met at Berchtesgaden, and on 22 September at Bad Godesberg. Each time Hitler increased his demands – eventually, Mussolini tried to moderate Hitler's stance. The French were not directly involved, though Britain and France informed the Czechoslovak government that they should hand the Sudetenland over to Germany, or risk fighting a war on their own. The Soviet Union, despite its commitments to Czechoslovakia, was not even consulted.

The Munich Agreement

Chamberlain met Hitler for the third time on 29 September, at Munich, where Germany, Britain, France and Italy finally agreed, on 30 September, that the Sudetenland should be handed to Germany, on the basis that self determination had been denied these German-speakers in 1919.

Once again, neither Czechoslovakia nor the Soviet Union was consulted. With no offer of help – despite the various treaties – the Czech government was forced to comply.

On 10 October, the Sudetenland became part of Germany. Once again, without firing a shot, Hitler obtained the part of Czechoslovakia which contained their border defences and the important Skoda armaments works – thus greatly reducing Czechoslovakia's ability to resist any future foreign aggression. In addition, Nazi Germany gained significant agricultural and industrial resources. In return, Hitler made vague promises to leave the rest of Czechoslovakia alone, and stated that the Sudetenland was his last territorial demand. He then signed a document with Chamberlain stating that Germany and Britain would never go to war against each other – the infamous 'peace in our time' pledge. Later that month, both Poland and Hungary seized land from Czechoslovakia.

> **ACTIVITY**
>
> Carry out some additional research on the Munich Conference. Then write a couple of paragraphs to answer the following questions:
>
> **a** How valid do you think Soviet Union fears were that their exclusion from the Munich Conference indicated British and French support for Hitler's eastwards expansion?
>
> **b** What other explanations are there for their exclusion from this Conference?

> **QUESTION**
>
> Why was losing the Sudetenland so significant in weakening Czechoslovakia's ability to defend itself?

> **SOURCE E**
>
> When Neville Chamberlain became British Prime Minister in May 1937 he gave a new impetus to appeasement. For Chamberlain, appeasement meant taking the initiative and showing Hitler that 'reasonable' claims could be achieved by negotiation and not force. Chamberlain and Daladier, the new French Prime Minister, feared that the Czech crisis could precipitate a wider conflict and decided that Czechoslovakia was simply not worth a European war. The Czech President, Benes, was urged therefore to make concessions to the Sudeten Germans. Chamberlain had three meetings with Hitler: at Berchtesgarden on 15 September, at Bad Godesberg on 22–23 September, and at Munich on 29–30 September. At the first meeting, Hitler stated his intention to annex the Sudetenland on the principle of self-determination. At Bad Godesberg he insisted on immediate German occupation, and finally at Munich he was persuaded to accept a phased occupation with an international commission to arbitrate over disputed boundaries … On 29 September 1938, an international conference was held at Munich. The participants were Germany, Italy, Britain and France. Conspicuous by their absence were Czechoslovakia, whose fate was to be decided, and the Soviet Union, which was not invited.
>
> Welch, D. 1998. *Hitler*. London. UCL Press. pp. 59–60.

Germany's and Italy's Actions

Invasion of Czechoslovakia, 1939

Meanwhile Hitler's foreign policy now centred on destroying the rest of Czechoslovakia. Within three weeks of occupying the Sudetenland, Hitler ordered his armies to get ready to invade the rest of Czechoslovakia. To begin with, the Slovaks were bullied into declaring their independence, while Poland and Hungary were encouraged to make their own territorial demands. By the end of 1938, Hitler was convinced that, because of its continued policy of appeasement, Britain would not oppose his plan to obtain *Lebensraum* in the east by invading the USSR – calculating correctly that Britain was more concerned about communism than his ambitions in the east. At the same time, Stalin came to believe that his attempts to build an anti-Nazi alliance with Britain and France were doomed to failure.

However, in February 1939, Britain at last began to move closer to France and signed a military alliance. Nonetheless, European diplomacy was still undecided – so, on 15 March, Hitler ordered the invasion of the rest of Czechoslovakia. This, too, was achieved without any opposition from Britain or France – despite it being a clear breach of the Munich Agreement.

Figure 6.11 Czechs protesting as German troops occupy Prague, March 1939

Though **Daladier** put France on a war footing, no actual action was taken by either Britain or France. Hitler now turned his attention to the Lithuanian port of Memel

Edouard Daladier (1884–1970)

He was a radical, and served as prime minister of France in 1933, 1934 and from 1938–40. He also signed the Munich Agreement in 1938, and declared war on Germany in September 1939. He was interned by the Vichy government in France (which, with German permission, ruled part of the country following France's defeat in 1940) and deported to Germany, where he remained a prisoner till the end of the war in Europe in 1945.

6 German and Italian Expansionism, 1933–40

where the German inhabitants had been demanding to be returned to Germany. In the end, Memel became a free port zone, effectively under Nazi control.

Though Hitler now turned his attentions to Poland, his plans to move against Poland without facing opposition were undermined later that month, when Britain and France announced they had signed a pact with Poland, guaranteeing its independence. To counter this, Hitler strengthened his military alliance with Fascist Italy in May 1939, with the signing of the Pact of Steel. More importantly, Hitler also decided to pursue negotiations with the USSR, so that there would be no ally for Britain and France in the east. Not until July/August did Britain begin, half-heartedly, to consider a pact with the USSR against Nazi aggression. To begin with, trade talks began between Germany and the Soviet Union in July 1939.

The Nazi–Soviet Non-Aggression Pact

The Soviet Union had been offering Britain and France an anti-Nazi alliance for some time but Chamberlain, a strong anti-communist, was opposed – in part because it might provoke Germany, and because Poland was opposed. The Soviet Union's Red Army could only get to Germany, in the event of a war, by crossing Polish

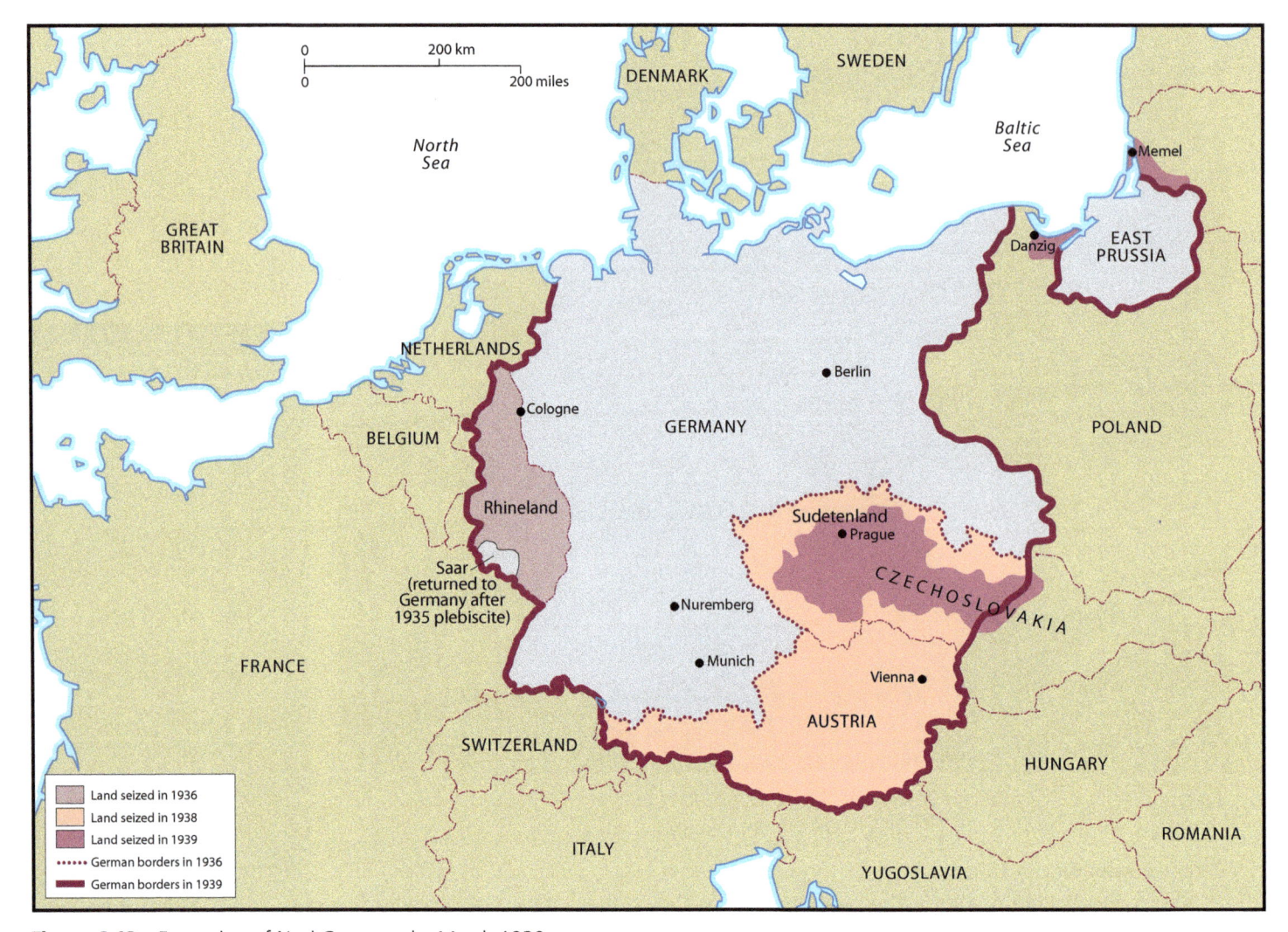

Figure 6.12 Expansion of Nazi Germany, by March 1939

territory. However, the Polish government feared that, once there, the Red Army would never leave – and neither Britain nor France was willing to persuade Poland to change its mind.

In fact, by the end of 1938, Poland was probably the most disliked and distrusted of the 'successor states'. Since 1926, Poland had had an authoritarian government which was increasingly pro-German and anti-Semitic, and which had its own 'revisionist' foreign policy, directed at some of its neighbours – including Czechoslovakia.

Despite a second British rejection of an alliance with the Soviet Union in May 1939, by mid-1939, there was strong public support in both Britain and France for such an alliance. So Chamberlain, reluctantly, agreed to open negotiations – but only at a low level. Eden, who had offered to conduct them, was excluded from the initial negotiations. Since the Munich Conference in September 1938, however, Stalin had come increasingly to suspect that Britain and France were prepared to accept German conquests in the east.

Fact: Poland's opposition to any alliance with the Soviet Union was partly because Poland had previously been part of the old Tsarist empire, and feared increased Russian influence. Poland's concerns were also partly because, in 1921, Poland – supported by Britain and France – had successfully taken land from Soviet Russia, following the Russo–Polish War of 1920–21. This land was in fact later re-taken by the Soviet Union after the end of the Second World War.

Figure 6.13 A Soviet cartoon about the Munich Agreement of 1938. The signpost says 'Western Europe' and 'USSR' – Britain and France (the 'policemen of Europe') are shown as directing the Nazis to the USSR

Britain's slow responses to these low-level negotiations in the summer of 1939 seemed to confirm this fear, so Stalin also began to respond to German requests for negotiations on a non-aggression pact. Hitler, who had already set the date for the invasion of Poland, saw such a pact as necessary – he calculated that, with no Soviet ally, Britain and

6

German and Italian Expansionism, 1933–40

France would not honour their pledges to Poland. Stalin saw such a pact, in the event of no firm alliance with Britain and France, as giving the Soviet Union more time to prepare defences against a German invasion which he expected to come in the very near future.

So while the negotiations with Britain seemed to stall (in part because of the continued refusal of Poland and the Baltic States to allow Russian troops to cross their territory), the **Molotov–Ribbentrop Pact of Non-Aggression** was concluded on 23 August 1939. This included secret clauses for the splitting of Poland and a Soviet takeover of the Baltic States.

Molotov–Ribbentrop Pact of Non-Aggression: This Nazi-Soviet Pact was, officially, a ten-year non-aggression pact between Germany and the USSR. However, it also contained a secret protocol, which contained clauses that divided Poland and large parts of Eastern Europe between the two powers. Germany was to have western Poland, while the USSR got eastern Poland, the three Baltic republics and part of Romania – all of which had previously been part of Tsarist Russia's empire before 1918.

SOURCE F

The notion of 'concept pluralism' – ... that there were a number of different views among the leaders of the Third Reich about the foreign policy Germany should pursue – has recently been taken further by Wolfgang Michalka in his analysis of Ribbentrop's own foreign policy ideas and influence upon Hitler. Michalka argues that from the mid-1930s onwards an anti-English rather than essentially anti-Russian policy provided the main thrust of Ribbentrop's own conception of foreign policy.... He demonstrates how, in the later 1930s, Hitler's increasing recognition of the failure to win over England allowed Ribbentrop a considerable scope for exerting influence, culminating in the signing of the Non-Aggression Pact with the Soviet Union in 1939.... None of the 'structural-functionalist', 'concept pluralist', or 'polycratic' approaches to foreign policy .... has shaken the conviction of the 'intentionalists' (or 'programmatists') that the character and consistency of Hitler's ideology was the crucial and determining element in the equation. Indeed, ... the leading studies of the varying centres of influence in the formation of foreign policy all come down ultimately to similar or compatible conclusions.

Kershaw, I. 1993. *The Nazi Dictatorship. Problems and Perspectives of Interpretation*. London. Arnold. p. 115.

KEY CONCEPTS QUESTION

Significance: According to Source F, how significant a role did Ribbentrop play in determining Nazi Germany's foreign policy in the mid-1930s?

ACTIVITY

Carry out some additional research on the reasons why Britain was so reluctant to ally with the Soviet Union before 1939. Then rank them in order of significance, and write a paragraph explaining your first choice.

Several historians, such as R. Henig, have pointed out how an important factor in determining the inter-war diplomacy of countries such as Britain and France was fear of the spread of communism – in part, this was the result of early Bolshevik propaganda, which had made no secret of its desire to see workers' revolutions take place throughout Europe. This revolutionary internationalism declined under Stalin, as he attempted to find allies in the 1930s for the war which he felt – especially after Hitler had become chancellor of Germany in 1933 – was bound to come. Nonetheless, the capitalist countries, in the context of the continuing impact of the Depression, still feared communism. Although by the late 1930s it was clear that only joint action by Britain, France and the Soviet Union could check Hitler's determination to expand Germany's frontiers, the preceding ideological warfare of the previous 20 years had created considerable mutual distrust between these potential allies. Especially after Munich, it was hardly surprising that Stalin eventually came to the conclusion that British and French leaders were not serious about checking Nazi Germany's eastward expansion.

End of unit activities

1. Carry out some additional research on Italy's foreign policy between 1935–39. Then construct a chart with three columns: 'Alliances'/'Actions', 'Aims', and 'Outcomes'. Then fill in brief details under each heading. Finally, write a short paragraph to explain to what extent you think that, overall, Mussolini's actions during this period were successful.

2. Design a poster to put Hitler's case for 'equality of treatment' at the World Disarmament Conference.

3. On the basis of what you have studied so far, what do you think was the significance of the Munich Conference of September 1938?

4. Draw a timeline showing the main foreign policy steps taken by Germany and Italy between 1933 and 1939.

6 End of chapter activities

Summary

You should now have a sound knowledge of the main foreign policy actions taken by Nazi Germany and Fascist Italy in the period 1933–39, prior to the outbreak of war in September 1939.

You should also understand the steps taken by Hitler after 1934 to ensure that Fascist Italy became an ally rather than remaining a possible opponent.

Summary activities

Using the example in this section, draw your own spider diagram and, using the information from this chapter and any other materials that you have available, make notes under each of the headings. Where there are differences over the relative importance of the actions of Germany and Italy in the period 1933–39, try to mention the views of specific historians.

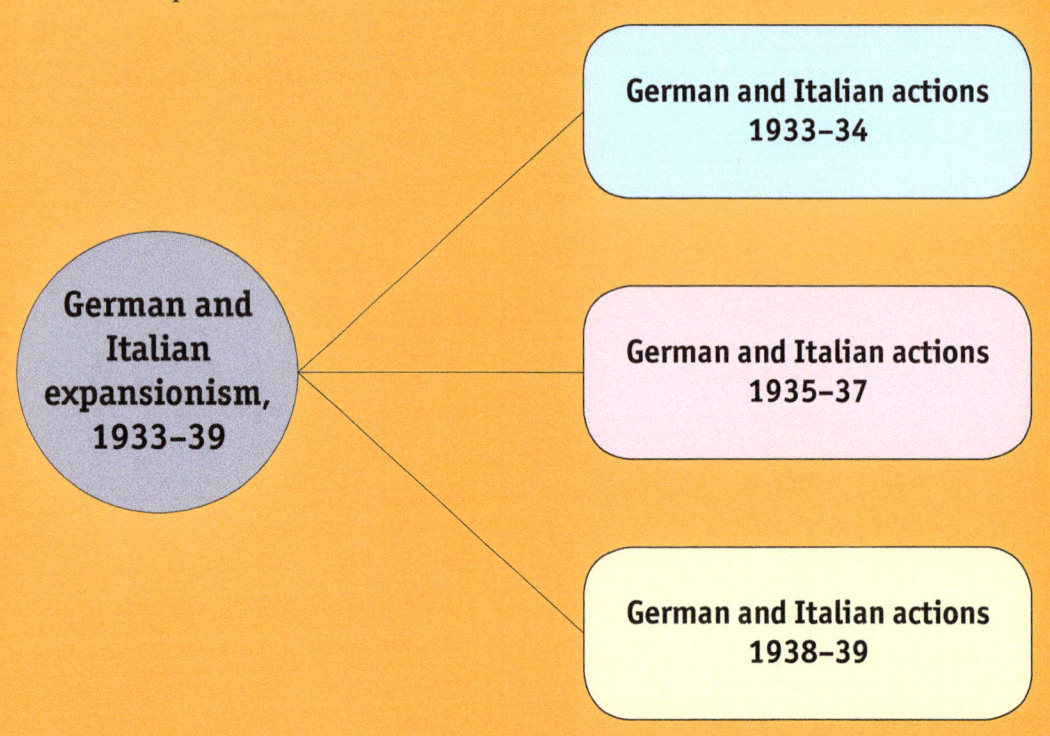

- **German and Italian expansionism, 1933–39**
  - German and Italian actions 1933–34
  - German and Italian actions 1935–37
  - German and Italian actions 1938–39

Paper 1 exam practice

Question

> **SOURCE A**
>
> The problem of Italian–Abyssinian relations has very recently shifted from a diplomatic plane to one which can be solved by force only. The object is nothing more or less than the complete destruction of the Abyssinian army and the total conquest of Abyssinia, in no other way can we build the Empire.
>
> The speedier our action the less likely the danger of diplomatic complications. In the Japanese fashion there will be no need whatever officially for a declaration of war and in any case we must always emphasise the purely defensive character of operations. No one in Europe would raise any difficulties provided the prosecution of operations resulted rapidly in an accomplished fact. It would suffice to declare to England and France that their interests would be recognised.
>
> Memorandum from Marshal Badoglio, Chief of General Staff to Mussolini, December 1934. Quoted in Hite, J. and Hinton, C. 1998. *Fascist Italy*. London. Hodder. p. 214.

With reference to its origin, purpose and content, analyse the value and limitations of **Source A** for a historian studying why Italy decided to invade Abyssinia in October 1935. **[4 marks]**

Skill

Value and limitations (utility/reliability) of a source

Before you start

Value and limitations (utility/reliability) of a source questions require you to assess a source over a range of possible issues – and to comment on its value to historians studying a particular event or period in history. You need to consider the **origin, purpose and content** of the source *and* then use these aspects to assess the **value and limitations** of the source. You should link these in your answer, showing how origin/purpose/content relate to value/limitations.

Before you attempt this question, refer to Chapter 9 for advice on how to answer these questions, and a simplified mark scheme.

Student answer

Source A, which is a memorandum, has a useful origin, as it was written by Marshal Badoglio, who was in charge of the army in Fascist Italy. It also has good value as it was written to Mussolini in December 1934 – less than a year before Italy invaded Abyssinia. In addition, it has good value as it is not something meant for publication; therefore its purpose is not for propaganda but for giving a genuine assessment.

Examiner comments

The response has some valid comments on the origin and thus the value of the source. In addition, there are also points about its purpose. However, there is nothing on its content, and nothing on the possible limitations of the source. The candidate has thus only done enough to get into Band 2, and so be awarded 2 marks.

Activity

Look again at the source, the simplified mark scheme, and the student answer above. Now try to write a paragraph or two to push the answer up into Band 1, and so obtain the full 4 marks. As well as assessing content and purpose, try to make developed comments on the limitations of the source as well as its value.

Paper 2 practice questions

1. Examine the significance of the failure of the World Disarmament Conference as a factor in the increasing tensions in Europe before 1939.
2. Compare and contrast the extent to which the foreign policies of Italy and Germany can be regarded as successful in the period 1933–39.
3. Evaluate the consequences of the Munich Conference in 1938 as regards Germany's expansion in Europe in the period 1938–39.
4. 'The main reason Hitler concluded the Non-Aggression Pact with the Soviet Union in 1939 was because he feared the power of Stalin's Red Army.' To what extent do you agree with this statement?

International Responses to German and Italian Expansionism

7

KEY QUESTIONS

- What was the international response to German aggression 1933–38?
- What was the international response to Italian aggression 1935–36?
- What was the international response to German and Italian aggression in 1939?

Overview

- During the 1920s, there had been some promising developments as regards upholding the peace treaties of 1919–20, and maintaining peace in Europe – these include the Locarno Treaty and the Kellogg-Briand Pact.
- Significantly, however, most of the diplomatic agreements made in the 1920s were done independently of the League.
- By 1933, as the impact of the Great Depression affected European states, the League became even more irrelevant as regards European diplomacy.
- However, the two main European powers – Britain and France – could not agree on how to react to the increasing violations of the peace treaties. In Britain in particular, the policy of appeasement became the main diplomatic approach to Italy and then to Germany in the second half of the 1930s.
- Despite several attempts to agree peaceful revisions of the peace treaties, both Italy and Germany resorted to increasingly aggressive actions after 1935. Each time, Britain and France took no real action – despite having made prior commitments to countries such as Czechoslovakia.
- With Britain and France apparently decided never to oppose their expansionist foreign policy, and the Soviet Union excluded from discussions, Germany and Italy felt confident in continuing their policies after 1936.
- Thus, by mid-1939, neither Germany nor Italy believed that Britain and France would honour their pledges to uphold Polish independence.

TIMELINE

1925 Locarno Treaty

1928 Kellogg-Briand Pact

1933 **Oct:** Germany leaves Disarmament Conference and League of Nations

1934 **Jul:** Hitler attempts *Anschluss* with Austria

Sept: Soviet Union joins League of Nations

1935 **Mar:** Hitler reintroduces conscription

Apr: Stresa Front

Oct: Italy invades Abyssinia

Nov: League of Nations applies sanctions against Italy

1936 **Mar:** German re-occupation of the Rhineland

July: Intervention in Spanish Civil War

Oct: Rome-Berlin Axis

Nov: Comintern Pact (Germany and Japan)

1937 **May:** Neville Chamberlain becomes British prime minister

Oct: Italy signs Anti-Comintern Pact (Rome-Berlin-Tokyo Axis)

Dec: Italy leaves the League of Nations

1938 **Mar:** *Anschluss* with Austria

Sept: Munich Conference

1939 **Mar:** German invasion of rest of Czechoslovakia; Lithuania forced to give up Memel to Nazi Germany

Apr: Italian annexation of Albania

May: Pact of Steel

169

7 German and Italian Expansionism, 1933–40

7.1 What was the international response to German aggression 1933–38?

In January 1933, with Hitler's appointment as chancellor of Germany and the impending destruction of the democratic Weimar Republic, the diplomatic situation in Europe was soon to change for the worse. The League of Nations – essentially Britain and France – had already experienced a serious failure over Japan's invasion of Manchuria in 1931. Further crises – resulting from the increasingly aggressive and expansionist actions of Germany and Italy – in the period 1933–39 would place such large stresses on the League that, by 1939, it had completely collapsed as an effective force. With the failure of the idea of collective security, Europe joined Asia in what, after 1939, is known as the Second World War.

Collective security 1933–36

When the League of Nations had been set up after the First World War, its main aims had been to uphold the peace settlements of 1919–20, and to avoid future wars of aggression by maintaining what was known as 'collective security'. Article 11 of the League's Covenant had attempted to give member – and non-member – states a sense of security after the horrors and destruction of the First World War by promising to

Figure 7.1 Cartoon about the Locarno Treaty – France on the left, Germany on the right

take collective action to preserve peace and international order. During the 1920s, some important steps had been taken to help maintain international peace: such as the Locarno Treaty of 1925 and the Kellogg–Briand Pact of 1928. In addition, the League seemed strengthened when, in 1926, Germany was allowed to join.

However the League had no army with which to effectively impose its decisions on states which resorted to aggression (see Chapter 1, The League of Nations). This had been only too clear in relation to the Japanese invasion of Manchuria. Despite diplomatic successes in the 1920s, the impact of the Great Depression resulted in the League facing increasingly difficult examples of expansionism by both Germany and Italy. An additional problem was that Britain and France, the two most important members of the League, increasingly followed national self-interests which further undermined the League and made it difficult to present a coherent, consistent and effective response to expansionism.

Figure 7.2 The signing of Kellogg-Briand Pact, 1928, outlawing war

7

German and Italian Expansionism, 1933–40

Fact: Mussolini's initial reaction to Nazi Germany's stated aim to unite all German-speakers was one of deep concern, as this would overturn important aspects of the peace settlements of 1919–20. He was also concerned that a Germany which had been increased in strength by the acquisition of Austria would be better able to block his own plans for Italian expansion into the Balkans.

Attempted *Anschluss* and the Stresa Front, 1934–35

The first potentially serious crisis occurred in July 1934, with Nazi Germany's attempt to force *Anschluss* with Austria. At this stage, however, members of the League were able to take action which prevented Hitler's first attempt at expansion. This was largely because one member – Italy – was opposed to it because, if Germany had been successful, it would have placed a powerful Germany on its borders. Despite their shared fascist ideology, Italy and Germany – Mussolini's hope was that by having closer relations with Britain and France, he might be able to get some aspects of the peace settlements altered in Italy's favour. Mussolini had also, in August 1933, met with Engelbert Dolfuss, the Austrian chancellor, to discuss Italian military support should there be an attack by Germany. In March 1934, he concluded the Rome Protocols with Austria and Hungary – this included an agreement for joint discussion and consultation of significant concerns. Although Hitler visited Italy in June 1934, in an attempt to win Mussolini over to his aims, he was unsuccessful.

Mussolini's initial reaction to Hitler coming to power in 1933 was one of caution. As early as June 1933, he proposed a Four-Power Pact between Britain and France. Hitler's failure to win Mussolini over was shown the following month, when Mussolini decided to take decisive action to prevent Hitler's attempted *Anschluss*. The presence of Italian troops on Austria's borders was enough to deter Hitler from his first aggressive foreign policy action. As Hitler then began to concentrate on German re-armament, Mussolini decided to move closer to Britain and France. In January 1935, the Rome Agreements saw France and Italy agree on aspects of European security. Then, in April 1935, the three countries met in Stresa to discuss the problems of German re-armament and its attempted *Anschluss* with Austria. The meeting resulted in confirmation of the Locarno Treaty and Austrian independence, and condemnation of the recent German attempt at aggression. In addition, the three countries then formed the Stresa Front, which saw all three agree to oppose 'by all means' any attempts at unilateral breaches of the peace settlements and any actions threatening the peace of Europe.

QUESTION
In what ways does the cartoonist suggest that the Stresa Front might not be very long-lasting?

Figure 7.3 A cartoon about the formation of the Stresa Front in 1935

International Responses to German and Italian Expansionism

Thus, in 1934–35, joint action by the three most important members of the League seemed to have prevented aggression and thus maintained collective security in Europe. However, there were some underlying weaknesses: apart from the fact that this was done outside of the League, events would soon show that Mussolini had expected to gain some tangible benefits for his cooperation with Britain and France. The most significant one was approval of his plan to invade Abyssinia. This action – and the reactions of Britain and France, and of the League – would be one of the developments which, within one year of the formation of the Stresa Front, would undermine the unity which had blocked Hitler's expansionism in 1934.

Re-armament

When Hitler announced publicly his intention to re-arm beyond the limits established at Versailles, and to re-introduce conscription, Britain and France – and as a result, the League – took no action. Instead, Britain's main response was to conclude the Anglo–German Naval Treaty, which allowed Germany to increase the size of its navy beyond the size laid down by the Treaty of Versailles – provided that the German navy was never more than 35% the size of the British navy. Once again, the international response was one of inaction; instead the major states failed to oppose this clear challenge to the peace settlements of 1919–20. One of its main effects was to encourage Hitler to pose even greater challenges – and the confidence that he would face no serious opposition.

Re-occupation of the Rhineland, 1936

By the time of Nazi Germany's next expansionist move in March 1936, the diplomatic situation in Europe had undergone significant changes. Although Hitler's announcement of German re-armament and conscription was a clear unilateral breach of the Treaty of Versailles, there was no combined attempt to prevent this. In fact, in June 1935, Britain concluded the Anglo-German Naval Agreement with Nazi Germany. This was significant as it was concluded without prior discussion with either France or Italy and it was therefore an action which began to undermine the recently-formed Stresa Front. The crisis over Italy's invasion of Abyssinia in October 1935 had an even greater impact on cooperation between the members of the Stresa Front (see section 7.2, Italy's invasion of Abyssinia, 1935).

As a consequence of Britain and France's inability to approve Mussolini's expansionist actions in Abyssinia, he had quickly begun to shift towards a more friendly diplomatic relation with Nazi Germany – especially when Hitler shifted his earlier position to one of support of Italy's invasion. Hitler was quick to take advantage of this new situation – and of the crisis of the Abyssinian war – to re-occupy the Rhineland. This was yet another act which was in clear violation of the Treaty of Versailles.

Yet, having lost Fascist Italy as an ally, Britain and France took no concerted action to prevent Hitler's actions. Although France wanted to oppose this move, Britain made it clear it would not support any French military action. The failure of the League – and its main members – to enforce such an important part of the peace settlements further undermined the League, and sent a clear message to Hitler that it was unlikely he would ever face serious opposition to his aims of territorial expansion. It also undermined the prospects of collective security, as Britain's refusal to support France drove a wedge between these two states. In addition, it drove Mussolini into an even stronger alliance with Nazi Germany.

Fact: With the collapse of the Stresa Front, Britain and France were now on their own – and yet continued to follow quite different policies. Eden, the British Foreign Secretary, was prepared to 'appease' what were seen as justified German grievances. Though Britain gave a promise to support France if there was an unprovoked German attack, France felt isolated. A request to US president Roosevelt to condemn this German action was ignored – thus France felt unable to oppose the re-occupation. The League took no action at all, and was becoming clearly irrelevant for international and European events.

7 German and Italian Expansionism, 1933–40

Figure 7.4 Photograph of the German re-occupation of the Rhineland in March 1936

International Responses to German and Italian Expansionism

Behind the scenes

However, although publicly Britain did little to show any intention of opposing German challenges to the peace settlements, behind the scenes things were beginning to change. In early 1936, Eden pointed out the need to buy time – which, according to historians such as D. Dilks, had been a strong element in British foreign policy for several years. Eden's recommendations to the British Cabinet were to reach agreements with Germany where they could be honourably reached; to be under no illusions that Nazi Germany would keep to them when they no longer served Hitler's purposes; and to speed up British re-armament. This did, in fact, take place later, in 1938 and 1939, with military expenditure in those years being far in excess of any previous British spending on weapons in peace time. However, Chamberlain, who came to power in 1937, had some genuine sympathy for German grievances concerning aspects of the Treaty of Versailles, and was especially keen to avoid, if at all possible, another world war with all its attendant destruction and loss of life.

The collapse of collective security 1936–38

Events during the next two years saw the eventual collapse of collective security. Although the Second World War did not break out in Europe until September 1939, it was clear by 1937 that the League of Nations – and its aim of collective security – was effectively dead.

Intervention and the Spanish Civil War, 1936–39

The Spanish Civil War – and, in particular, the intervention by Nazi Germany and Fascist Italy – had important consequences for collective security. The two main countries of the League, Britain and France, proposed that all countries should agree not to intervene in the Spanish Civil War. In September 1936, the Non-Intervention Committee met in London to draw up a pact, which was signed by several countries – including Germany, Italy, the USSR and the US. In reality, though the Non-Intervention Committee effectively blocked the purchase of war materials by the republicans, the nationalists found it relatively easy to purchase such materials from many of the democracies who had signed the Pact. These included the USA and Britain – according to R. Whealey, in July 1938 alone, Franco bought over 30% of his material from British companies, without any attempt by the British government to prevent this. While US oil firms, with the knowledge of Roosevelt's government, supplied large quantities of oil to the rebel forces in Spain. This was noted by Hitler, and arguably helped him come to the conclusion that there would be no serious opposition to his plans for expansion in central and Eastern Europe.

As previously stated, the Spanish Civil War was also of great importance to Nazi Germany in other ways. In return for military assistance, Hitler got Franco to provide raw materials which greatly aided German re-armament. In addition, Hitler's intervention provided an opportunity to test out military tactics. This was especially important for the Luftwaffe, which gained valuable experience from the Condor Legion's bombing missions, while the importance of anti-tank and anti-aircraft guns was also established. However, in some ways, the most important benefit to Nazi Germany was the conviction that the appeasement policies which led to non-intervention by Britain and France meant that Hitler's plans for territorial expansion were not likely to be met by war. As well as confirming his views about Britain and France, the experience of the Spanish Civil War also gave Hitler a greater hold over Mussolini. Fascist Italy's intervention further weakened its previous relations with Britain, and instead pushed

---

KEY CONCEPTS ACTIVITY

Causation and consequence: Carry out further research on developments in the period 1933–36, and then write a couple of paragraphs to explain the reasons for, and the immediate consequences of, the undermining of the Stresa Front.

Historical debate: According to W. C. Frank, Hitler's earlier regard for Britain evaporated as a result of its 'lack of backbone' in regard to the Spanish Civil War, and he became increasingly determined to expand – even if such expansion was eventually opposed by Britain. In particular, it gave him the confidence to annex Austria and move against Czechoslovakia in 1938. In fact, Frank believes that it was the experiences gained in the Spanish Civil War that encouraged Hitler to risk war as early as he did.

7 German and Italian Expansionism, 1933–40

it firmly into Hitler's camp – setting it on course for involvement in the Second World War. The first important step in this was the signing of the Rome-Berlin Axis in October 1936. The following month, Hitler signed the Anti-Comintern Pact with Japan, designed to confront the Soviet Union.

The policy of 'non-intervention', though in many ways an attempt to appease the dictators, failed and mainly served to expose the weaknesses of Britain and France. However, non-intervention only postponed the outbreak of the Second World War – and France was left facing a hostile neighbour, allied to Nazi Germany, south of the Pyrenees. At the same time, the Soviet Union, which had intervened initially to show its support for a democratic republic – and its opposition to any revolution in Spain – in the hope that this would result in an anti-fascist alliance with Britain and France, had its hopes dashed. On the contrary, according to G. Roberts, it came to the conclusion that the non-intervention policy, and appeasement in general, meant that Britain and France would not oppose any eastwards expansion by Hitler. Although, even as late as April 1939, Stalin continued to press for a Grand Anti-fascist Alliance, he also began to consider some temporary deal with Nazi Germany to buy time.

SOURCE A

The Spanish Civil War, non-intervention and intervention had an impact on the subsequent fortunes of the world powers. Non-Intervention failed to appease the dictators. Intervention hardly benefited Italy and the Soviet Union. Only Germany really gained an advantage, both economically and militarily, from its participation in the Spanish war. Above all, the Civil War can be seen as a rehearsal for, or at least a prelude to, the Second World War... The weaknesses of the democracies were neatly exposed by their refusal to intervene in Spain. According to Mary Habeck, the Spanish war prevented Franco-British unity against the dictators in that it distracted attention from far greater dangers…

Britain's policy of compromise, rather than calming the international situation, only heightened tension between the European powers. The British government failed to understand that Spain was another arena where Germany and Italy were testing how far their aggressive stance could be taken… The Civil War also alienated the Soviet Union from the West. Receiving no response to appeals for collective security, Stalin became increasingly convinced that appeasement would channel Hitler's attention towards the East.

Durgan, A. 2007. *The Spanish Civil War*. Basingstoke, UK. Palgrave MacMillan. pp. 74–6.

QUESTION
How did the policy of non-intervention further weaken the League and attempts to achieve collective security?

Fact: In addition, the bombing of civilian populations in Guernica, Barcelona, Lerida and Madrid, and the horrors engendered by bitter ideological conflict, gave a taste of the modern and horrific type of war just round the corner for the various peoples of the world.

Ultimately, the policies of non-intervention and appeasement failed to calm the international situation. Instead, the Spanish Civil War only confirmed the growing ideological divisions in Europe between left and right, and democracies and dictatorships. In addition, Hitler and Mussolini's early fears that Britain would enforce non-intervention were soon dispersed, and were replaced by the conviction there would be no response to further aggression, as the British government seemed determined to avoid another European war.

Although European tensions over Austria, Abyssinia, the Rhineland and the Sudetenland arguably had a more direct impact on the eventual outbreak of the Second World War, the Spanish Civil War certainly contributed to the growing

International Responses to German and Italian Expansionism

Figure 7.5 A cartoon, published on 14 December 1936 in the British newspaper, the *Evening Standard*, commenting on the League's inaction during the Spanish Civil War

European crisis. By the end of the Civil War, in April 1939, the division of Europe into two opposed power blocs which would eventually go to war against each other was largely confirmed.

Anschluss with Austria, 1938

As a result of diplomatic developments in 1935–36, Hitler had managed not only to detach Italy from Britain and France, but had even gained Italy as an ally. Encouraged by this – and by the passive reaction of Britain and France in relation to the Spanish Civil War, Hitler calculated he could carry out his next unilateral 'revision' of the peace settlements without much likelihood of military opposition from Britain or France. Knowing that Italy would no longer oppose *Anschluss* with Austria – as it had in 1934 – Hitler's calculations about British and French reactions proved correct. This was despite the fact that the Austrian chancellor had called on both countries for help. Thus Hitler was able to send troops to occupy Austria without a shot being fired. As well as confirming his views that British and French intervention to block his further plans for territorial expansion was unlikely, the *Anschluss* made his next target – Czechoslovakia – even more achievable.

The Sudetenland Crisis, 1938

To many people, it was soon obvious that Hitler's next target would be Czechoslovakia – or at least the border areas where 3.5 million German-speakers

Theory of knowledge

History, emotion and bias:
The American writer William Faulkner (1897–1962) once wrote: *'The past is never dead. It's not even past.'* The Spanish Civil War – at least in part – involved a life-and-death struggle between fascism and its opponents, and seemed to many to be a precursor for the Second World War. Given that Franco's dictatorship only ended just 40 years ago, and neo-fascist groups are still active in several countries, are historians who write about the Civil War able to avoid bias? Should such controversial topics even be taught in schools – or is it important that young people are given the chance to study such events?

7

German and Italian Expansionism, 1933–40

Fact: In fact, many people in Britain believed union between Germany and Austria was a valid aim, and that self-determination had been denied these two populations in 1919. Thus they saw the *Anschluss* of 1938 as basically righting a wrong.

Figure 7.6 A David Low cartoon, printed in October 1938, commenting on the implications of the Anschluss of 1938. Hitler's sack reads: 'Germany over all', and the caption is: '"Europe can look forward to a Christmas of peace", says Hitler.'

lived. Such suspicions were borne out in May 1938, when Hitler stated that he was prepared to go to war against Czechoslovakia over the Sudetenland's German-speaking population. The Czech president, Benes, appealed to Britain and France for help. France was, in fact, committed to help Czechoslovakia by the treaties it had signed with the 'successor states' in the 1920s – including one specifically with Czechoslovakia in 1924. Significantly, however, Britain had made no such treaties and was not prepared to make any guarantees. Given this attitude, France felt unable to act alone; yet another example of how the two main members of the League were not able – or not willing – to pursue a joint policy to prevent aggression and so preserve collective security in Europe.

This Czech Crisis seemed so serious that war in central Europe was seen as an imminent possibility. This led Britain and France to consider ways of dealing with Hitler's expansionist aims which would avoid war.

Fact: In the summer of 1938, several countries actually began preparing for war.

However, it was at this point especially that political developments in Britain played a crucial role. For, in May 1937, the Conservative politician Neville Chamberlain had become prime minister. He was extremely committed to the policy of appeasement – and came to power at a tense period in diplomatic relations, which – as a result of various recent crises – such as Abyssinia, Austria, Japan's invasion of China, the continuing civil war in Spain, and the growing threat of aggression by Nazi

International Responses to German and Italian Expansionism

WHAT, NO CHAIR FOR ME?

Figure 7.7 A David Low cartoon, commenting on the exclusion of the Soviet Union from the Munich Conference

Germany – had led to a rapid decline in peaceful international cooperation. With the League of Nations now clearly defunct in practice by 1937, Chamberlain hoped a policy of appeasement would calm international relations and bring about a lasting peace.

Consequently, instead of any joint attempt to block this latest example of Nazi Germany's expansionist aims – which threatened yet another independent country that had been created by the peace settlements of 1919–20 – a series of meetings took place. In September 1938, Chamberlain flew three times to Germany, to have meetings with Hitler. At first, Hitler's aims seemed moderate, but he then increased his demands. At the suggestion of Mussolini, a Four-Power Conference was held at Munich on 29 September 1938 between Britain, France, Italy and Germany. The Czechs – who were not present to discuss the fate of their country – were abandoned by Britain and France, who both made it clear they would not come to Czechoslovakia's aid if it decided to resist. Instead, they were told that Germany's claims on the Sudetenland were legitimate and so the area should be handed over. As well as confirming Hitler's belief that he would never be opposed, the Munich Agreement also had important repercussions as regards the Soviet Union and eventually paved the way for the Nazi–Soviet Non-Aggression Pact the following year, which included secret clauses for the joint dismemberment of Poland.

Fact: For some time, Stalin had been pushing for an alliance with Britain and France to curb the growing threat from a clearly expansionist Nazi Germany – hence he had been opposed to any revolutionary workers' government coming to power in Spain. However, some Soviet advisers had begun to suggest that Soviet security would be best served by a temporary pact with Germany, in order to give the Soviet Union time to prepare its defences for a war that had been expected for several years since 1933. After Munich, Stalin was more prepared to listen to these advisers – by the time Britain belatedly began to respond to Soviet calls for an anti-fascist Grand Alliance, it was too late: Britain and France thus lost a potentially-powerful ally at a critical time in international relations.

7 German and Italian Expansionism, 1933–40

Fact: In 1889, the Treaty of Wuchale between Italy and Menelik II, the emperor of Ethiopia, had seemed to give Italy control over Ethiopia's foreign policy – in effect, making Ethiopia an Italian protectorate. However, this was disputed by the Ethiopians; Italy's response was to launch what became known as the First Italo–Ethiopian War of 1895–96. In March 1896, a smaller Italian force was decisively beaten by the Ethiopian army at Adowa, and suffered heavy losses. This defeat led to riots in many Italian cities against the Italian government, which collapsed. In October 1896, Italy was forced to agree to the Treaty of Addis Ababa, which established clear borders between Abyssinia and Italian Eritrea, and the independence of Ethiopia.

7.2 What was the international response to Italian aggression 1935–36?

While Italy faced some opposition from the League – and Britain and France – over its early expansionist aims, it was not serious opposition. Furthermore, the inadequate attempts to limit Fascist Italy's expansionist aims served only to drive Mussolini into an ever-closer relationship with Nazi Germany. This would have serious repercussions in the critical years 1936–39.

Italy's invasion of Abyssinia, 1935

The invasion of Abyssinia by Italian forces on 3 October 1935 was the first unprovoked attack by any European power since the establishment of the League of Nations. It was not, however, unexpected, as Italian nationalists had long wanted an opportunity to avenge its defeat by Abyssinian forces at Adowa in 1896 – as well as a chance to expand Italy's empire. Despite the expectations of such an invasion, when it actually happened, it caused real problems for Britain and France as regards how to respond. To begin with, both Ethiopia and Italy were members of the League; in fact, Italy was actually a member of the Council – the League's ruling body. Both Britain and France were reluctant to take action against Italy, for a variety of reasons.

Initially, despite publicly stating its support for the League, the British government thought in terms of offering Italy some territory elsewhere. This was because, by 1935 – as a result of the increasingly aggressive foreign policies being pursued by Japan and Germany – the British government had begun to consider how rearmament and appeasement could be used to maintain Britain's security against the threats to British interests posed by both Japan and Germany. In this context, the impending Italian invasion of Abyssinia was seen as a 'most inconvenient dilemma'. On 11 September 1935, Britain's foreign secretary, Sir Samuel Hoare, made a speech at the League of Nations concerning the tensions building up between Italy and Abyssinia. In it, he re-stated Britain's support of the League and its Covenant – though the speech included the 'wiggle-room' phrase 'within the measure of [Britain's] capacity'.

Britain's stance was designed to keep Italy within the Stresa Front – but, though it came as a surprise to Mussolini, it did not stop him carrying on with Italy's invasion plans. France was particularly reluctant to provoke an argument with Mussolini, as it too wished to maintain the Stresa Front in order to resist future German threats to Austria, the 'successor states' and, ultimately, to itself. Consequently, as the tension built during the first half of 1935, following the Wal-Wal Incident of December 1934, France was keen to reassure Mussolini of French support – in fact, even when the Italian invasion had begun, France actually communicated its initial support to Italy.

Before October 1935, the League – effectively Britain and France – had set up a commission to investigate the Wal-Wal Incident and had decided that it was a disputed border issue – even though the oasis lay 70km (34 miles) within Abyssinian territory. In January 1935, Haile Salassie, the emperor of Abyssinia had appealed to the League for arbitration, but the League's Arbitration Committee decided that neither side was to blame. As the tension continued to build, and Mussolini mobilised Italian forces, both Britain and France tried to settle the problem by offering Italy land from its neighbouring colonies. But Mussolini rejected these offers, and it became increasingly clear that he was intent on launching a full-scale invasion. Britain then imposed an embargo on arms sales to both sides. However, this hit Abyssinia harder than it did Italy – and Britain also decided to withdraw its warships from the Mediterranean, thus giving Mussolini a clear way to east Africa.

Fact: The embargo on arms sales probably came about as a result of Mussolini's announcement that he would view arms sales to Abyssinia as an act of unfriendliness against Italy.

Fact: In the end, the League agreed to ban the import of Italian goods, and to place an embargo on arms sales and financial aid to Italy. However, because of the Depression, and fears that the US – which was not a member of the League – would step in to supply Italy with the goods included in the sanctions, League members did not include a range of vital supplies. These included oil, steel and coal, all of which were necessary for conducting modern warfare. Mussolini later admitted that if full economic sanctions had been applied, it would have halted his invasion within a week.

SOURCE B

Five months before the pretext found in December [1934] in the Wal-Wal incident, Italy had begun the armament of her colonies, armament which since has been intensified and increased by the continuous sending of troops, mechanical equipment and ammunition during the entire duration of the work of the Council of the League of Nations and the work of the arbitration board.

Now that the pretext on which they planned to make war upon us has vanished, Italy, after having obtained from the powers their refusal to permit us to purchase and armaments and ammunition which we do not manufacture and which are necessary to our defence, seeks to discredit the Ethiopian people and their government before world opinion.

They characterize us as a barbarous people whom it is necessary to civilize. The attitude of Italy will be judged by history.

Haile Selassie's appeal, 13 September 1935. Quoted in Copeland, L. 1942. *The World's Great Speeches*. New York. Garden City Publishers. pp. 450–1.

Once the invasion had begun, the League immediately declared Italy to be in breach of Article 12 of the Covenant and, a few days later, declared Italy to be the aggressor. The League then began to consider what sanctions to apply against Italy. On 18 October, the League voted to impose economic sanctions against Italy. However, it took over a month for the members of the League to agree to impose what were very limited sanctions.

In addition, Britain refused to close the Suez Canal to Italian supply ships. Although these were the strongest sanctions the League had ever imposed on another country, their limited nature effectively demonstrated the weaknesses of the League and its irrelevance in solving serious crises. In addition, many non-League members continued to trade with Italy. In fact, as feared by many League members, the US actually greatly increased its exports – including oil – to Italy during the invasion.

SOURCE C

Yes, we know that World War began in Manchuria fifteen years ago. We know that four years later we could easily have stopped Mussolini [over Abyssinia] if we had taken the sanctions against Mussolini that were obviously required, if we had closed the Suez Canal to the aggressor and stopped his oil.

Extract from a speech made by the British diplomat and politician, Philip Noel Baker, to the last session of the League of Nations in April 1946. Quoted in Fellows, N. 2012. *Peacemaking, Peacekeeping: International Relations 1918–36*. Cambridge. Cambridge University Press. p. 195.

7 German and Italian Expansionism, 1933–40

In addition, Britain and France, who were desperate to keep Italy from moving closer to Nazi Germany, began to consider a way of ending the crisis which would satisfy Mussolini. In December 1935, their foreign ministers – Samuel Hoare and Pierre Laval, respectively – secretly drew up what became known as the Hoare-Laval Pact. This would have given Italy over half of Abyssinia, by splitting the more prosperous northern and southern areas away from Abyssinia and awarding them to Italy's existing east African colonies. Mussolini was prepared to accept this – however, details were leaked and led to public outcries in both Britain and France which forced the two countries to drop the plan. This 'behind-the-scenes' action by Britain and France also further undermined the credibility of the League, as it seemed as if aggression was being rewarded rather than being punished.

After the secret Hoare-Laval Pact was dropped, the League – supported by Britain and France – began to take a tougher line. In March 1936, it decided to ban the sale of oil and petrol to Italy. However, this was not fully operable until May 1936. By then, the Italian conquest was virtually complete. In addition, Hitler's re-occupation of the Rhineland in March had made France in particular reluctant to further antagonise Mussolini. Despite these concerns, British and French reactions to the invasion had succeeded both in finally alienating Mussolini (and so destroying the Stresa Front), and in discrediting the idea of collective security and the League itself which, in July 1936, finally ended all sanctions against Italy. To powerful states, intent on following aggressive and expansionist foreign policies, it seemed clear that the League could be ignored with impunity. Significantly, all future European crises would be dealt with outside the structures of the League.

SOURCE D

The real death of the League was in December 1935, not in 1939 or 1945. One day it was a powerful body imposing sanctions, seemingly more effective than ever before; the next day it was an empty sham, everyone scuttling from it as quickly as possible. What killed the League was the publication of the Hoare-Laval plan. Yet this was a perfectly sensible plan, in line with the League's previous acts of conciliation from Corfu to Manchuria. It would have ended the war; satisfied Italy; and left Abyssinia with a more workable, national territory.... For the League action against Italy was not a common sense extension of practical policies; .... No concrete 'interest' was at stake in Abyssinia – not even for Italy; Mussolini was concerned to show off Italy's strength, not to acquire the practical gains (if any such exist) of Empire.

Taylor, A. J. P. 1963. *The Origins of the Second World War*. Harmondsworth. Penguin Books. p. 128.

Italy, Spain and the Rome-Berlin Axis

One of the results of the League's ineffectiveness over Abyssinia was to convince Mussolini that leaving the orbit of Britain and France and, instead, joining up with Nazi Germany would be in Italy's interests. Consequently, in the summer of 1936, with the war in Abyssinia over, Mussolini was easily persuaded by Hitler to join Nazi Germany in aiding the nationalists in the Spanish Civil War. Their cooperation in this – and the weakness of Britain and France's Non-Intervention Committee – resulted in the Rome-Berlin Axis of October 1936. The ways in which both Britain and France had reacted to aggression in the period 1931–36 had resulted in Fascist Italy being now clearly allied with Nazi Germany. Both of these countries had plans for expansion which were increasingly put into effect in the years after 1936. However, as far as Italy was concerned, the next attempts at territorial expansion did not come until 1939.

Figure 7.8 Mussolini and Hitler photographed after the signing of the Rome-Berlin Axis in October 1936

7.3 What was the international response to German and Italian aggression in 1939?

Between 1935 and 1938, the reactions of Britain and France to German and Italian aggression and expansion had resulted in the League of Nations being totally undermined as, very often, the public statements of these two countries had been shown to be at odds with what they were doing behind the scenes. In particular, this period saw Britain increasingly following a foreign policy known as appeasement. Though this had begun as early as 1935, it is particularly associated with Neville Chamberlain, who became British prime minister in 1937. With the League effectively defunct by then, this policy was to become the dominant international reaction to expansionism in 1939.

The final steps

During 1939, although many believed war was now inevitable, it is possible to argue that a general war might still have been avoided – if there had been different international responses to the events which took place in the spring of 1939.

German invasion of Czechoslovakia, March 1939

Despite having pledged at Munich, in September 1939, that he had no more territorial demands – and even making vague promises to leave the rest of Czechoslovakia alone,

7 German and Italian Expansionism, 1933–40

Hitler waited only six months before breaking all his promises and invading the rest of Czechoslovakia in March 1939. As in previous crises, Britain and France took no action to stop this – although France was put on a war footing. By then, several things were clear: the League and its idea of 'collective security' were both finished, while the policy of appeasement had clearly failed.

Italian invasion of Albania, April 1939

Mussolini was quick to take advantage of Germany's unopposed success in Czechoslovakia. Less than a month later, Italian troops had overrun Albania. As with Germany's invasion of Czechoslovakia, Britain and France once again took no direct action against Italy.

The League and the Soviet Union

The many instances of the League's – and its most important members' – inaction in the face of aggression and expansion by Germany and Italy in the period 1938–39 had an important effect on Soviet foreign policy. Soviet foreign policy underwent a significant change in this period, which was one of the crucial factors in the final steps to what soon became an extremely destructive global war.

Evidence released since the collapse of the Soviet Union in 1991 suggests that a military alliance with Britain and France was Stalin's favoured option. This was the policy which was pursued by Litvinov, the Soviet commissar for foreign affairs, in the years up to 1939. Litvinov believed that these two countries could be persuaded to defend collective security by joining with the USSR in an alliance to block Nazi Germany's expansionist aims. However, Stalin was also increasingly drawn to those officials – such as Molotov – who advised him that Britain and France would never join the Soviet Union in any alliance. As Britain and France continued with their policy of appeasement, Stalin began to see a temporary agreement with Hitler might be a way of at least postponing a war with Germany. To Stalin, this alternative seemed increasingly more realistic after the Munich Conference of September 1938. In May 1939, he thus replaced Litvinov with Molotov, who was then instructed to pursue a new diplomatic policy.

The US and the League

As well as the Soviet Union's role, US reactions to Germany and Italy's expansionist policies in the period 1933–39 were also important. After the First World War, the US had followed a policy of isolationism and neutrality – though, as has been seen, this was mainly in relation to Europe. This policy continued through the early 1930s, under the presidency of Franklin D. Roosevelt – despite the growing tensions resulting from Germany's expansionist foreign policy in the years before 1936. The US ambassador in London in 1938, **Joseph Kennedy**, supported Britain's policy of appeasing Nazi Germany, and was strongly opposed to the idea of any alliance with the Soviet Union. Instead, he tended to support the views of US 'hardliners' such as George Kennan and the **'Riga Axiomists'**.

Kennan's ideas and advice would later play an important part in the early stages of the Cold War which began almost immediately after the end of the Second World War in 1945.

However, Kennedy's views were opposed by Joseph Davies, the US ambassador in Moscow from 1937 to 1938, who believed the USSR was genuinely interested in cooperation in order to stabilise Europe against Nazi aggression.

This US policy meant, for most of the 1930s, Britain and France felt they would be on their own in the event of another war with Germany; while Nazi Germany was

---

Historical debate:
Historians remain divided as to the real aims and motives of Soviet Union foreign policy in the 1930s. Beginning with A. J. P. Taylor's *The Origins of the Second World War*, many have argued that Stalin's policy, as pursued by Litvinov, was genuine. Opposed to this view are those historians who argue that Stalin's approach to the West was a screen behind which the Soviet Union followed its main policy of maintaining the close links with Germany established in 1922 by the Treaty of Rapallo. These 'Germanist' historians believe negotiations with the West were just ploys to put pressure on Nazi Germany to sign an agreement with the USSR. A third group of historians, however, stress the importance of 'internal politics' in understanding the two different strands of foreign policy pursued by Stalin from 1933–39. They have pointed out the genuine policy differences which existed between the pro-western Litvinov (his wife was English) and Molotov, who placed his faith in the independent strength of the Soviet Union; and the fact that Stalin wavered between these two options.

International Responses to German and Italian Expansionism

confident that there would be no US involvement as in 1917, should war break out again in Europe. Eventually, though, Roosevelt came to the view that Nazi Germany was more expansionist than the Soviet Union: he gave diplomatic recognition to the Soviet Union in 1933 and, in the late 1930s, US foreign policy began to change. By then, however, the Soviet Union had despaired of obtaining an alliance with the West, while Hitler was convinced his expansionist plans would not be opposed by any major state.

Appeasement and the road to war

Despite the roles of the US and the Soviet Union, the policy of appeasement, pursued by Britain and France from the mid-1930s, is often seen as the international 'response' which was most responsible for leading Europe and the rest of the world into another global war.

Reasons for appeasement

Despite the aims of Chamberlain's policy of appeasement, the years after 1937 saw Hitler taking an increasingly aggressive approach to foreign policy objectives. For decades, this appeasement policy has been criticised for being short-sighted and an encouragement to Hitler to continue his aggressive policies, and so a significant contribution to the outbreak of the Second World War. Yet many contemporaries saw it as the only practical policy for averting another war.

Some contemporaries, such as Churchill, advocated an alternative policy of forming a grand anti-fascist alliance. However, the only significant European power capable of resisting Nazi Germany was the Soviet Union. Many western politicians rejected Stalin's Russia as a potential ally – partly because it was going through the turmoil of the 'Great Purges', which saw Stalin execute large numbers of suspected rivals – including many of the officers in the Soviet Union's armed forces. This seriously affected the capability of the Soviet Red Army in the short term; in addition, many western politicians feared the Soviet Union because of its stated commitment to communism and world revolution. Chamberlain was not alone in being extremely anti-communist.

> **SOURCE E**
>
> I must confess to a most profound distrust of Russia. I have no belief whatever in her ability to maintain an effective offensive, even if she wanted to. And I distrust her motives which seem to me to have little connection with our ideas of liberty, and to be concerned only with getting everyone by the ears. Moreover, she is both hated and suspected by the smaller states, notably, Poland, Rumania and Finland.
>
> An extract from Chamberlain's diary entry for 26 March 1939. Quoted in Feiling, K. 1946. *The Life of Neville Chamberlain*, London. Macmillan. p. 403.

Another alternative – reviving the collective security role of the League of Nations – seemed totally unrealistic, given the League's failure to act effectively in the years since 1929 and, since 1937, the non-membership of Germany, Italy and Japan; as well as the continued non-membership of the USA. Thus, by 1937, the League was weak and extremely discredited. Many British politicians therefore saw only France as a possible ally – yet this was not very feasible either: the Stresa Front had collapsed, Germany was openly ignoring Versailles and the Treaty of Locarno, and it now seemed likely that, because of German and Italian help, a pro-Axis Spanish state would soon be in existence on France's southern borders.

Joseph Kennedy (1888–1969)

He was a wealthy businessman and politician, who, from 1938 to 1940, was the US ambassador in Britain. He was right-wing and strongly anti-communist, and so opposed democracies joining in an alliance with the Soviet Union. He was a strong supporter of the right-wing nationalist forces in the Spanish Civil War, and held anti-Semitic views. He unsuccessfully tried to arrange unofficial meetings with Hitler – even after war had begun – in order to effect a 'better understanding' between the US and Nazi Germany. He was the father of J. F. Kennedy, who was US president from 1961 to 1963.

Riga Axiomists: Since the Bolshevik Revolution, the US had followed a foreign policy of outright opposition to Soviet Russia. US troops had intervened in the Russian Civil War, on the side of the Whites; and had then initially followed an anti-Soviet policy of economic boycott. They had quickly formed the Division of Russian Affairs (DRA) which was at first based in Riga, in Latvia. It was headed by Charles Bohlen and George Kennan who, influenced by White Russian exiles, drew up a set of conclusions – the 'Riga Axioms' – about Soviet intentions. These claimed that the USSR was intent on world domination, and their views helped shape US policy during the 1930s.

7 German and Italian Expansionism, 1933–40

More importantly, Chamberlain was informed by military advisers that British armed forces were in no state in 1937 to give effective military support to France, or even to defend British cities from air-raids. In addition, he was told that the British Navy could not give effective protection to British colonies in the Far East, in view of Japan's expanding military strength. Furthermore, the majority of British citizens were opposed to Britain re-arming, and many believed that some revision of the peace settlements was legitimate. Those who, like Chamberlain, had lived through the horrors of the First World War, did not want to risk another war.

SOURCE F

Country	January 1938	August 1939
Germany	81	130
Great Britain	2	4
France	63	86
Italy	73	73
Soviet Union	125	125
Czechoslovakia	34	0
Poland	40	40

Army strength (fully equipped army divisions)

Country	January 1938	August 1939
Germany	1,820	4,210
Great Britain	1,050	1,750
France	1,195	1,234
Italy	1,301	1,531
Soviet Union	3,050	3,361
Czechoslovakia	600	0
Poland	500	500

Air force strength (number of available aircraft)
Military strength of the European powers, 1938–39.

SOURCE G

It is our opinion that no pressure that Great Britain and France can bring to bear, either by sea, on land, or in the air, could prevent Germany from overrunning Bohemia and from inflicting a decisive defeat on Czechoslovakia. The restoration of Czechoslovakia's lost integrity could only be achieved by the defeat of Germany and as the outcome, which from the outset must assume the character of an unlimited war.

The intervention of Italy and/ or Japan on the side of Germany would create a situation which the Chiefs of Staff in the *'Mediterranean and Middle East Appreciation'* described in the following language: 'Moreover, war against Japan, Germany and Italy simultaneously in 1938 is a commitment which neither the present nor the projected strength of our defence forces is designed to meet, even if we were in alliance with France and Russia, and which would, therefore, place a dangerous strain on the resources of the [British] Empire …'

Extracts from Chiefs of Staff Report: 'Appreciation of the Situation in the Event of War against Germany', 14 September 1938. Quoted in Dickenson, M. 2009. *Historical Controversies and Historical Significance*. Harlow. Heinemann. p. 71.

> **QUESTION**
> How far do sources F and G explain why Chamberlain persisted with his policy of appeasement?

Consequently, most British government ministers supported Chamberlain's policy of appeasement, designed to avoid war by negotiating mutually-acceptable revisions of the Treaty of Versailles. In November 1937, Lord Halifax was sent to Germany to meet Nazi officials and to tell them that Britain would support legitimate German claims in Europe, provided they were negotiated peacefully. However, Eden, the Foreign Secretary, objected to this, and later resigned.

Appeasement and the historical debate

There has been considerable debate about appeasement and the role of Chamberlain. The earliest classic or 'orthodox' view was offered as early as 1940, when 'Cato' (a collective pseudonym for several left-wing critics of appeasement) published their *Guilty Men* booklet. It condemned Chamberlain as a 'guilty man', and portrayed appeasement as a shameful combination of deliberate deception of British public opinion, incompetent leadership and diplomacy, and extremely poor military planning. One of the first post-war historical studies of appeasement appeared in 1948, when J. Wheeler-Bennett judged Chamberlain as a leader whose appeasement policy was morally bankrupt and politically ineffective – this was essentially the stance of most historians from the late 1940s. Then, in the 1950s and 1960s, several memoirs from contemporary British politicians, diplomats and officials – such as Winston Churchill and Anthony Eden – seemed to support such a view.

However, from the late 1960s, various 'revisionist' historians, such as D. Dilks, M. Cowling and J. Charmley, portrayed Chamberlain as having a good grasp of Britain's economic and military weaknesses, and trying to maintain peace while preparing for war, whereas K. Feiling, amongst others, focused on Chamberlain's doubts about the USSR as a potential ally. Instead of seeing Chamberlain as a 'guilty man', they depicted the policy of appeasement as a realistic way of dealing with the situation in the period 1937 to early 1939 – in particular, because of Britain and France's inability to fight a war in Europe with any realistic chance of success. These revisionist historians based their arguments on the structural problems facing Britain in the late 1930s; the threat posed by Japanese expansion in Asia, which occurred at the same time as Hitler and Mussolini were becoming increasingly aggressive; the strength of public opinion against re-armament; and documents, relating to the late 1930s, which had become available from 1967, under the thirty-year rule. All this, they argued, showed that the British government did not have any choice but to pursue appeasement.

> **KEY CONCEPTS ACTIVITY**
>
> **Significance:** How important do you think the results of this opinion poll are in explaining the foreign policy pursued by Britain in the late 1930s?

SOURCE H

Question 2: Are you in favour of an all-round reduction of armaments by international agreement?

Yes: 10,058,026 votes

No: 815,365 votes

Votes in favour as a percentage of all answers (Yes, No, Doubtful, Abstentions): 90.7

Published by the League of Nations Union, 1935

Results of the 'Peace Ballot', 1934. Quoted in Dickenson, M. 2009. *Historical Controversies and Historical Significance*. Harlow. Heinemann. p. 70.

German and Italian Expansionism, 1933–40

These views came under attack by post-revisionists, who argued that one of the main weaknesses of revisionist interpretations was that they had placed too much reliance on official documents, which had been drafted, collected and selected by the supporters of appeasement. In addition, with the exception of Cowling, revisionist interpretations had tended to ignore alternative policies, and had overlooked intelligence reports which warned Chamberlain and the British Foreign Office of Hitler's intention to dominate Europe by the use of military means. K. Middlemas and R. A. C. Parker, for example, see Chamberlain as persisting in a misguided policy, deliberately misleading public opinion and ignoring or rejecting viable alternatives. Some – such as A. Adamthwaite – see the decision not to seriously consider a 'Grand Alliance' with the USSR (which even Churchill, a strong anti-communist, suggested to counter the growing threat from Nazi Germany) until it was too late, as part of the elite's ingrained hostility to communism.

SOURCE I

It has become almost axiomatic in assessments of British and French leaders to see them as realistic statesmen, oppressed by the knowledge of their countries' weaknesses and the strengths of potential enemies. The uncritical premise of these assessments is that the policy pursued was the only practicable one at the time. In fact there were many variables, and ministerial appraisals were the product of prejudice and opinion …

The feebleness and timidity of British and French foreign policies in the late 1930s were symptomatic of the shortsighted selfishness of a ruling class set on self-preservation.

Adamthwaite, A. 1977. *The Making of the Second World War*. London. Allen & Unwin. p. 95.

Later views have accepted the validity of some of the structural constraints on Chamberlain; while R. J. Overy and others have argued that when the circumstances changed, so did Chamberlain's policy. For instance, pointing out that when the international circumstances changed concerning the possibility of allies, Chamberlain dropped appeasement.

SOURCE J

Throughout 1939 Hitler entirely misread western intentions. After Munich, Britain and France rallied at last to the armed defence of the status quo. Both states speeded up military preparations, until by the summer their combined aircraft and tank production exceeded Germany's. There developed a popular nationalist revival which turned public opinion in both states strongly against Germany and in favour of firmer action. In the summer of 1939, 87% of Britons and 76% of Frenchmen, subjects of earlier opinion polling, recorded a firm commitment to fight if Germany invaded Poland and seized Danzig. Hitlerism was now regarded as a profound threat to the survival of western values and interests, and Poland was chosen as an issue not for its own sake, but to demonstrate to Hitler the west's determination to defend those interests when threatened. Their empires rallied to the cause too. Canada abandoned neutrality; Australia and New Zealand pledged support; colonial armies were raised in French North Africa, India and Indo-China. Even neutral America began to give encouragement to the western cause, though Roosevelt was too wary of isolationist opinion to commit the United States to a more active or military policy.

Overy, R. 1994. *The Inter-War Crisis 1919–1939*. Harlow. Longman. p. 89.

Such arguments, though, have been criticised on the grounds that the delay in declaring war on Germany after its invasion of Poland showed that Chamberlain was still looking for Polish 'Munich' in order to keep Britain out of a new war. Furthermore, the 'phoney war' is taken to show that, even after the declaration of war in 1939, Chamberlain was still attempting to keep appeasement alive.

At the time, however, many believed that Chamberlain's policy of appeasement had peacefully revised an unfairness of the 1919–20 peace settlements – and Chamberlain was nominated for the 1938 Noble Peace Prize. However, in November 1938, the anti-Jewish violence of the event known as *Kristallnacht* added to growing concern over Hitler's real intentions (intelligence reports suggested a possible invasion of the Netherlands) so, in February 1939, Britain promised to support France. Britain then began to create a large British Expeditionary Force and discussions took place between British and French military leaders. Thus, by the end of the 1930s, Britain and France were beginning to shape a different response to German and Italian expansionism.

Activities

1 Write a newspaper article which summarises the strengths and weaknesses of the Stresa Front; and, in your final paragraph, explain which one factor you consider was most significant in its break-up.

2 Draw up a summary chart, with Britain on the left-hand side, and France on the right, showing their different foreign policy concerns and aims in the 1930s.

3 Find out more about Britain's attitude to forming an alliance with the Soviet Union to oppose Germany's expansionist foreign policy. Then write a couple of paragraphs to show how significant this was as a far in the eventual outbreak of war in 1939.

4 'Change or continuity?' Write a couple of paragraphs to argue which of those two key concept terms you think most accurately applies to the British policy of appeasement in the 1930s.

7 End of chapter activities

Summary

You should now have a good understanding of how Britain and France – and other countries responded to the expansionist foreign policies pursued by Germany and Italy in the 1930s.

You should also be able to explain the reasons for the various responses and inactions – and why appeasement increasingly came to the fore.

Finally, you should be able to understand why Germany and Italy interpreted those responses – or lack of responses – as indicating that Britain and France would never oppose their expansionist policies.

Summary activities

There has been much historical debate about why Britain and France did little to oppose the increasingly expansionist foreign policies pursued by Germany and Italy in the 1930s. There has also been much debate about the role of appeasement in the eventual outbreak of war in September 1939.

Copy the diagram below and, under each heading, try to summarise the main historical viewpoints and arguments – and, where possible, try to include names of specific historians.

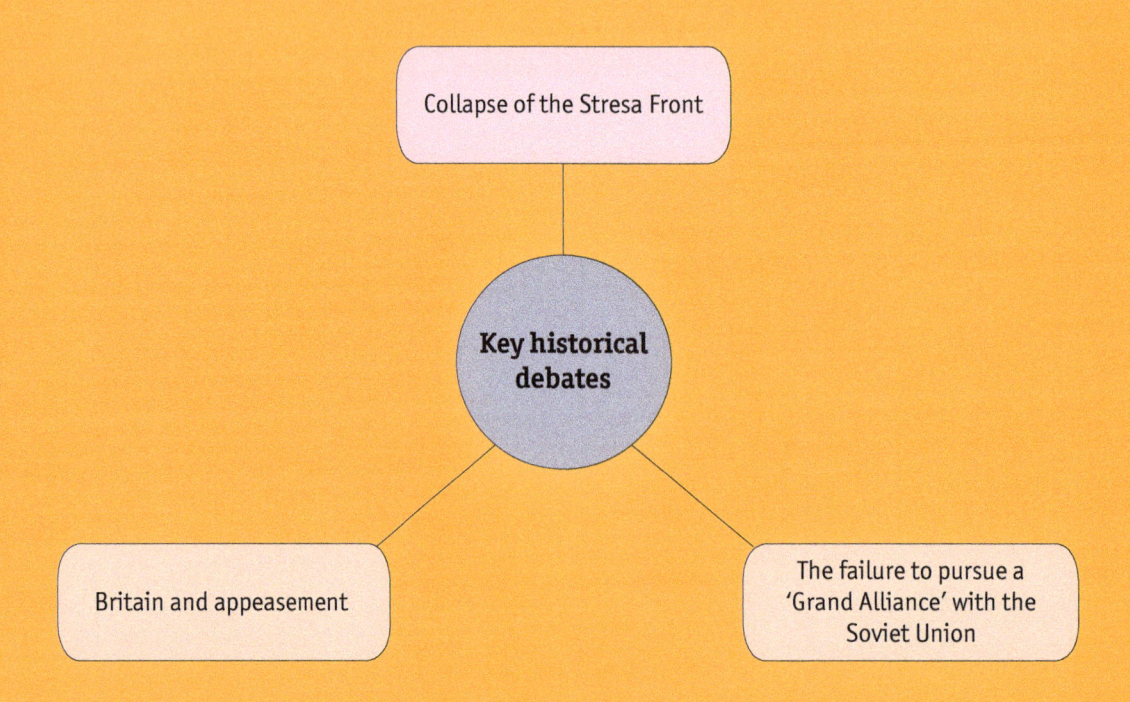

- Collapse of the Stresa Front
- **Key historical debates**
- Britain and appeasement
- The failure to pursue a 'Grand Alliance' with the Soviet Union

Paper 1 exam practice

Question

> **SOURCE A**
>
> Yes, we know that World War began in Manchuria fifteen years ago. We know that four years later we could easily have stopped Mussolini [over Abyssinia] if we had taken the sanctions against Mussolini that were obviously required, if we had closed the Suez Canal to the aggressor and stopped his oil.
>
> Extract from a speech made by the British diplomat and politician, Philip Noel Baker, to the last session of the League of Nations in April 1946. Quoted in Fellows, N. 2012. *Peacemaking, Peacekeeping: International Relations 1918–36*. Cambridge. Cambridge University Press. p. 195.

> **SOURCE B**
>
> It has become almost axiomatic in assessments of British and French leaders to see them as realistic statesmen, oppressed by the knowledge of their countries' weaknesses and the strengths of potential enemies. The uncritical premise of these assessments is that the policy pursued was the only practicable one at the time. In fact there were many variables, and ministerial appraisals were the product of prejudice and opinion …
>
> The feebleness and timidity of British and French foreign policies in the late 1930s were symptomatic of the shortsighted selfishness of a ruling class set on self-preservation.
>
> Adamthwaite, A. 1977. *The Making of the Second World War*. London. Allen & Unwin. p. 95.

Compare and contrast the views expressed in Sources A and B about the wisdom of British and French foreign policies during the period 1935–39. **[6 marks]**

Skill

Cross-referencing of two sources

Before you start

Cross-referencing questions require you to compare **and** contrast the information/content/nature of **two** sources.

Before you attempt this question, refer to Chapter 9 for advice on how to tackle these questions, and a simplified mark scheme.

Student answer

Sources A and B both seem to agree that the policies followed by Britain and France were mistaken. Source A, written in 1946, states that the Second World War really began 'in Manchuria fifteen years ago' and that, in 1935, Britain and France 'could easily have stopped Mussolini' if they 'had taken the sanctions against Mussolini that were obviously required'. The view of this source is clearly that the foreign policy Britain and France adopted was inadequate.

The view of Source A is supported by the view given in Source B, which refers to the 'feebleness and timidity of British and French foreign policies in the late 1930s'. According to this source, the actions of Britain and France were the result of 'the shortsighted selfishness of a ruling class set on self-preservation'. They thus both agree that the policies pursued by Britain and France were not wise.

Examiner comments

There are clear/precise references to both sources, and a clear similarity/comparison is identified. Also, the sources are clearly linked, rather than being dealt with separately. The candidate has thus done enough to get into Band 2, and so be awarded 4 or 5 marks. However, as no differences/contrasts are made, this answer fails to get into Band 1.

Activity

Look again at the two sources, the simplified mark scheme, and the student answer above. Now try to write a paragraph or two to push the answer up into Band 1, and so obtain the full 6 marks.

Paper 2 practice questions

1. Evaluate the significance of the response of Britain and France to Nazi Germany's re-occupation of the Rhineland in 1936.
2. 'The main reason for Britain and France's non-intervention policy during the Spanish Civil War was fear of a socialist revolution in Spain.' To what extent do you agree with this statement?
3. Compare and contrast the reactions of the Soviet Union and the US to Italian and German expansionism between 1935 and 1939.
4. Examine the most significant consequences of Germany's invasion of Czechoslovakia in March 1939.

The Final Steps to Global War, 1939–41

8

Nazi Germany's invasion of Poland

Soon after the Munich Conference, Germany had begun to request the return of Danzig (run by the League of Nations as an International Free City), and the building of road and rail links across the Polish Corridor to East Prussia. Once Czechoslovakia and then Memel had been taken in March 1939, it became clear to most people that Poland was Hitler's next target. As a result, by the end of March 1939, both Britain and France had made a significant policy change, and had guaranteed to protect Polish independence (similar promises were made to Greece, following Italy's invasion of Albania in April 1939). Hitler, however, was not convinced these would be acted on – even when the US moved a battle fleet from the Atlantic to the Pacific (allowing British and French fleets to move to the North Sea), or when Britain announced conscription for all males aged 20–21.

Initially, Hitler had intended to invade Poland at the end of August. However, Mussolini warned Hitler that Italy was not yet ready for a serious European war. Instead, he informed Hitler that Italy needed at least three years of peace in order to recover sufficiently from the effects of the Abyssinian and Spanish Wars. Thus Hitler had to postpone the planned attack on Poland. Despite this short delay, on 29 August, Hitler – confident that he would face no serious opposition – 'offered' Poland a choice: dismemberment either by peaceful negotiation, or by war. Poland refused, and on 1 September 1939 Germany invaded Poland.

Figure 8.1 German tanks entering Poland on 1 September 1939

TIMELINE

1939 Sept: Nazi Germany invades Poland: Britain and France declare war on Germany

1940 April: Germany invades Demark and Norway

May: Germany invades the Netherlands, Belgium and France

June: Italy enters the Second World War; France surrenders

Aug: Italy invades British Somaliland

Sept: Italy attacks Egypt

Oct: Italy invades Greece

1941 Apr: Germany invades Greece and Yugoslavia

June: Germany invades the Soviet Union

Dec: Pearl Harbor; US enters the Second World War

193

8 The Final Steps to Global War, 1939–41

> **SOURCE A**
>
> On 23 August Hitler gave instructions for the invasion of Poland to begin at 4.30 a.m. on 26 August. Two things caused him to countermand the order. On 25 August Britain ratified the Anglo–Polish Agreement of 31 March and Mussolini informed Hitler that Italy was not ready to fight. That afternoon Hitler postponed the attack. But on 26 August he again ordered the invasion to take place, this time on 1 September. The intervening delay of five days can be interpreted as a final attempt on Hitler's part either to secure a compromise or to split Britain and France from Poland, or simply as a loss of nerve on Hitler's part. According to A. J. P. Taylor, war broke out because Hitler launched 'on 29 August a diplomatic manoeuvre which he ought to have launched on 28 August' (*Origins of the Second World War*, 1964, p. 336). The manoeuvre in question was an offer on Hitler's part to negotiate directly with the Poles, provided that a plenipotentiary arrived in Berlin within twenty-four hours. The Poles refused to be coerced, and on this occasion neither Britain nor France (unlike the case of Czechoslovakia) were prepared to abandon Poland.
>
> Simpson, W. 1991. *Hitler and Germany*. Cambridge. Cambridge University Press. p. 110.

Fact: Mussolini had boasted that Fascist Italy had enough planes to 'blot out the sun', and 8 million reservists, along with 150 army divisions well-supplied with modern weapons. The reality was that, in September 1939, Italy only had 10 divisions (about 700,000 men) ready to fight. Many troops had no rifles, and the army had less than 100 heavy tanks; while the airforce had no long-range bombers. In addition, the Italian navy – meant to control the Mediterranean – had no aircraft carriers; and, although it had more submarines than Britain, they were mostly inferior.

Alpine War: Even though France was on the verge of total defeat at the hands of the Germans, Italian forces did not do well in the Alpine War – instead, they were forced to withdraw, without any extra territory being obtained. To make matters worse, Hitler (who had expected Italy to attack the British in Malta), refused to let Italy have France's North African colonies – instead, he allowed Vichy France to retain control.

War in Europe

To Hitler's surprise, Britain and France did honour their commitments to Poland and, two days later, on 3 September 1939, Britain and France declared war on Germany. Thus the Second World War had begun – at least as far as Europe was concerned. However, Germany's Four-Year Plan and re-armament programme had still not achieved full economic and military preparedness. Hitler thus found himself facing a war in September 1939 which he had not foreseen, and for which Germany was not fully ready. Evidence suggests that the leading Nazis did not expect Germany's economy and military to be really ready for war until at least 1943.

Nonetheless, for the first eight months, the war – which became known as the 'phoney war' – presented no immediate problems for Nazi Germany on its western borders as, despite declaring war on Germany, Britain and France took no action. While, in the east, Germany's army was able to grab 'Germany's share' of Poland after only three weeks of devastating *Blitzkrieg*. On 17 September, Stalin – further convinced by the 'phoney war' that Britain and France would never act against Nazi Germany – ordered the Red Army to takeover the 'Soviet half' of Poland.

Mussolini had been taken by surprise when Hitler invaded Poland. Despite Mussolini's boasting about Fascist Italy's military strength, and the various agreements signed between Germany and Italy from 1936 to 1939, Mussolini did not join Hitler in his attack on Poland. In part, this was because the Italian commission on war production warned Mussolini that Italy would not be ready to wage war until 1949! So, instead, he demanded that Germany give Italy huge supplies of strategic resources. When these were not given, Mussolini said that Italy could not participate in the war – but that it would send agricultural and industrial labourers to Germany. Italy did not finally enter the war until 10 June 1940, when it declared war on France – Italian troops were sent into France, in order to seize land along the French Riviera, in what became known as the **Alpine War**.

By then, Hitler had already launched a successful *Blitzkrieg* on Germany's western frontiers, with the aim of conquering France and so leaving Britain with no choice but to agree to further German expansion in the east, and to accept German hegemony in continental Europe. Although some of his military commanders were reluctant, Hitler ordered attacks against several west European states in April and May 1940. Within three months, Denmark, Norway, the Netherlands and Belgium had been invaded and occupied. While, by the end of June 1940, France too had been defeated and partially occupied.

Global War

However, the Second World War was still essentially a European war until August 1940, when it spread to Africa. In that month, Mussolini – thinking that Britain was near defeat – decided to invade British Somaliland. The following month, Italian forces attacked British-controlled Egypt. Back in Europe, in October 1940, Mussolini ordered the invasion of Greece – in part, to block German influence in the Balkans (that same month, Germany had sent troops into Romania which, in July 1940, had become an ally of Nazi Germany). However, determined Greek resistance meant that this war, too, went badly for Italy.

The Italian war effort continued to go badly and, in April 1941, Nazi Germany invaded both Greece and Yugoslavia – partly in order to help Italian forces.

It became even more of a truly 'world war' in the second half of 1941 when, as well as Germany invading the Soviet Union, Japan attacked the US naval base in Pearl Harbor. Once the US had declared war on Japan in December 1941, Hitler declared war on the US. This was despite the fact that, after early successes, Nazi Germany's invasion of the Soviet Union – which had begun in June 1941 – was already running into serious problems. As a consequence, Germany – having failed to defeat Britain – was faced with a war on two fronts: just as it had in the First World War. Despite doing so badly in the war, Mussolini decided to join in the invasion of the Soviet Union – sending troops and equipment that Italy could ill afford.

While 1941 is thus often seen as the date when the Second World War began in earnest, for many countries in Asia and the Pacific, war – i.e. the early stages of the Asian–Pacific War – had been going on for a whole decade before 1941.

Who was to blame?

Much of the post-war historical debate about the responsibility for the Second World War had centred on the roles of the League of Nations, the appeasement policy followed by countries such as Britain and France, the foreign policy of the Soviet Union, and the isolationist stance of the US. However, another crucial factor to be considered is the extent to which imperial Japan, Nazi Germany and Fascist Italy can be blamed. As regards Nazi Germany in particular, there has been considerable debate, with some historians claiming that Hitler had deliberately planned this war, even before he came to power in 1933.

There was certainly a widespread belief that after 1933 he followed some *Stufenplan* (or master plan) which he consistently pursued up to and beyond the start of the war.

Fact: In 1940, Italy suffered defeats in Egypt; and, in 1941, also lost control of the Mediterranean, following defeats at the hands of the British navy. In 1942, it was driven out of Italian East Africa, and only managed to hang on to Libya because of German assistance.

Fact: Nazi Germany's invasion of the Soviet Union – code-named 'Operation Barbarossa' – had originally been planned for the spring of 1941, but was delayed until June because Germany had to divert troops to North Africa, Greece and the Balkans in order to assist the Italian forces which were encountering serious problems in those theatres of war.

Fact: Mussolini's decision to join in the invasion of the Soviet Union was, in part, because Mussolini feared that his forces' poor performances would lead Hitler to refuse to honour earlier agreements about spheres of influence.

Fact: The view that Hitler had deliberately planned the Second World War is a view that is, in part, based on a study of Hitler's book, *Mein Kampf*; and was one of the assumptions behind the Nuremberg war trials that followed the end of the Second World War.

8 The Final Steps to Global War, 1939–41

Figure 8.2 Italian troops trying to take a Greek village, where they encountered fierce resistance

Initially, most historians shared such a view, pointing out how Hitler began attempts to drive wedges between Poland and France, and between Italy and its Stresa Front partners, Britain and France. As early as 1934, H. Trevor-Roper, for instance, argued that Hitler had systematically followed a foreign policy which, step by step, was designed to achieve his long-term aims. The examination of specific crises tended to confirm this view: during the Czech Crisis in 1938, for instance, Hitler had set a date for the invasion (1 October) as early as May 1938. Similarly, once the whole of Czechoslovakia had been invaded, and Memel taken from Lithuania, Hitler then set 1 September 1939 as the date for the invasion of Poland – *before* he had secured the Non-Aggression Pact with the Soviet Union.

However, this 'orthodox' view – usually known as the intentionalist school – was first strongly criticised by the historian A. J. P. Taylor in *The Origins of the Second World War*, published in 1961. His claims that Hitler had *not* followed a pre-determined master plan for war, and his questioning of the reliability of the Hossbach Memorandum as historical evidence, provoked heated historical debate. Taylor argued that Hitler's foreign policy was essentially improvised and based on simply making the most of opportunities when they arose. The furious historical arguments which this 'opportunist' or 'structuralist' position unleashed led Taylor to issue a foreword to a second edition of Origins in 1963, entitled 'Second Thoughts' – in part, to reject claims that his book somehow 'vindicated Hitler'. He stressed that simply directing 'his generals to prepare for war' did not mean that Hitler was actively intending to start a war. He pointed out that from 1935 British and French governments also directed their generals to prepare for a possible war. Taylor's argument was that such plans 'were precautions, not "blueprints for aggression"'. Taylor also stressed how Hitler's desire to overturn the Treaty of Versailles and also to restore German greatness was an aim 'shared by all German politicians, by the Social democrats who ended the war in 1918 as much as by Stresemann'. Taylor also claimed that German rearmament after 1936 was not as great as Hitler claimed, to the extent that by 1939, Germany's armed forces were not strong enough to sustain a world – or even a European – war.

Since then, the debate has continued, with historians divided into two broad schools of thought: the 'Orthodox/Intentionalist' school, and the 'Revisionist/Structuralist' school. The former – including historians such as H. Trevor-Roper, A. Bullock, A. Hillgruber and K. Hildebrand – have argued that Hitler had deliberately planned for such a war – even before he came to power – and that he had some programme which he consistently pursued. Such historians have pointed to his statements in *Mein Kampf*, and to the Hossbach Memorandum. However, Intentionalists are themselves divided, with 'globalists' arguing that he aimed for world domination, while 'continentalists' see his aim as being restricted to *European* hegemony.

Revisionist/Structuralist historians – such as A. J. P. Taylor, K. D. Bracher, M. Broszat and T. Mason – have criticised these 'Intentionalist' views. Later historians have also pointed out how Hitler's foreign policy was at times a response to internal economic problems, as well as external opportunities.

The Second World War after 1941

Once Japan had attacked the US in December 1941, the Second World War became a truly global struggle: linking the European, Asian, American and African sectors of war, and thus spreading to affect people in all the world's continents.

At first, the Axis powers achieved rapid victories but, after Hitler's decision to invade the Soviet Union in June 1941, Germany began to suffer a series of setbacks and defeats – mainly at the hands of the Soviet Union. In June 1944, the Western Allies invaded mainland Europe and, as Germany was invaded by the Soviet Union's Red Army from the east, and by British and US troops from the west, Hitler committed suicide. On 8 May, the war in Europe came to an end. However, the war continued for eight more months in the Pacific, until the dropping of US atomic bombs on Japan in August 1945. The Second World War turned out to be the most destructive war in

8 The Final Steps to Global War, 1939–41

Fact: In reality, while the USA's great economic and military strength ensured it was a world superpower, the Soviet Union – which, for most of the Cold War, lacked any credible allies either in or outside Europe – was more of a regional superpower in Europe, rather than a truly global superpower.

history; with over 80 million deaths for war and war-related disease and famine. Of these deaths, over 50 million were of civilians.

After 1945, the rapidly-emerging tensions between the US and the Soviet Union saw the world enter a long period of nuclear arms races and the Cold War. While no direct 'hot war' broke out between these two superpowers, all the regions of the world experienced crises and/or local wars. It was not really until the collapse of the Soviet Union at the end of 1991 that the Cold War finally came to an end.

Exam Practice

Introduction

You have now completed your study of the main aspects and events of *The Move to Global War* – in relation to Japan's actions, and to those of Italy and Germany. In the previous chapters, you have had practice at answering some of the types of source-based questions you will have to deal with in Paper 1. In this chapter, you will gain experience of dealing with:

- the longer Paper 1 question, which requires you to use both sources and your own knowledge to write a mini-essay
- the essay questions you will meet in Paper 2.

Exam skills needed for IB History

This book is designed primarily to prepare both Standard and Higher Level students for the Paper I *The Move to Global War* topic (Prescribed Subject 3), by providing the necessary historical knowledge and understanding, as well as an awareness of the key historical debates and perspectives. However it will also help you prepare for Paper 2, by giving you the chance to practise writing essays. The skills you need for answering both Paper 1 and Paper 2 exam questions are explained in the following sections.

Paper 1 exam practice

Paper 1 skills

This section of the book is designed to give you the skills and understanding to tackle Paper 1 questions. These are based on the comprehension, critical analysis and evaluation of different types of historical sources as evidence, along with the use of appropriate historical contextual knowledge.

For example, you will need to test sources for value and limitations (i.e. their reliability and utility, especially in view of their origin, purpose and content) – a skill essential for historians. A range of sources has been provided, including extracts from official documents, tables of statistics, memoirs and speeches, as well as visual sources such as photographs and cartoons.

9 Exam Practice

In order to analyse and evaluate sources as historical evidence, you will need to ask the following **'W' questions** of historical sources:

- **Who** produced it? Were they in a position to know?
- **What** type of source is it? What is its nature – is it a primary or secondary source?
- **Where** and **when** was it produced? What was happening at the time?
- **Why** was it produced? Was its purpose to inform or to persuade? Is it an accurate attempt to record facts, or is it an example of propaganda?
- **Who** was the intended audience – decision-makers, or the general public?

You should then consider how the answers to these questions affect a source's value.

The example below shows you how to find the information related to the 'W' questions. You will need this information in order to evaluate sources for their value and limitations.

Comments WHAT? (type of source)

Shidehara Kijuro WHO? (produced it)

1931 WHEN? (date/ time of production)

setting out his views WHY? (possible purpose)

Chinese diplomat Ch'en Yu-jen WHO? (intended audience)

> **SOURCE A**
>
> Chinese seem to think Manchuria is part of China but it used to be Russian. There is no doubt that if the situation had been left alone, Manchuria would soon have ceased to be under Ch'ing authority. The only reason the Manchu regime was able to hold this vast fertile region was a Japanese military presence. Since the Russo-Japanese War, Manchuria has enjoyed peace and prosperity unparalleled in any other Chinese area. Japanese are convinced that the development of the northeast region is at least partly due to our businesses and investment there.
>
> **Comments** made by **Shidehara Kijuro**, in a meeting with the **Chinese diplomat Ch'en Yu-jen** in **1931**, **setting out his views** concerning Japanese influence in Manchuria. These comments were made a month before the Manchurian Incident; at the time, Shidehara was Japan's foreign minister and did not support an expansionist foreign policy.

This approach will help you become familiar with interpreting, understanding, analysing and evaluating different types of historical sources. It will also aid you in synthesising critical analysis of sources with historical knowledge when constructing an explanation or analysis of some aspect or development of the past. Remember – for Paper 1, as for Paper 2, you need to acquire, select and deploy relevant historical knowledge to explain causes and consequences, continuity and change. You also need to develop and show (where relevant) an awareness of historical debates, and different perspectives and interpretations.

Paper 1 contains four types of question:

1. Comprehension/understanding of a source (2 or 3 marks)
2. Assessing the value and limitations of a source (4 marks)

3   Cross-referencing/comparing or contrasting two sources   (6 marks)
4   Using and evaluating sources and knowledge to reach a judgement (9 marks)

Comprehension/understanding of a source

Comprehension questions require you to understand a source and either extract two or three relevant points that relate to the particular question, or make one or two comments about the message of a source.

Examiner's tips

Step 1: Read the source and highlight/underline key points.

Step 2: Write a concise answer. Just a couple of brief sentences are needed, giving the information necessary to show that you have understood the message of the source – but make sure you make three clear points for a 3 mark question and two clear points for a 2 mark question. If relevant, also try to make some brief overall comment about the source. Make it as easy as possible for the examiner to give you the marks by clearly distinguishing between the points.

Common mistakes

Make sure you don't comment on the wrong source! (Mistakes like this are made every year. Remember – every mark is important for your final grade.)

Simplified mark scheme

For each item of relevant/correct information identified, award 1 mark – up to a maximum of 2 or 3 marks.

> **EXAMINER'S COMMENT**
>
> **Timing:** For a 3 mark question you ought not to spend more than about 7 minutes, and for a 2 mark question no more than about 5 minutes. Don't spend too long on these questions or you will run out of time!

> **EXAMINER'S COMMENT**
>
> Examples of a comprehension question can be found at the end of Chapter 2 and Chapter 5.

Assessing the value and limitations of a source

Value and limitations (utility/reliability) questions require you to assess **one** source over a range of possible issues/aspects – and to comment on its value to historians studying a particular event or period of history.

Examiner's tips

The main areas you need to consider in relation to the source and the information / view it provides are:

- **origin**, **purpose** and **content**
- value and limitations.

These areas need to be linked in your answer, showing how the value and limitations of the source to historians relate to the source's origin, purpose and content

For example, a source might be useful because it is primary – the event depicted was witnessed by the person producing it. But was the person in a position to know? Is the view an untypical view of the event? What is its nature? Is it a private diary entry

origin: The 'who, what, when and where?' questions

purpose: This means 'reasons, what the writer/creator was trying to achieve, who the intended audience was'

content: This is the information or explanation(s) provided by the source

Remember: a source doesn't have to be primary to be useful. Remember, too, that content isn't the only aspect to have possible value. The context, the person who produced it, and so on, can be important in offering an insight.

9 Exam Practice

(therefore possibly more likely to be true), or is it a speech or piece of propaganda intended to persuade? The value of a source may be limited by some aspects, but that doesn't mean it has no value at all. For example, it may be valuable as evidence of the types of propaganda put out at the time. Similarly, a secondary – or even a tertiary – source can have more value than some primary sources: for instance, because the author might be writing at a time when new evidence has become available.

Step 1: Read the source and highlight/underline key points.

Step 2: Then draw a rough chart or spider diagram to show the origin/purpose/content of the source, and how it links to that source's value/limitation.

Step 3: Write your answer, remembering to deal with **all** the aspects required: **origin, purpose, content, value and limitations**. To do this, you will need to make **explicit** links between a source's origin/purpose/content **and** its value/ limitations to an historian.

Common mistakes

- Don't just comment on content and ignore the nature, origin and purpose of the source.
- Don't say 'a source is/ isn't useful because it's primary/ secondary'.

Simplified mark scheme

Band		Marks
1	**Explicit/ developed** consideration of **BOTH** origin, purpose and content **AND** value and limitations.	3–4
2	**Limited consideration/ comments** on origin, purpose and content **AND** value and limitations. **OR** more developed comments on **EITHER** origin, purpose and content OR value and limitations.	0–2

> **EXAMINER'S COMMENT**
> Examples of value and limitations questions can be found at the end of Chapters 3 and 6.

Cross-referencing/comparing or contrasting two sources

Cross-referencing questions require you to compare **and** contrast the information/content/nature of **two** sources, relating to a particular issue.

Examiner's tips

For cross-referencing questions, you need to provide an integrated comparison, rather than dealing with each source separately.

Step 1: Read the sources and highlight/underline key points.

Step 2: Draw a rough chart or diagram to show the **similarities** and the **differences** between the two sources. That way, you should ensure you address both elements of the question.

Step 3: Write your answer, ensuring that you write an integrated comparison. For example, you should comment on how the two sources deal with one aspect, then compare and contrast the sources on another aspect. Avoid simply describing/ paraphrasing each source in turn – you need to make **clear and explicit** comparisons and contrasts, using precise details from the sources.

Common mistakes

- Don't just comment on **one** of the sources! (Such an oversight happens every year – and will lose you 4 of the 6 marks available.)
- Make sure you comment on the sources identified in the question – don't select one (or two) incorrect sources!
- Be careful to make **explicit** comparisons – do not fall into the trap of writing about the two sources separately and leaving the similarities/differences implicit.

Simplified mark scheme

Band		Marks
1	Both **sources linked**, with detailed references to **BOTH** sources, identifying both **similarities and differences**.	6
2	Both **sources linked**, with detailed references to **BOTH** sources, identifying **either similarities or differences**.	4–5
3	**Comments on both sources**, but treats each one separately.	3
4	Discusses/ comments on **just one source**.	0–2

> **EXAMINER'S COMMENT**
>
> Examples of a cross-referencing question can be found at the end of Chapters 4 and 7.

Using and evaluating sources and knowledge to reach a judgement

The fourth type of Paper 1 question is a judgement question. Judgement questions are a synthesis of source evaluation and own knowledge.

Examiner's tips

- This fourth type of Paper 1 question requires you to produce a mini-essay – with a clear/relevant argument – to address the question/statement given in the question. You should try to develop and present an argument and/or come to a balanced judgement by analysing and using these **four** sources **and** your own knowledge.
- Before you write your answer to this kind of question, you may find it useful to draw a rough chart to note what the sources show in relation to the question. This will also make sure you refer to all or at least most of the sources. Note, however, that some sources may hint at more than one factor/result. When using your own knowledge, make sure it is relevant to the question.

9

Exam Practice

- Look carefully at the simplified mark scheme – this will help you focus on what you need to do to reach the top bands and so score the higher marks.

Common mistakes

- Don't just deal with sources **or** your own knowledge! Every year, some candidates (even good ones) do this, and so limit themselves to – at best – only 5 out of the 9 marks available.

Simplified mark scheme

Band		Marks
1	**Consistently focused** on the question. Developed and **balanced analysis**, with precise use of BOTH sources AND relevant/accurate own knowledge. Sources and own knowledge are used **consistently and effectively** together, to support argument/judgement.	8–9
2	**Mostly focused** on the question. Developed analysis, with relevant use of BOTH sources AND some detailed own knowledge. But sources and own knowledge **not always combined** to support analysis/judgement.	6–7
3	**Some focus** on the question. **Some analysis**, using some of the sources OR some relevant/accurate own knowledge.	4–5
4	**No/limited focus** on the question. Limited/ **generalised comments** on sources AND/ OR some **limited/inaccurate/irrelevant** own knowledge.	0–3

Student answers

The student answers below have brief examiner's comments in the margins, as well as a longer overall comment at the end. Those parts of the answers which make use of the sources are highlighted in purple. Those parts that deploy relevant own knowledge are highlighted in red. In this way, you should find it easier to follow why particular bands and marks were – or were not – awarded.

Question 1

Using Sources A, B, C, and D, **and** your own knowledge, evaluate the reasons for Japan's expansionist foreign policy after 1933. [9 marks]

[Handwritten notes in margin: 1) read Question 4 first 2) Plan Qu4 after first writing]

SOURCE A
Figure 9.1

EASTERN MONROE DOCTRINE.

[Cartoon depicting figures with a sign reading "ASIA FOR THE ASIATICS" and a box labelled "RUSSIA".]

SOURCE B

Japan may be regarded, along with Germany and Italy, as one of the three major dissatisfied 'have-not' powers of the world. It was in Italian Fascist intellectual circles that the idea first found expression that there could just as logically be a 'class struggle' between rich and poor nations as between the 'bourgeoisie' and the 'proletariat' in a single nation. German National Socialist [Nazi] leaders have displayed an increasing tendency to attribute their countries economic difficulties largely to the lack of colonial sources of essential raw materials. Japan sees itself confronted with a similar problem, despite the acquisition of Manchukuo. So the spokesman of the Foreign Ministry, Mr. Amau, recently remarked:

'Unfortunately the territories which now feed Japan's population are too small. We are advised to practice birth control, but this advice comes too late, since the population of the Japanese Empire is already about 100,000,000. Japanese work harder and longer than people in Western countries; their opportunities in life are more restricted. Why? We need more territory and must cultivate more resources if we are to nourish our population.'

Extract from Chamberlain, W. H. 1938. *Japan over Asia*. Quoted in Overy, R. J. 1994. *The Inter-War Crisis 1919–1939*. Harlow. Longman. p. 124.

9 Exam Practice

SOURCE C

Article 1. Japan recognizes and respects the leadership of Germany and Italy in the establishment of a new order in Europe.

Article 2. Germany and Italy recognize and respect the leadership of Japan in the establishment of a new order in Greater East Asia.

Article 3. Japan, Germany, and Italy agree to co-operate in their efforts on aforesaid lines. They further undertake to assist one another with all political, economic and military means if one of the Contracting Powers is attacked by a Power at present not involved in the European War or in the Japanese-Chinese conflict.

The first three articles of the Tripartite Pact of September 1940.

From: http://avalon.law.yale.edu/wwii/triparti.asp

SOURCE D

1. Our Empire is determined to follow a policy that will result in the establishment of the Greater Asia Co-Prosperity Sphere and will thereby contribute to world peace….

2. Our Empire will continue its efforts to effect a settlement of the China Incident [Japan's invasion of China] and will seek to establish a solid basis for the security and preservation of the nation. This will involve steps to advance south.

3. Our Empire is determined to remove all obstacles in order to achieve the above-mentioned objectives.

In order to achieve the above objectives, preparations for war with Great Britain and the United States will be made…. In carrying out the plans outlined above, our Empire will not be deterred by the possibility of being involved in a war with Great Britain and the United States.

Extract from the minutes of the Japanese government's Imperial Conference, held in Tokyo on 2 July 1941. Quoted in Overy, R. J. 1987. *The Origins of the Second World War.* London. Longman. p. 114.

> **EXAMINER'S COMMENT**
>
> This is a good, well-focused, start, with a clear argument – Source A is examined, with a clear link to the question, along with some relevant own knowledge. Although not specifically identifying individual sources, the candidate has flagged up their intention to use the other three sources.

Student answer

There are a number of reasons why Japan pursued an expansionist foreign policy after 1933, and these are all shown by the four sources. One reason is shown by Source A, which shows a weak China being 'supported' by Japan. The cartoon is about the announcement by Japan in 1933 about its 'Eastern Monroe Doctrine'. The poster talks of 'Asia for the Asiatics'. Japan – which had completed its occupation of Manchuria in 1932, and had already taken over the Chinese province of Rehe (Jehol) – saw its version of the Monroe Doctrine as a way of expanding its own territory and influence in China and elsewhere in Asia. In particular, China – distracted by civil war between the Nationalist and the Communists – presented an easy target for Japanese expansion, and thus an important reason for making such expansion seem possible. After several encroachments and 'incidents', Japan finally invaded China in 1937, thus beginning the Second Sino-Soviet War.

This aim of expanding Japanese territory is also shown by the other three sources. Source B, which was written in 1938, refers to Japan as a 'have-not' power which saw its 'economic difficulties' being the result of its 'lack of colonial sources of essential raw materials'. In addition, Source B contains comments made by a spokesperson of Japan's Foreign Ministry, who stated that Japan needs 'more territory'. Japan's nationalists and many of its military leaders wanted to expand the Japanese empire as a way of overcoming the economic problems caused by the Great Depression. By 1931, over half of Japan's factories had closed, and exports had also dropped by half. Japan's important silk industry was hit particularly badly.

Source C – which shows some of the main articles of the Tripartite Pact of September 1940 – is closely linked to Sources A, B and D, as it comments on Japan's aim of 'establishing a new order in Greater East Asia' (this idea is also specifically mentioned in Source D). This was similar to the ideas of the earlier Eastern Monroe Doctrine, and would help achieve the extra territory Japan felt it needed after the Depression. By 1940, imperial Japan had moved close to two other expansionist powers – Nazi Germany and Fascist Italy. By joining with them, Japan felt more able to risk war with Britain and the US, as the Tripartite Pact included promises to help each other if they were 'attacked by a Power at present not involved in the European War or in the Japanese-Chinese conflict'. As Britain was already at war with Germany and Italy, this was clearly aimed at the US – the power most likely to object to further Japanese expansion in Asia and the Pacific as it too had its own important interests in those areas.

Finally, Source D – an extract from the Minutes of Japan's Imperial Conference of July 1941 – also relates to the aim of expanding Japanese territory. Point 2 actually talks about Japan's intention to 'advance south', and even mentions that the Japanese Empire was prepared to get 'involved in a war with Great Britain and the United States' to achieve this territorial expansion. The signing of the Tripartite Pact (as shown in Source C) the year before would have given Japan greater confidence to risk such a war. The Greater East Asia Co-Prosperity Sphere, which Japan first announced in 1940, was meant to be a loose alliance between Japan and other nations in Asia to overcome the control of European colonial powers such as Britain, France and the Netherlands which had extensive colonies in the region. However, in practice, it was essentially a way of Japan extending its own empire.

So, in conclusion, these four sources touch on all the main reasons why Japan followed an expansionist foreign policy after 1933.

Overall examiner's comments

There is a clear argument, and good use of the sources, with clear references to them. However, although there is a mixture of some precise and general own knowledge, which is mainly integrated with comments on the sources, there are some omissions. For instance, own knowledge could have been used to give other reasons not touched on by the sources – such as the impact of US sanctions imposed following Japan's aggression in China, or the problem of overpopulation (which is actually mentioned in Source B). Additionally, something could have been said about the growing control of Japan's military leaders over civilian governments. Also, there is no real attempt to assess the relative importance of these factors. Hence, this answer fails to get into Band 1 – but this is a reasonably sound Band 2 answer and so probably scores 6 marks out of the 9 available.

> **EXAMINER'S COMMENT**
>
> Sources B and C and are clearly referred to and used, showing good understanding, and there is some own knowledge about how the Great Depression's impact on Japan led to increased pressure for expansion. In addition, Sources B, C, D and A are explicitly linked, and there are comments about why the Tripartite Pact was seen as useful by Japan's expansionists.

> **EXAMINER'S COMMENT**
>
> As before, Source D is clearly used, and is linked to Source C. There is also some relevant own knowledge. However, the student has not really made an attempt to evaluate the relative importance of the reasons mentioned in the sources. Nor are any other reasons – not mentioned by the sources – examined.

* begin each paragraph with own knowledge.

9

Exam Practice

Activity

Look again at the all sources, the simplified mark scheme, and the student answer above. Now try to write a few paragraphs to push the answer up into Band 1, and so obtain the full 9 marks. As well as using all/most of the sources, and some precise own knowledge, try to integrate the sources with your own knowledge, rather than dealing with sources and own knowledge separately. And don't lose sight of the need to use the sources and your own knowledge to explain which reason you think was most important.

Question 2

'Japan's invasion of Manchuria in 1931 was the most important reason for the collapse of collective security in the period 1929–39.' Using Sources A, B, C, and D, **and** your own knowledge, to what extent do you agree with this statement? [9 marks]

SOURCE A

In February 1933, the League of Nations declared that the State of Manchukuo could not be recognised. Although no sanctions were imposed upon Japan, nor any other action taken, Japan, on March 27, 1933, withdrew from the League of Nations. Germany and Japan had been on opposite sides in the [First World] war; they now looked upon each other in a different mood. The moral authority of the League was shown to be devoid of any physical support at a time when its activity and strength were most needed.

Churchill, W. 1948. *The Gathering Storm.* London. Cassell and Co. p. 80.

SOURCE B
Figure 9.2

SOURCE C

The Spanish Civil War, non-intervention and intervention had an impact on the subsequent fortunes of the world powers. Non-intervention failed to appease the dictators. Intervention hardly benefited Italy and the Soviet Union. Only Germany really gained an advantage, both economically and militarily, from its participation in the Spanish war. Above all, the Civil War can be seen as a rehearsal for, or at least a prelude to, the Second World War… The weaknesses of the democracies were neatly exposed by their refusal to intervene in Spain. According to Mary Habeck, the Spanish war prevented Franco-British unity against the dictators in that it distracted attention from far greater dangers…

Britain's policy of compromise, rather than calming the international situation, only heightened tension between the European powers. The British government failed to understand that Spain was another arena where Germany and Italy were testing how far their aggressive stance could be taken… The Civil War also alienated the Soviet Union from the West. Receiving no response to appeals for collective security, Stalin became increasingly convinced that appeasement would channel Hitler's attention towards the East.

Durgan, A. 2007. *The Spanish Civil War*. Basingstoke, UK. Palgrave MacMillan. pp. 74–6.

SOURCE D

In 1936 when Hitler ordered German troops into the demilitarized Rhineland there was little international protest,… Few in Germany bothered to read Mein Kampf to discover Hitler's real motives and his obsession with territorial expansion. Nazi propaganda portrayed Hitler as a man of peace pursuing justifiable revisions of the humiliating Versailles Treaty.

The treaty that led to the Rome-Berlin Axis in November 1936 had changed the balance of power in Europe, and Austria, in particular, was left isolated as a result. Previously, Austria had depended on an alliance with Britain, France and Italy to secure her independence in the face of German demands. With Italy now on Germany's side, the balance of power in central Europe had shifted dramatically. …. As a result of the Rome-Berlin Axis, Hitler was now in a stronger position… The German invasion of Austria [on 12 March 1938] was Hitler's first move outside German territory in defiance of the Treaty of Versailles…. The Anschluss of Austria not only revealed the extent of Hitler's imperial ambitions, it also dealt a strategic blow at Czechoslovakia which could now be attacked from the south as well as from the west and north.

Welch, D. 1998. *Hitler*. London. UCL Press. pp. 58–9.

Student answer

There were several reasons for the collapse of collective security during the 1930s. These include the impact of the Great Depression, Japan's invasion of Manchuria in 1931, the failure of the Disarmament Conference in 1934, Italy's invasion of Abyssinia in 1935,

9

Exam Practice

Germany's re-occupation of the Rhineland in 1936 and its Anschluss with Austria in 1938. Also important was the Munich Conference in 1938, the US policy of isolation, and the failure of Britain to form an anti-Nazi alliance with the Soviet Union. The four sources mention several of these, but not all of them.

> **EXAMINER'S COMMENT**
> This is a good introduction, showing a clear understanding of the topic and the factors relevant to the question.

The most important reason for the collapse of collective security was the economic and political impact of the Great Depression – and none of the sources mentions this. *The Depression began as a result of the Wall Street Crash in the US and had important economic and political impacts across the world. Because of the resulting poverty and unemployment in Germany, Hitler and the Nazis were able to come to power in Germany in 1933. This was crucial as Hitler's foreign policy aims – such as grabbing land in the east for Lebensraum ('living space'), and overturning aspects of the peace treaties of 1919–20 – were bound to lead to conflicts in Europe. The Depression also impacted on Japan, and played a large part in the emergence of a militaristic and expansionist foreign policy there. However, because the Depression caused serious economic problems, many of the democratic countries – including Britain – adopted austerity policies by cutting government expenditure. This included spending on armed forces. This meant they felt unable to resist the aggressive foreign policies adopted by imperial Japan and by the fascist dictatorships of Italy and Germany. In addition, many countries – including the US – were not prepared to impose economic sanctions on aggressor countries, as they didn't want to lose any trade. Amongst other things, this pursuit of self-interest undermined the ability of the members of the League of Nations to work effectively together, in the way they had done before 1929 and the Depression. In particular, France felt increasingly abandoned by Britain when it came to opposing Hitler's actions in the period 1935–38.*

> **EXAMINER'S COMMENT**
> There is good use of relevant own knowledge, some of which is precise, and the candidate is clearly aware of the need to make a judgement about which reason was most important. Although, so far, there has been no use of – or even reference to – any of the sources, this is OK as the candidate has begun with a factor not dealt with by any of the sources.

Although Japan's invasion of Manchuria in 1931 was important in showing how an aggressor nation could ignore the League, Italy's invasion of Abyssinia in 1935 (Source A) was probably more important. *This is because it led to the break-up of the Stresa Front between Britain, France and Italy. This had been formed in 1935, after these three countries had joined together to oppose Hitler's attempt in 1934 to push through Anschluss with Austria. This was proof that collective security could work. However, these three countries – which were the main members of the League of Nations – then fell out over the Abyssinian crisis. Although Britain and France had tried, by the Hoare-Laval Pact, to give Mussolini most of Abyssinia, this had caused public outcry and was dropped. Even though the sanctions that Britain and France had then got the League to impose on Italy were very limited, they were enough to anger Mussolini. More importantly, Hitler moved quickly to get Italy on his side. The following year, they formed the Rome-Berlin Axis (Source D) – once Japan joined in 1937, there were three Axis powers, all of which were determined to pursue expansionist foreign policies. Abyssinia was also important for the collapse of collective security because – like with Manchuria – it showed aggressors that Britain and France were not prepared to take strong action to prevent conflict.*

> **EXAMINER'S COMMENT**
> There is more good use of relevant and mostly-precise own knowledge, linked to the question. However, although there are very brief references to two sources, these sources have not been used, nor has their content been analysed/evaluated. This is a serious weakness in a question that requires both own knowledge AND sources to be used.

This impression was confirmed in many ways in the years after 1936. *For instance, despite setting up a Non-Intervention Committee when civil war broke out in Spain (Source C), Britain and France did nothing when both Fascist Italy and Nazi Germany sent weapons and troops to aid the right-wing rebels. They maintained this line even when British and French merchant ships were attacked by Axis submarines and planes. This lack of action to protect a democratically-elected government from fascist aggression confirmed Hitler's belief that, whatever he did, there would be no serious practical opposition from the democracies.*

Although Hitler had walked out of the Disarmament Conference (Source B) in 1933, and had begun to re-arm, it was his foreign policy actions from 1936 onwards that did more to further undermine collective security than the actual collapse of the Disarmament Conference. These included the re-occupation of the Rhineland in 1936 and the Anschluss with Austria in 1938 (Source D). Though more important than Hitler's actions was the reaction – or, rather, the lack of reaction – of Britain and France to these breaches of the Treaty of Versailles. The successful Anschluss with Austria shows how important Abyssinia and the break-up of the Stresa Front was: in 1934, Italy had joined with Britain and France to block Hitler's first attempt in 1934. This time, with Italy joined to Nazi Germany in the Rome-Berlin Axis, Austria was taken without a shot being fired.

All this encouraged Hitler to go further – his first target was Czechoslovakia. At first, he demanded the Sudentenland: unlike the Rhineland and Anschluss with Austria, this had nothing to do with the terms of the Treaty of Versailles as, previously, this land had been part of the Austro-Hungarian Empire, not of Germany. As on previous occasions, Britain and France decided to let Hitler take possession of this land at the Munich Conference in September 1938. This Conference was important in undermining collective security because, as well as convincing Hitler and Mussolini that Britain and France would never oppose their actions, it began to convince the Soviet Union that, if anything, Britain and France were in effect giving Hitler a free hand to expand eastwards. This was significant as, for some time, the Soviet Union (which had been a member of the League since 1934) had been suggesting a joint pact to oppose Nazi Germany's growing aggression. By August 1939, Stalin had instead made a Non-Aggression Pact with Nazi Germany to buy time for building up Soviet defences.

Finally, another important reason for the collapse of collective security by 1939 was how USA and the Soviet Union reacted to the aggressive foreign policies of Imperial Japan and the fascist dictators in Europe. The US which, certainly since the end of the First World War, had become the most powerful nation in the world – both economically and militarily – had refused to join the League of Nations. Instead, it mainly followed a policy of isolation: at least as far as Europe was concerned. In fact, during most of the 1930s, some of its leading politicians and statesmen – such as Joseph Kennedy, the US ambassador to Britain – were actually opposed to taking action against Hitler, as his fierce anti-communism made him seem a useful block against the Soviet Union. In addition, while the Soviet Union had, up until the Munich Conference in 1938, been prepared to work with Britain and France to block Hitler's growing aggression in Europe, it eventually gave up on this. Instead, Stalin replaced Litvinov (who had favoured an alliance with Britain and France) with Molotov, and then tried to stay out of any possible war by signing the Nazi-Soviet Non-Aggression Pact in August 1939.

Although all these factors were important reasons for the collapse of collective security, I think the Abyssinian crisis was the most important one as it was this which broke up the Stresa Front and pushed Fascist Italy into the arms of Nazi Germany. Given that Britain would not join with the Soviet Union, collective security was effectively mortally wounded in 1935: it just took a few more years to die.

> **EXAMINER'S COMMENT**
> The own knowledge approach has, unfortunately, been continued. Although the own knowledge is relevant, mostly precise and pinned to the question, yet again there are only the very briefest references to two sources.

9

Exam Practice

Overall examiner's comments

There is good and precise own knowledge, which is focused on the question. In addition, there is a clear attempt to come to a balanced judgement about relative importance. However, there are only minimal references to – **and no real use of** – the sources. Hence, as Paper 1 is mainly a source-based exam, the candidate has only done enough to be awarded the top of Band 3 – so gaining only 5 marks of the 9 available.

Activity

Look again at all the sources, the simplified mark scheme, and the student answer above. Now try to write your own answer to this question – and see if you can analyse the sources in relation to the question, and integrate this with own knowledge. You can, of course, decide that another reason is more important that Abyssinia.

Question 3

'Fear and hatred of communism was the main reason why Britain preferred appeasing Nazi Germany rather than forming an alliance with the Soviet Union to oppose Hitler's aggressive foreign policy in the period 1937–39.' Using the sources *and* your own knowledge, to what extent do you agree with this statement? [9 marks]

SOURCE A

It is our opinion that no pressure that Great Britain and France can bring to bear, either by sea, on land, or in the air, could prevent Germany from overrunning Bohemia and from inflicting a decisive defeat on Czechoslovakia. The restoration of Czechoslovakia's lost integrity could only be achieved by the defeat of Germany and as the outcome, which from the outset must assume the character of an unlimited war.

The intervention of Italy and/ or Japan on the side of Germany would create a situation which the Chiefs of Staff in the '*Mediterranean and Middle East Appreciation*' described in the following language: 'Moreover, war against Japan, Germany and Italy simultaneously in 1938 is a commitment which neither the present nor the projected strength of our defence forces is designed to meet, even if we were in alliance with France and Russia, and which would, therefore, place a dangerous strain on the resources of the [British] Empire … '

Extracts from Chiefs of Staff Report: 'Appreciation of the Situation in the Event of War against Germany', 14 September 1938. Quoted in Dickenson, M. 2009. *Historical Controversies and Historical Significance.* Harlow. Heinemann. p. 71.

SOURCE B

When Neville Chamberlain became British Prime Minister in May 1937 he gave a new impetus to appeasement. For Chamberlain, appeasement meant taking the initiative and showing Hitler that 'reasonable' claims could be achieved by negotiation and not force. Chamberlain and Daladier, the new French Prime Minister, feared that the Czech crisis could precipitate a wider conflict and decided that Czechoslovakia was simply not worth a European war. The Czech President, Benes, was urged therefore to make concessions to the Sudeten Germans. Chamberlain had three meetings with Hitler: at Berchtesgarden on 15 September, at Bad Godesberg on 22–23 September, and at Munich on 29–30 September. At the first meeting, Hitler stated his intention to annex the Sudetenland on the principle of self-determination. At Bad Godesberg he insisted on immediate German occupation, and finally at Munich he was persuaded to accept a phased occupation with an international commission to arbitrate over disputed boundaries … On 29 September 1938, an international conference was held at Munich. The participants were Germany, Italy, Britain and France. Conspicuous by their absence were Czechoslovakia, whose fate was to be decided, and the Soviet Union, which was not invited.

Welch, D. 1998. *Hitler*. London. UCL Press. pp. 59–60.

SOURCE C
Figure 9.3

9 Exam Practice

> **SOURCE D**
>
> I must confess to a most profound distrust of Russia. I have no belief whatever in her ability to maintain an effective offensive, even if she wanted to. And I distrust her motives which seem to me to have little connection with our ideas of liberty, and to be concerned only with getting everyone by the ears. Moreover, she is both hated and suspected by the smaller states, notably, Poland, Rumania and Finland.
>
> An extract from Chamberlain's diary entry for 26 March 1939. Quoted in Feiling, K. 1946. *The Life of Neville Chamberlain*. London. Macmillan. p. 403.

Student answer

These sources only partly support the view that British fear and hatred of communism was the main reason appeasement was pursued rather than an anti-Nazi alliance with the Soviet Union. There were several other reasons behind the policy of appeasement, and the sources show some of these – but not all of them.

EXAMINER'S COMMENT
This is a brief – but good – introduction, which shows a clear understanding of the topic and the demands of the question.

Fear and hatred of communism was certainly an important factor behind the refusal to make common cause with the Soviet Union to stop Nazi Germany's expansionist foreign policy. Source D shows this most clearly – while Sources B and C also seem to confirm this view. Source D – which, because it is from Chamberlain's private diary (and therefore not meant for immediate publication) – seems a reliable and thus useful indication of attitudes to the Soviet Union. This source is also useful because appeasement is mainly associated with Chamberlain who, as Source B states, became British prime minister in 1937. This source shows he had a 'most profound mistrust of Russia'; the diary entry then goes on to show that he distrusted Soviet 'motives which seem to me to have little connection with our ideas of liberty'.

As well as 'liberty' meaning a democratic multi-party system, Chamberlain – as a Conservative – would also have meant a capitalist economy. Ever since the Bolshevik Revolution in Russia in November 1917, the main countries of Europe – and the US and Japan – had been opposed to the Soviet Union. In fact, immediately after the revolution, these states – including Britain – had sent armed forces to intervene on the side of the Whites in the Russian Civil War. When, unexpectedly, the Reds won the civil war, these capitalist states had imposed economic blockades and sanctions against the Soviet Union in the hope – as expressed by Churchill (a Conservative politician) – that Bolshevism could be 'strangled in its cradle'. When the Great Depression hit in the 1930s, the mass unemployment and poverty saw a growth in support for Communist Parties across Europe. *This only increased long-standing fears of communism amongst conservative politicians and capitalist bankers and industrialists.*

EXAMINER'S COMMENT
There is good and balanced use – including brief evaluative comments on value/usefulness – of Source D, along with links to Sources B and C. There is also relevant own knowledge, which is mostly precise, focused on the question, and integrated in the answer – along with some awareness of historical debate.

The significance of anti-communism as an important factor behind the adoption of appeasement, rather than allying with the Soviet Union, is something post-revisionist historians have stressed. Even Churchill – who was fiercely anti-communist – criticised the continuance of appeasement and, instead, advocated an alliance with the USSR. Post-revisionist historians have pointed out that Chamberlain ignored intelligence warnings about Hitler's intentions and often deliberately misled public opinion. According to such historians as Adamthwaite, this was because of the anti-communist prejudices of the British ruling class – *something that can be seen as confirming the view expressed in the Soviet cartoon (Source C).*

Exam Practice

As well as Source D indicating that fear of communism was a factor, both Sources C and B can be read as confirming this. Source C shows Britain and France directing a clearly-aggressive Nazi Germany towards the Soviet Union. This was published after the Munich Conference, and reflects the growing belief in the USSR that Britain and France were not just opposed to an alliance with Stalin's Russia, but were actively hoping that Hitler would attack the USSR, and so destroy the only non-capitalist country in the world. This was a genuine Soviet fear – especially given the context of the Great Depression which had had such a negative impact on the economies of capitalist states. This was why the Soviet Union was worried – as well as angry – that they were not invited to the Munich Conference. Especially given the fact that they had promised military aid to Czechoslovakia to prevent Nazi Germany taking the Sudetenland.

Source B, which is an extract from a history book written in 1998, confirms that the Soviet Union 'was not invited' to the Munich Conference. However, Source B does not offer an explanation of why the Soviet Union was not invited. In fact, one reason – which is touched on by Source D – was that the Soviet Union was 'both hated and suspected by the smaller states, notably, Poland, Rumania and Finland' (Source D). Poland, in particular, hated the Soviet Union. As well as having had an authoritarian conservative and anti-communist government for some time, Poland was afraid that, if it allowed the Red Army to cross their territory in order to help Czechoslovakia, the Soviet Union might then attempt to take back the land Poland had taken from Soviet Russia as a result of the 1920–21 Russo-Polish War.

Source D also gives another reason why Britain was reluctant to form an alliance with the Soviet Union. In his diary, Chamberlain states that he did not believe in the Soviet Union's 'ability to maintain an effective offensive'. This was written in 1939, after the Great Purge and Terror had been taking place in Stalin's USSR. These had begun in 1936 – though the first victims were leading members of the Communist Party, from May 1937, they had also been directed at important officers of the Red Army and the Soviet Air Force. The Great Terror then spread to the lower ranks – by the end of 1938, almost 50% of the entire officer corps had been either executed, imprisoned or sacked. Consequently, many analysts believed the Red Army had been seriously weakened. This would be confirmed later on in 1939, when Soviet forces performed badly in the 'Winter War' against Finland. *This factor is perhaps why, in Source A, the Chief of Staff Report says that 'even if we were in alliance with France and Russia' Britain could not cope with a war against the three Axis powers. Significantly, this source is dated 14 September 1938 –* just two weeks before the Munich Conference at which Britain and France 'gave' Hitler the Sudetenland.

However, as well as reasons connected to attitudes to the Soviet Union, there are also other reasons why appeasement was followed. Source B shows one of these: which was to avoid war. According to Source B, Chamberlain saw appeasement as a way of 'showing Hitler that "reasonable" claims could be achieved by negotiation and not force'. As well as the advice he had received from the British military (Source A), that Britain was not militarily-ready to fight a major war, Chamberlain – like many Europeans – was very reluctant to risk another war. In fact, Source B also states that France thought 'Czechoslovakia was simply not worth a European war.'

In fact, according to opinion polls, during much of the 1930s, most Britons were against re-armament and, instead, in favour of disarmament. A League of Nations opinion poll, found 90% of Britons thinking like this. *So it can be argued that appeasement was something the public*

> **EXAMINER'S COMMENT**
> There is clear use and assessment of Sources B and C, which is also linked to Sources A and D. In addition, there is good use of relevant own knowledge, which is mostly precise, and focused on the question. The candidate also identifies another reason.

> **EXAMINER'S COMMENT**
> The candidate offers two more possible reasons, with good synthesis of sources and some precise own knowledge.

wanted. Although, after Munich, there was a rapid shift in public attitudes – yet Chamberlain continued with appeasement. In fact, there is some evidence to suggest that, even after the declaration of war in September 1939, he was still prepared to do a deal with Hitler. This could be interpreted as being the result of anti-communism.

Although there are several reasons why an alliance with the Soviet Union was rejected, I believe the main one was fear and hatred of communism. Many of the upper classes in Britain and elsewhere even had a slight admiration of the fascist dictators precisely because of their fierce anti-communism.

Overall examiner's comments

There is good and clear use of sources throughout, and constant integration of precise own knowledge to both explain and add to the sources. In addition, there is also some awareness of historical debate. The overall result is a sound analytical/evaluative explanation, focused clearly on the question, and with a clear and supported judgement. The candidate has done more than enough to be awarded Band 1 and the full 9 marks.

Activity

Look again at the all sources, the simplified mark scheme, and the student answer above. Now try to write your own answer to this question – and see if you can make different points with the sources, and use different/additional own knowledge, to produce an answer that offers an alternative judgement.

Paper 2 exam practice

Paper 2 skills and questions

For Paper 2, you have to answer **two** essay questions – chosen from two **different** topics from the 12 options offered. Very often, you will be asked to comment on two states from two different IB regions of the world. Although each question has a specific mark scheme, you can get a good general idea of what examiners are looking for in order to be able to put answers into the higher bands from the general 'generic' mark scheme. In particular, you will need to acquire reasonably precise historical knowledge in order to address issues such as cause and effect, or change and continuity, and to learn how to explain historical developments in a clear, coherent, well-supported and relevant way. You will also need to understand and be able to refer to aspects relating to historical debates, perspectives and interpretations.

Make sure you read the questions carefully, and select your questions wisely. It is important to produce a rough essay plan for each of your essays before you start to write an answer, and you may find it helpful to plan both your essays before you begin to write. That way, you will soon know whether you have enough own knowledge to answer them adequately.

Remember, too, to keep your answers relevant and focused on the question. For example, don't go outside the dates mentioned in the question, or answer on individuals/

states different from the ones identified in the question. Don't just describe the events or developments – sometimes, students just focus on one key word or individual, and then write down all they know about it. Instead, select your own knowledge carefully, and pin the relevant information to the key features raised by the question. Also, if the question asks for 'causes/reasons' and 'consequences/results', or two different countries/leaders, make sure you deal with **all** the parts of the question. Otherwise, you will limit yourself to half marks at best.

Examiner's tips

For Paper 2 answers, examiners are looking for clear/precise analysis, and a balanced argument, linked to the question, with the use of good, precise and relevant own knowledge. In order to obtain the highest marks, you should be able to refer, where appropriate, to historical debate and/or different historical perspectives, interpretations, or historians' knowledge, making sure it is both relevant to the question AND integrated into your answer.

Common mistakes

- When answering Paper 2 questions, try to avoid simply describing what happened. A detailed narrative, with no explicit attempts to link the knowledge to the question, will only get you half marks at most.
- If the question asks you to select examples from **two** different regions, make sure you don't choose two states from the same region. Every year, some candidates do this, and so limit themselves to – at best – only 8 out of the 15 marks available for each question.

Simplified mark scheme

Band		Marks
1	**Consistently clear focus** on the question, with all **main aspects addressed**. Answer is **fully analytical** and **well-structured/organised**. There is **sound understanding** of historical concepts. The answer also integrates **evaluation** of different historical debates/perspectives, and reaches a **clear/consistent judgement/conclusion**.	13–15
2	**Clear understanding** of the question, and **most** of its main **aspects are addressed**. Answer is mostly **well-structured and developed**, with supporting own knowledge **mostly relevant/accurate**. Answer is mainly **analytical**, with attempts at a **consistent conclusion**; and shows some **understanding of historical concepts and debates/perspectives**.	10–12

continued

9 Exam Practice

Band		Marks
3	**Demands** of the question are **understood** – but some aspects not fully developed/addressed. **Relevant/accurate** supporting own knowledge, but attempts at analysis are limited/inconsistent.	7–9
4	**Some understanding** of the question. Some relevant own knowledge, with some factors identified – but with **limited explanation**. Some attempts at analysis, but answer is **mainly description/narrative**.	4–6
5	**Limited understanding** of the question. Short/general answer, with very **little accurate/relevant** own knowledge. Some **unsupported assertions**, with **no real analysis**.	0–3

Student answers

Those parts of the student answer which follow will have brief examiner's comments in the margins, as well as a longer overall comment at the end. Those parts that are particularly strong and well-focused will be highlighted in red. Errors/confusions/loss of focus will be highlighted in blue. In this way, you should find it easier to follow why marks were – or were not – awarded.

Question 1

'Appeasement was the main reason why Nazi Germany followed an aggressively expansionist foreign policy from 1933 to 1939.' To what extent do you agree with this statement? [15 marks]

Skill

Analysis/argument/evaluation

Examiner's tip

Look carefully at the wording of this question, which asks you to show **to what extent** you agree with the statement. To do this, you will need to examine a **range** of reasons – including appeasement – *and* evaluate their **relative** importance as causes of the foreign policy adopted by Nazi Germany in this period. Just focusing on one reason will not allow you to score the highest marks.

Student answer

There are many reasons why Nazi Germany followed an expansionist foreign policy from 1933–39. Apart from appeasement, many orthodox historians have argued that such policies were the result of Hitler's long-term foreign policy aims for 'Lebensraum' in eastern Europe. However, revisionist historians have instead insisted on the importance of a variety of other factors: such as the peace treaties of 1919–20, the impact of the Great Depression, and the weaknesses of the League of Nations.

Appeasement contributed to the foreign policy followed by Hitler after he came to power in 1933, because it led him to think that Britain and France would never oppose him, whatever

> **EXAMINER'S COMMENT**
>
> This is a clear introduction which is focused on the question, and which identifies a range of different reasons. It also shows some awareness of relevant historical debates connected to the topic.

218

he did. The problem of appeasement in the 1930s was mainly associated with Britain, which had always favoured a revision of some aspects of the peace treaties which ended the First World War. France, which was more prepared to resist Nazi Germany's actions, was only willing to do so if Britain supported it. This was because France had been badly weakened by the First World War, and needed Britain's military strength to be able to stand up to Hitler's Germany. But this was something that Britain's Conservative governments in the 1930s were not prepared to do. This was especially true of Neville Chamberlain's government which was in power from 1937–40. Because Britain and France decided to do nothing to stop him, Hitler was encouraged to keep breaking aspects of the Treaty of Versailles and expand German territory.

There were several reasons why British governments followed appeasement: as well as being weakened by the effects of the Great Depression, Chamberlain – like many of his generation – did not want to see another war like that of 1914–18. In addition, for much of the 1930s, opinion polls showed that the British public favoured disarmament; while Britain's Conservative government feared possible socialist revolution in parts of Europe – such as Spain – and so tended to see Nazi Germany as a block to such developments. This was why Britain pushed France into setting up a Non-Intervention Committee during the Spanish Civil War, instead of aiding the democratically-elected Popular Front government in Spain resist the military rising against it. Amongst other things, this policy prevented the government of Republican Spain from buying weapons: even when it was clear that Fascist Italy and Nazi Germany were both giving weapons and troops to help Franco and his Rebel army. This fear of communism was also why, when the Soviet Union proposed an alliance to resist Nazi Germany's breaches of the Treaty of Versailles, Britain refused to join such an alliance – even though France was prepared to do so, as long as Britain did too.

Hitler's policy of gaining 'Lebensraum' was another reason behind the foreign policy followed by Germany after 1933. This aim had been stated by him early on – well before he came to power in 1933 – in his book, Mein Kampf, which he began writing as early as 1924 when he was in prison. This stated that Germany needed to expand in eastern Europe, in order to gain extra resources, and to provide land for German settlers. This long-term aim was behind the 1936 Four-Year Plan which he ordered Goring to carry out – this was to get Germany ready for war by 1940. Hitler's aggressive foreign policy was also shown by the Hossbach Memorandum of 1937. These were the notes of a meeting at which Hitler told his ministers and commanding officers to get Germany ready for invading countries in eastern Europe.

Another reason for Hitler's expansionist foreign policy was to do with aspects of the Treaty of Versailles. As well as Hitler – and many Germans – seeing this treaty as being too harsh on Germany, Britain also felt it had been unfair. In fact, during the 1920s, British governments were prepared to consider revisions – which were put forward by democratic German politicians such as Stresemann. As a result, relations with Germany had improved after the invasion of the Ruhr by France and Belgium in 1923. There was the Locarno Treaty of 1925, by which Germany accepted its western borders – but said nothing about its eastern borders. Then, in 1928, Germany was one of many nations which signed the Kellogg-Briand Pact, by which those countries promised not to use war as a way of settling disputes.

In addition, the League of Nations was weak – in part, because it had no armed force of its own, and in part because the USA and the Soviet Union were not members. As a result, the League depended on Britain and France to uphold the terms of the peace treaties. Italy was also a member – but, in the 1930s, Mussolini's Fascist Italy also began to follow an increasingly-expansionist foreign policy. This led to the break-up of the Stresa Front in 1935, after Italy's invasion of Abyssinia.

> **EXAMINER'S COMMENT**
>
> The candidate has made a link to the question, and has provided some relevant and accurate supporting own knowledge to explain how appeasement encouraged Hitler to follow an expansionist foreign policy after 1933. However, there then follows a paragraph explaining the reasons for appeasement – although the own knowledge is accurate, it has not been made relevant by linking it to the question. Thus the candidate gains no marks for this second paragraph – and has also wasted valuable time.

> **EXAMINER'S COMMENT**
>
> Again, there is some relevant focus, with some accurate own knowledge. However, although two other valid reasons are identified, there is no real attempt – so far – to evaluate their relative importance. In addition, although there is quite a lot of accurate information, it is not effectively tied to the question. As a result, the answer is beginning to become a list of reasons, rather than an analysis/evaluation of the relative importance of these reasons.

9

Exam Practice

The Great Depression had a big negative impact on the countries of Europe. This began with the Wall Street Crash in the US in 1929, and was the result of speculation and over-production. As well as causing economic chaos in the US, it led the US to impose tariffs on foreign imports. This badly affected world trade, and led other countries to do the same. By 1932, there were over 6 million unemployed people in Germany – this was one of the reasons Hitler was able to come to power in 1933, because the Nazi Party was able to gain large votes in elections, making them the largest party in the German parliament. Britain and France were also badly affected; this led Britain to cut government spending – including on armaments. Also, all countries tended to follow their own interests, rather than cooperate with each other. Some then became increasingly aggressive as regards their foreign policies.

EXAMINER'S COMMENT

This answer has now become even more of a list of reasons – with little or no explicit attempts to link the points to the question. For instance, the League of Nations' paragraph doesn't explicitly state that this was a reason for Hitler's foreign policy. Also, the information about the effects of the Depression could have been linked to (a) Hitler's attempt to solve Germany's problems by increased spending on armaments and attempts to gain extra territories; and on Britain's decision to cut spending on weapons and so being less able to fight a war. This is a shame, as there is some relevant and precise own knowledge. In addition, there is no conclusion – this is where the candidate should have attempted an overall judgement about which reason was the most important one.

Overall examiner comments

This answer makes only a few attempts to explicitly address the question of which reason(s) was/were the most important one(s). There is plenty of precise/correct own knowledge – though some is irrelevant. The approach has been mainly to present a 'list' of reasons, with much of the supporting information not being 'pinned' to the question. Consequently, the answer is not good enough to go higher than Band 3 – probably getting 7 marks. To reach the higher Bands, more **explicit analysis of reasons – and evaluation of their relative importance –** are needed. Frustratingly, the candidate clearly has good knowledge, and some of the information needed to produce a good answer is already present.

Also, for Band 1, it would be necessary to have a little more **mention of relevant specific historians / historical interpretations** – there are several to choose from on this topic.

Activity

Look again at the simplified mark scheme and the student answer above. Now try to write a few extra paragraphs to push the answer up into Band 1, and so obtain the full 15 marks. As well as making sure you explicitly address **both** aspects of the question, try to integrate some references to relevant historians / historical interpretations.

Further information

Japan

Barnhart, M. A., 1987, *Japan Prepares for Total War: The Search for Economic Security 1919–1941*, Ithaca (NY), Cornell University Press

Beasley, W. G., 1987, *Japanese Imperialism 1894–1945*, New York, Oxford University Press

Chamberlain, W., 1938, *Japan Over Asia*, London, Duckworth

Gruhl, W., 2007, *Imperial Japan's World War Two*, New Brunswick (USA), Transaction Publishers

Hane, M., 2013, *Japan: A Short History*, London, Oneworld Publications

Henig, R., 1995, *The Origins of the Second World War 1933–1939*, London, Routledge

Ienaga, S., 1978, *The Pacific War 1931–1945*, New York, Pantheon Books

Large, S. S., 1992, *Emperor Hirohito and Showa Japan*, London, Oxford University Press

McDonough, F., 1997, *The Origins of the First and Second World Wars*, Cambridge, Cambridge University Press

Mitter, R., 2013, *China's War with Japan 1937–1945: The Struggle for Survival*, London, Penguin Books

Morris, I., 1960, *Nationalism and the Right Wing in Japan*, London, Oxford University Press

Nish, I., 1977, *Japanese Foreign Policy 1869–1942,* London, Routledge & Kegan Paul

Taylor, A. J. P., 1963, *The Origins of the Second World War,* Harmondsworth, Penguin Books

Italy and Germany

Adamthwaite, A., 1992, *The Making of the Second World War*, London, Routledge

Adamthwaite, A., 1980, *The Lost Peace – International Relations in Europe 1918–1939*, London, Edward Arnold

Blinkhorn, M., 2006, *Mussolini and Fascist Italy,* London, Routledge

Carr, W., 1991, *A History of Germany 1815–1990,* London, Edward Arnold

Clark, M., 2005, *Mussolini,* Harlow, Pearson/Longman

Clavin, Patricia, 2000, *The Great Depression in Europe 1929–39,* New York, St Martin's Press

Craig, G. A., 1981, *Germany 1886–1945*, Oxford, Oxford University Press

Henig, R., 1984, *Versailles and After 1919–1933,* London, Methuen

Henig, R., 1995, *The Origins of the Second World War 1933–1939*, London, Routledge

Hobsbawm, Eric, 1994, *Age of Extremes,* London, UK, Abacus

Layton, G. 1995, *From Bismarck to Hitler: Germany 1890–1933*, London, Hodder and Stoughton

Lowe, C. J. and Mazari, F., 1975, *Italian Foreign Policy 1870–1940,* London, Routledge and Kegan Paul

McDonough, F., 1997, *The Origins of the First and Second World Wars*, Cambridge, Cambridge University Press

McDonough, F., 2002, *Hitler, Chamberlain and Appeasement,* Cambridge, Cambridge University Press

Overy, R. J., 1994, *The Inter-War Crisis 1919–1939,* London, Longman

Robson, M., 1992, *Italy: Liberalism and Fascism 1870–1945,* London, Hodder & Stoughton

Taylor, A. J. P., 1963, *The Origins of the Second World War,* Harmondsworth, Penguin Books

Williamson, D., 1994, *War and Peace: International Relations 1914–45*, London, Hodder

Wood, A., 1986, *Europe 1815–1960,* London, Longman

Index

Abyssinia 10, 65, 84, 86, 122, 152, 180–2
Africa 102–4, 111, 156, 195
Albania 151, 157–8, 184
Anglo-German Naval Treaty 137, 146, 152, 173
Anglo-Japanese Alliance 7, 27, 29
Anti-Comintern Pact 62, 87, 89, 91, 147, 148, 155, 176
appeasement 89, 138, 160, 173
    historical debate and 187–9
    reasons for 10–11, 178–9, 185–7
arditi 106
Asiatic Monroe Doctrine 61–2, 72
Austria (*Anschluss*) 145–6, 147, 149–50, 155, 158, 172, 177
Austro-Hungarian empire 7, 14, 104
autarchy 122
Axis Powers 30

Belgium 6
Benes, Edvard 158
Bolshevik Revolution 8, 30, 121
Boxer Rebellion 27, 42, 44, 91

Chamberlain, Neville 138, 162
    appeasement policy 10, 138, 174, 178–9, 185–9
    peace in our time pledge 159, 160
China *see also* Manchuria, China; Second Sino-Japanese War
    Chinese Republic, early years 44–5
    civil war 48–50
    communist rebellions 48, 49–50, 59, 89
    Double Tenth, Nationalist Revolution 43, 44, 91
    extermination campaigns 50, 59, 88
    First Sino–Japanese War 26–7, 44
    German concessions in Shandong 30, 45
    GMD (People's National Party) 45, 46–9, 87
    Japanese in Northern China 59–60, 86–7, 91–2
    Manchu Qing dynasty 43–4
    May Fourth Movement 45–6, 47
    Northern Campaigns 48, 49
    Opium Wars 21, 43
    pinyin system, Chinese names 43
    Russian/Soviet support for 46–8, 87, 89
    Second Sino-Japanese War 61–7
    Second United Front 50, 87
    Sino-German cooperation 91
    Sino-Soviet Non-Aggression Pact 87
    Twenty-One Demands 29–30, 47
    'unequal treaties' 43, 45
    and USA 42, 43–4, 89
    Warlord period 45–8

Chinese Communist Party (CCP) 46–50, 67, 87
Churchill, Winston 5, 185, 187, 188
collective security 11, 130–3, 137–8, 170–9
communism 11, 164
Condor Legion 147, 175
Conference of Ambassadors 9, 12, 109, 132
Corfu Incident 109, 151
Czechoslovakia 158–62, 163, 177–8

D'Annunzio, Gabriele 105, 107

Edouard Daladier 161

fascism 12, 101–2 *see also* Italian fascism
First Sino–Japanese War 26–7, 44
First World War
    Chinese labour battalions 45
    economic impact on Germany 124–5
    economic impact on Italy 120–1
    and German nationalism 115
    and Italian nationalism 105
    and Japanese nationalism 29–31
    Ypres, Belgium 6
Four-Power Pact 42, 152, 172, 179
France 112, 114
    and German aggression 135–7, 170–3
    and the Great Depression 90, 135
    and invasion of Czechoslovakia 161
    and the Manchurian crisis 82, 84
    Popular Front 135
    relations with Italy 148
    Second Opium War 43
Franco, Francisco 136, 147, 175

Gentile, Giovanni 107
German expansionism
    Anschluss with Austria 145–6, 147, 149–50, 155, 158, 172, 177
    in Czechoslovakia 158–62, 177–8, 184
    Eastern Europe (Hossbach Memorandum) 149
    economic policies and 128–9
    and Manchurian crisis 84
    map, March 1939 162
    Molotov–Ribbentrop Pact of Non-Aggression 164
    Munich Agreement 160, 161, 163, 179, 184
    overview of 2, 3
    in Poland 162, 193–4
    pre-1914 115
    re-armament and conscription 146, 173
    re-occupation of the Rhineland 147, 148, 173–4, 182
    in the Soviet Union 195, 197

German militarism
    alliance with Italy 155
    Anglo-German Naval Treaty 137, 146, 152, 173
    Condor Legion (Spanish Civil War) 147, 175–6
    de-militarisation of the Rhineland 11, 15
    economic policies and 128–9
    European responses to 135–7
    military strength 186
    pre-1914 114–15
    Schlieffen Plan 115
German nationalism
    and the 'diktat' 117–18, 144
    early form of 112
    German unification 112–14
    and imperialist expansion 115
    and Nazism 119–20
    and peace treaties 115–16
    and Treaty of Versailles 16, 116–17, 118, 124, 125, 143, 144, 146
    and WWI 115–16
    Zollverein 112
German Nazism
    economic policies 128
    foreign policies 143–4, 149
    and Italian fascism 118–19, 172
    and nationalism 119–20
    Pact of Steel 158
    rise of 126, 127–8
    Rome-Berlin Axis 182–3
    Social Darwinism 108
Germany
    Dual Alliance 104
    economy, 1900–33 124–9
    Four-Year Plan 128, 129–30, 148–9, 160
    German Centre Party 128
    and the Great Depression 126–7
    Locarno Treaty 10, 132
    mefo bills 128, 129
    non-aggression pact with Poland 145
    relations with Russia 115, 117
    Shandong concessions 30, 45
    Sino-German cooperation 91
    Tripartite Pact 72–4
    Triple Alliance 104
gold standard 135
Great Britain
    Anglo-German Naval Treaty 137, 146, 152, 173
    Anglo-Japanese Alliance 7, 27, 29
    and the Great Depression 90, 134–5
    gun-boat diplomacy 21
    and Italy 156

Index

Great Britain (continued)
   and the Manchurian crisis 82, 84
   Opium Wars 21, 43
   reaction to invasion of Czechoslovakia 161
   responses to German aggression 135–7, 170–4
   and the Soviet Union 163–4
   Washington Conference 33, 42–3, 90
Great Depression
   and Europe 133–5
   and Germany 126–7
   global effects 9, 82, 84, 89–90, 120
   and Great Britain 90, 134–5
   and Italy 123–4
   and Japan 31, 33–4, 35–7
   and the Soviet Union 133
Greater East Asia Co-Prosperity Sphere 22, 30, 72, 77
gun-boat diplomacy 21

'have not' nations 37, 61, 69, 72, 87
Hiranuma Kiichi 32
Hirohito, Emperor 14, 32
Hirota Koki 62, 63, 69
Hitler, Adolf 118, 119, 136, 143–4, 147
Holy Roman Empire 112

Ikezaki Tadakata 33–4
Indo-china 74–6, 94–5
Inukai Tsuyoshi 34, 37, 40, 59
Inuoe Nissho 39, 40
Ishiwara Kanji 57, 63
Itagaki Seishiro 57
Italian expansionism
   in Abyssinia 10, 65, 84, 86, 122, 147, 152–4, 180–2
   in Albania 151, 157–8, 184
   in Austria 152
   emergence of 151–2
   and the Manchurian crisis 84
   in the Mediterranean and Africa 156
   overview of 2, 3
   spazio vitale ('vital space') 110–11
Italian fascism
   diplomacy, 1922–35 151–2
   doctrine 107–8
   economic policies 121–3
   and German Nazism 118–19, 172
   imagery of 101, 106, 109, 110
   and invasion of Poland 194
   and nationalism 101, 102, 108
   Pact of Steel 158
   Romanità movement 109–10
   Rome-Berlin Axis 182–3
   Social Darwinism 108
   spazio vitale ('vital space') 110–11
Italian militarism
   alliance with Germany 155
   military strength 186, 194
   and the Spanish Civil War 154, 175–6
Italian nationalism
   before 1933 102–6
   Associazione Nazionalista Italiana (ANI) 104
   and fascism 101, 102, 108
   Italia irridenta and empire 102–5

Risorgimento 102
unification of 102, 103
WWI and peace treaties 8, 30, 105–6
Italy
   economy, 1900–33 120–4
   and the Great Depression 123–4
   Locarno Treaty 151
   new international order, calls for 37
   reaction to *Anschluss* 145, 147, 152, 155, 172, 177
   relations with Britain 156
   relations with France 148
   Tripartite Pact 72–4
   Triple Alliance 105

Japan
   Anglo-Japanese Alliance 7, 27, 29
   economy, 1868–1929 35–6
   Fundamental Principles of National Policy 69–70, 72
   and the Great Depression 31, 33–4, 35–7
   imperial periods, 1868–1989 24
   Japanese-Soviet Neutrality Pact 74, 76, 89, 90
   Minseito political party 36
   new international order, calls for 37
   parliamentary democracy 38
   political developments, post-1918 38–43
   relations with USA 21–2, 29–30, 42, 61–2, 77, 91–2, 93–5
   samurai clans 21, 31
   Shogunate period 13, 20–1
   and the Soviet Union 71–2, 84, 88
   Tanggu Truce 40–2
   Tripartite Pact 72–4
   Twenty-One Demands 29–30, 47
Japanese expansionism
   Asiatic Monroe Doctrine 61–2, 72
   conquests in Asia and the Pacific, 1941 95
   in Indo-china 74–6, 94–5
   in Korea 26–7
   League of Nations response to 82–6, 170, 171
   in Manchuria 34, 38, 49, 50, 57
   need for raw materials 31–2, 33–4, 35, 36, 37, 42
   into Northern China 59–60, 86–7, 91–2
   overview of 1–3, 19
   in Russia 30
   Shandong concessions 30, 45
Japanese militarism
   Control Faction (Strike-South faction) 68–9, 74, 89, 94
   and the Great Depression 33–4
   Imperial Way (Strike-North faction) 68–9, 74, 89, 94
   industrial production 39, 69–70
   kamikaze suicide missions 31, 32
   military modernisation 25–6
   political influence, post-WWI 31–2, 33, 34–5, 39–40, 42, 43
   samurai legacy and bushido code 31
   South Sea advances 69
   and the Washington Conference 30, 33, 38, 42–3, 90

Japanese nationalism *see also* Second Sino-Japanese War
   anti-Westernization sentiments 24–5, 31, 35
   Blood Brotherhood League 34, 39, 40
   First Sino-Japanese War 27
   and the Great Depression 33–4, 37–8
   hakko ichiu principles 72
   and imperialist expansion, 1894–1914 26–9
   Meiji Restoration, 1868 23, 24–5, 26
   and modernisation 25–6
   opposition to liberalism and democracy 34–5, 39–40
   Pan-Asia Mission 62
   pre-1900 20–6
   Russo-Japanese War 27
   seclusionism 20–1
   sense of racial superiority 30, 31, 65, 70
   state nationalism 25
   sun goddess, symbolism 23–4
   ultranationalism 22, 32–3, 35, 39
   and 'unequal treaties' 8, 21–2, 26, 30
   and WWI 29–31
Japanese-Soviet Neutrality Pact 74, 76, 89, 90
Jiang Jieshi 34, 57, 87
   and the communists 48, 49–50, 59, 89
   extermination campaigns 50, 88
   and the Japanese 43, 49, 50, 59
   Northern Campaigns 48

Kellogg-Briand Pact 10, 92, 171
Kennedy, Joseph 184, 185
Konoe Fumimaro 61, 63, 66, 69, 72
Korea 26–7, 44
Kwantung Army 12, 34, 40–2, 57–9, 62, 71

League of Nations
   collective security 11, 130–3, 137–8, 170–9
   formation of 10
   German withdrawal from 144–5
   and invasion of Abyssinia 153–4, 180–2
   Lytton Commission 82–3, 92
   and the Manchurian crisis 59, 82–6, 170, 171
   'Racial Equality' clause 31
   response to *Anschluss* 172
   and the Soviet Union 184, 185
   and the USA 184–5
   weaknesses of 10, 12, 130–3, 135–7, 170–2, 185
   World Disarmament Conference, 1932 143, 144–5
left-wing politics 12–13
Lenin, Vladimir 11, 121
Locarno Treaty 10, 132, 151, 170, 171
Lytton Commission 82–3

MacDonald, Ramsay 133, 134
Manchuria, China
   Boxer Rebellion 27, 42, 44, 91
   Chinese response to 43, 49, 50, 59
   Japanese expansionism 34, 38, 49, 50, 57
   Japanese interests in 27, 29
   League of Nations and 59, 82–6, 170, 171
   as Manchuko 42, 59, 83
   Mukden incident 58–9
   raw materials in 36, 42, 57

Index

Russia in 27
South Manchurian Railway 27, 40, 57, 58
Tanggu Truce 40–2
USA and 82, 84, 92
Mao Zedong 47, 49
Marx, Karl 11
Matsuoka Yosuke 84
Mazaki Jinzaburo 68
Meiji Restoration 13, 32, 35–6
militarism 13
Molotov–Ribbentrop Pact of Non-Aggression 164
Munich Agreement 160, 161, 163, 179, 184
Mussolini, Benito
  aggressive foreign policy 109, 111
  and fascism 12, 101, 106–7, 108, 119
  as Il Duce 109, 110

Napoleon, Bonaparte 102, 112
nationalism 13–14
Nazi-Soviet Non-Aggression Pact 179
Netherlands 94–6
new international order 37
Nine-Power Treaty 87, 90–1, 93
non-intervention policies 175–7

Okawa Shumei 32
open door policies 42
Opium Wars 21, 43
Orlando, Vittorio 9, 105–6
Ottoman empire 7, 104–5

Pact of Steel 158
peace treaties, 1919-20 see also Treaty of Versailles
  and German nationalism 115–16
  and Italian nationalism 8, 30, 105–6
  overview of 8–9, 11, 137
  territorial changes under 15
  as 'unequal treaties' 8, 21–2, 26, 30, 43, 45
Pearl Harbour attack
  invasion of Indo-china and 74–6
  Japanese foreign policy and 69–70
  Japanese military factions and 68–9
  as knock-out attack 77
  Tripartite Pact and 72–4
  US regional influence 70, 95
Perry, Commodore 21, 22
Philippines 27, 44, 70
Poland 145, 162–4, 179, 193–4

revolutions, pre WWI 7–8
Ribbentrop, Joachim von 148
Riga Axiomists 184
right-wing politics 12–13
Rome-Berlin Axis 182–3
Roosevelt, Franklin D. 184
Roosevelt, Theodore 70, 87, 91–2, 173
  Quarantine Speech 90, 92, 93
Russia see also Soviet Union (USSR)
  Bolshevik Revolution 8, 30, 121
  Japanese expansionism in 30
  in Korea 27
  in Manchuria 27
  March Revolution 7
  Russo–Japanese War, 1904–05 27–9, 35
  support for China 46–8
  Treaty of Brest-Litovsk 117, 118
Russo–Japanese War, 1904–05 27–9, 35

Sadao Araki 39, 40, 42, 59, 68
samurai clans 21
Schacht, Hjalmar 128, 129
Second Sino-Japanese War, 1937–41
  after Pearl Harbour 88
  Beijing (Beiping) 62–3
  build-up to 60–2
  Chongqing bombings 67
  continuation of 66–7
  map showing Japanese conquests 66
  Marco Polo Bridge Incident 63
  Rape of Nanjing 65
  Shanghai incident 64–5
Second World War
  after 1941 197–8
  Alpine War 194
  as European war 194–5
  as global war 195, 197–8
  historical debate 195–7
  Japanese invasion of Manchuria and 84
  phoney war 194
self-determination 14
Shidehara Kijuro 37, 38
Shogunate period 13, 20–1
Sino-Indo-china Railway 75
Sino-Soviet Non-Aggression Pact 87
Social Darwinism 108
socialism 11
sources 4, 200–4
Soviet Union (USSR) see also Russia
  German expansionism into 195, 197
  and the Great Depression 133
  Japanese-Soviet Neutrality Pact 74, 76, 89, 90
  and the League of Nations 184, 185
  Molotov–Ribbentrop Pact of Non-Aggression 164
  and the Munich Conference 160, 179
  Nazi-Soviet Non-Aggression Pact 162–4
  Poland's distrust of 163
  relations with Japan 71–2, 84, 88
  relations with Britain 163–4
  relations with USA 185
  Sino-Soviet Non-Aggression Pact 87
  support for China 87, 89
Spanish Civil War 147–8, 154, 175–7
Stalin, Joseph 11, 50, 74, 84, 87, 89, 164, 184
state nationalism 25
Stresa Front 146, 147, 152, 172–3, 180
Stresemann, Gustav 125, 126, 144
successor states 14, 15
Sudetenland 158, 160, 177–8

sun goddess, symbolism 23–4
Sun Yixian 44–5, 48

Taisho democracy 14
Tanaka Giichi 33, 36, 57
Tanggu Truce 40–2
Theory of Knowledge (ToK) 4, 5, 25, 66, 96, 109, 152, 177
three-way alliance 72
Tokugawa Yoshinobu 21
Toyama Mitsuru 32
Treaties of Rapallo and Berlin 143
Treaty of Amity and Commerce 21–2
Treaty of Brest-Litovsk 117, 118
Treaty of Portsmouth 27, 91
Treaty of Versailles 8, 10, 11, 30, 45
  equality of treatment, German 144
  German disarmament under 143, 146
  German reparations under 16, 116, 118, 124, 125
  German territory losses under 116–17, 118
Tripartite Pact (Three-Power/Berlin Pact) 72–4, 76
Triple Alliance 7, 8, 105, 115
Triple Entente 7, 8, 115
Triple Intervention 27

United States of America (USA) see also Pearl Harbour attack
  and China 42, 43–4, 89
  Dawes Plan 125
  expansionist approach 44, 70–1
  gun-boat diplomacy 21
  interests in East Asia 44
  and Japanese aggression 91
  and Japanese invasion of Northern China 91–2
  and the League of Nations 130, 184–5
  and the Manchurian crisis 82, 84, 92
  open door policy 42
  relations with Japan 29–30, 42, 61–2, 77, 91–2, 93–5
  relations with the Soviet Union 185
  trade relations with Japan 21–2, 92, 93
  Treaty of Portsmouth 27, 91
  Washington Conference 33, 42–3, 90

Wakatsuki Reijiro 58
Wall Street Crash 16, 120, 126
Washington Conference 30, 33, 38, 42–3, 90
Wilson, Woodrow 14, 30, 91, 115, 130
World Disarmament Conference, 1932 143, 144–5

Yoshida Shoin 23
Yuan Shikai 44–5, 47

zaibatsu 16, 39, 69–70
Zhang Xueliang 49, 50, 57
Zhang Zuolin 36, 49, 57

Acknowledgements

The author and publishers acknowledge the following sources of copyright material and are grateful for the permissions granted. While every effort has been made, it has not always been possible to identify the sources of all the material used, or to trace all copyright holders. If any omissions are brought to our notice, we will be happy to include the appropriate acknowledgements on reprinting.

Text

Extracts on pages 27, 32, 65 reproduced with permission of Curtis Brown, London on behalf of the Estate of Sir Winston Churchill. © Winston S. Churchill.

Extracts on pages 83, 85, 98, 182 © Taylor, A. J. P., 1964, The origins of the Second World War, Harmondsworth, Penguin Books.

Images

p 6 © Photos 12/Alamy; p 7 © WorldPhotos/Alamy; p 9 Trinity Mirror/Mirrorpix/Alamy; p 10 © World History Archive/Alamy; p 12 © Pictorial Press Ltd/Alamy; p 14 © Archive Pics/Alamy; p 22 Free Library of Philadelphia/Print and Picture Collection – Jackson Collection of American Lithographs/Bridgeman Images; p 23 © JTB MEDIA CREATION, Inc./Alamy; p 24 © Bettmann/CORBIS; p 26 © FALKENSTEINFOTO/Alamy; p 32 Hulton Archive/Getty Images; p 40 Private Collection/Peter Newark Military Pictures/Bridgeman Images; p 46 Sovfoto/UIG via Getty Images; p 48 © Hulton-Deutsch/Hulton-Deutsch Collection/CORBIS; p 49 Archiv Gerstenberg/ullstein bild via Getty Images; p 58 Scherl/Sueddeutsche Zeitung Photo; p 63 © Bettmann/CORBIS; p 64 © CORBIS; p 65 Pictures From History/Bridgeman Images; p 67 Keystone-France/Gamma-Keystone via Getty Images; p 71 Boston Globe; p 73 ullstein bild/ullstein bild via Getty Images; p 76 2942/Pictures From History/Bridgeman Images p 85 David Low/Solosyndication; p 93 New York Times Co./Getty Images; p 101 TopFoto.co.uk; p 107 Amerigo Petitti/Mondadori Portfolio via Getty Images; p 109 © 2006 Alinari/Topfoto; p 110 Keystone-France/Gamma-Keystone via Getty Images; p 118 Willi Ruge/ullstein bild via Getty Images; p 119 Luce/Keystone/Getty Images; p 122 Paul Popper/Popperfoto/Getty Images; p 126 Walter Ballhause/akg-images; p 131 © Punch Limited; p 136 ullstein bild/ullstein bild via Getty Images; p 149 © Keystone Pictures USA/Alamy; p 150 Solo Syndication;

Acknowledgements

p 153 Solo Syndication; p 155 © Punch Limited; p 157 Heinrich Hoffmann/ullstein bild via Getty Images; p 158 © CTK/Alamy; p 159 John Frost Newspapers; p 161 ullstein bild/ullstein bild via Getty Images; p163 David King Collection; p 170 fotoLibra/Paul Dwight-Moore; p 171 Keystone/Getty Images; p172 ©Associated Newspapers/Solo Syndication; p 174 Universal History Archive/Contributor; p 177 Solo Syndication; p 178 Solo Syndication/British Cartoon Archive; p 179 Solo Syndication; p 183 Mondadori Portfolio via Getty Images; p 193 © Bettmann/CORBIS; p 196 http://www.comandosupremo.com; p 208 Solo Syndication; p 213 David King Collection.